PRAISE FOR *C'MON, GET HAPPY*

"Thank you for your insightful and loving book about the movie *Summer Stock*. I'm sure that, without a doubt, it will make your readers forget their troubles and just Get Happy!"

—LORNA LUFT, singer, author, and daughter of Judy Garland

"Just like the dance Gene Kelly does on a squeaky board and newspaper that builds from a hesitating start to an explosive finish, Dave and Tom expertly chronicle the making of *Summer Stock* from uncertain beginnings to its ultimate triumph on the screen."

—TOMMY TUNE, ten-time Tony Award–winning director, choreographer, and dancer

"This very special book is entertaining and meticulously researched. It offers a clear sense of how they created a musical during the Golden Age of Hollywood and connects the dots of the process, combining the strands of many important voices, leaving the modern reader agog at the wonders of the MGM factory and the studio system. I thoroughly enjoyed it!"

—MICHAEL FEINSTEIN, singer, songwriter, and ambassador of the Great American Songbook

"Shout 'HALLELUJAH!'—Fantle and Johnson have given us a rare peek into the miracle that is filmmaking. Their love for movie musicals of the Golden Age comes through in every glorious and riveting detail."

—ROB MARSHALL, film and Broadway director and choreographer of *Chicago*, *Nine*, and *Into the Woods*

"I know every step in *Summer Stock* like the back of my hand, and David and Tom have done a brilliant job capturing the magic of this beloved classic. What a thrill to be taken behind the scenes to glimpse the extraordinary talents who brought to life one of the all-time greats from the MGM era. An absolute must-read!"

—SUSAN STROMAN, five-time Tony Award–winning choreographer and director of the Broadway and film versions of *The Producers*

"Whenever a film scoring assignment took me to MGM, I looked forward to eating lunch in the studio café where Gene Kelly and Judy Garland dined, peeking into soundstages 26 and 27 where they rehearsed and filmed the great musicals of MGM's Golden Age. 'If only these walls could talk,' I wondered. Well, it's as if they spilled all they had seen and heard to David Fantle and Tom Johnson who have given me and all you lucky readers this fascinating, meticulously researched, mega-readable book. I ate it up and couldn't wait to watch *Summer Stock* again, only this time as a privileged insider."

—DAVID SHIRE, Oscar-winning songwriter, composer, and arranger for *The Taking of Pelham One Two Three, The Conversation,* and *All the President's Men*

"The authors have done us a great service. They bring us into the world of the creation of an MGM musical, *Summer Stock*, in the waning days of the studio system and let us see the process in ways we seldom get to know. They take us behind the scenes and show us what went into creating these moments, and all the others, while at the same time giving us a glimpse into the lives of the wildly talented actors and artists—people who were doing the creating. This is the present the authors have given us in this remarkable and delightful book—a full tour of how an MGM musical was really made. In Fantle and Johnson's hands, the making of *Summer Stock* is touching—and ultimately moving."

—RICHARD MALTBY JR., Tony Award–winning director and lyricist of such shows as *Ain't Misbehavin', Fosse,* and *Miss Saigon*

"The book brings to life every detail of the making of this movie, and I enjoyed it immensely. The research and the result should be applauded."

—ALAN BERGMAN, multiple Oscar-, Emmy-, and Grammy-winning songwriter

C'MON, GET HAPPY

C'MON, GET HAPPY

The Making of *Summer Stock*

DAVID FANTLE and TOM JOHNSON

Foreword by SAVION GLOVER

UNIVERSITY PRESS OF MISSISSIPPI / JACKSON

The University Press of Mississippi is the scholarly publishing agency of the Mississippi Institutions of Higher Learning: Alcorn State University, Delta State University, Jackson State University, Mississippi State University, Mississippi University for Women, Mississippi Valley State University, University of Mississippi, and University of Southern Mississippi.

www.upress.state.ms.us

The University Press of Mississippi is a member of the Association of University Presses.

Manufactured in the United States of America

First printing 2023
∞

Library of Congress Control Number: 2023021778
Hardcover ISBN 978-1-4968-3839-1
ePub Single ISBN 978-1-4968-4658-7
ePub Institutional ISBN 978-1-4968-4659-4
Web PDF Single ISBN 978-1-4968-4660-0
Web PDF Institutional ISBN 978-1-4968-4661-7

British Library Cataloging-in-Publication Data available

To all the men and women in front of the camera and behind the scenes that made the heyday of American film musicals a unique gift to the world

I'd like to say one word about the people the public has never seen who knocked themselves out so we could look good. No one knows their names! They made us strive to do better things.

—GENE KELLY, AMERICAN FILM INSTITUTE LIFE ACHIEVEMENT AWARD 1985

CONTENTS

FOREWORD

SAVION GLOVER

I'M SO GLAD THE AUTHORS TURNED ME ON TO THIS JEWEL OF A FILM, *Summer Stock*; at the same time I was disappointed to know that until I first saw it a few months ago, I wasn't aware of it. I started dancing on Broadway back in 1984 as the titular *Tap Dance Kid*. I was eleven years old then and *A Chorus Line* was playing in the theater right next door. Of course I had heard of *Singin' in the Rain*, *Stormy Weather* with the great "Bojangles" and the soaring Nicholas Brothers who I came to know personally, and I remember Gene Kelly dancing with Jerry the Mouse, but *Summer Stock*? Wow!

The musical is one of those great vintage movies that follows all the rules; has all the ingredients that define a hit, a master "piece"—great story, memorable music, star power with Judy Garland and Gene in the leads, hilarious secondary characters, and more.

I got to know Fred Kelly, Gene's brother, when I was hanging out with Gregory Hines and Honi Coles back in the day. I was still being taught tap by Honi and Gregory, Lon Chaney (the dancer, not the actor), and Jimmy Slyde and the other great black hoofers, but I remember Fred and Gregory arguing good-naturedly about the origin of tap dancing. Fred said tapping stemmed from Irish clogging and Gregory said that it was born from African American dancing and rhythms. They didn't agree, but it was a friendly disagreement. I was young so I just listened and absorbed.

And that's just it—we are all part of that ongoing tradition. We learn and absorb from who came before us. I know that Gene, when he was working on Broadway in the late 1930s, would visit Harlem and the Cotton Club, Small's Paradise and the Apollo Theater to learn . . . study . . . steal, and that he must've loved every minute of it. All these great artists: Gene

Kelly, Sammy Davis Jr., Steven Spielberg, whoever they are, deliver the goods and then it's up to us not to change it, exactly, but rather to explore what they were doing and put our own stamp on it—absorb it—and then pass that legacy on.

When you examine the numbers themselves—"Dig-Dig-Dig Dig for Your Dinner," the challenge dance in the barn with that wonderful frisson between Judy and Gene, the newspaper dance, and Judy's "Get Happy"—they are so advanced, rhythmic, syncopated. I listened intently to what was being put down on the floor and dug all of them. I realized how groovy those numbers were and, therefore, how groovy and timeless they still are. And to capture it all on film—amazing!

And I want to say something about Eddie Bracken, who plays Orville Wingait, Judy's fiancé in the film. He's fantastically funny and the whole emotional blackmail thing he does holding the tractor he gifted Judy over her head really resonated with me. It's a kind of bondage she was being held in that is topical to any era in history.

Another thing about all that connectedness: Nick Castle helped Gene out with the dances on *Summer Stock*. He also helped the Nicholas Brothers on *Stormy Weather* and other films they did. Decades later, his son, Nick Castle Jr., wrote and directed the movie *Tap* which I appeared in along with Gregory and Sammy. Again, that legacy.

David and Tom, in their own way, are following in the tradition—adding to the legacy—by chronicling how *Summer Stock* got made and the afterlife, as such, that it had. I think that you'll appreciate the movie even more after you've read their book.

Savion Glover is a Tony Award–winning choreographer and dancer.

C'MON, GET HAPPY

INTRODUCTION

WHY *SUMMER STOCK*?

THAT'S THE QUESTION (GREETED WITH RAISED EYEBROWS OR EVEN GREATER degrees of incredulity) we received from many people—directors, actors, musicologists, even hardcore fans of the genre—when we told them we were writing a book about the making of this 1950 Metro-Goldwyn-Mayer Studios Technicolor musical, a movie many felt was a bit old-fashioned even upon its release more than seventy years ago. In fact, no less a legend than Broadway producer/director Hal Prince, in an email to us not long before he died in 2019, questioned our choice of *Summer Stock* as the subject for a book. We had reached out for comments to Prince's wife, Judy, the daughter of Saul Chaplin, who served as a music director and composer on *Summer Stock*.

"I saw *Summer Stock* and I'm fascinated that you should want it as a centerpiece in your book," Prince wrote. "Obviously, or perhaps obviously for us, 'Get Happy' was essentially an appendage to that film, and in every respect a brilliant one. Saul's work was consummate, Judy Garland looked glorious, and the staging looked perfect. It's a sort of schizoid project, is it not?"[1]

Admittedly, *Summer Stock* is not in the same league as other MGM musicals from the storied studio's heyday: *Meet Me in St. Louis* (1944), *Easter Parade* (1948), *An American in Paris* (1951), *Singin' in the Rain* (1952), *The Band Wagon* (1953), and *Gigi* (1958), all produced by the studio's preeminent producer of musicals, Arthur Freed. *Summer Stock* was produced by Joe Pasternak, a jovial Hungarian immigrant who gifted the world some musical trifles starring Deanna Durbin, a few Mario Lanza operatic confections and who rarely made a movie where the end credits didn't scroll without a "feel-good" conclusion having just played out. Nonetheless, we've always felt *Summer Stock* has been unduly unheralded, slighted with the vague and dismissive moniker of being "perhaps" underrated. And that, taking into account *Summer Stock*'s stellar cast clocking in with brilliant performances and the sheer *joie de vivre* on display throughout the film, is a gross disservice, especially considering the troubled atmosphere surrounding the movie.

The backstory of how this film starring Judy Garland and Gene Kelly in their third and final pairing was brought to the screen contains enough drama, heartache, and genuine selflessness to fuel the plots of a score of MGM melodramas. It took a herculean effort and the bottomless empathy of Kelly, co-stars Phil Silvers, Eddie Bracken, Carleton Carpenter, and director Charles Walters to "pull" a performance out of a drug-addled and emotionally spent Garland who was the locus of some production delays, and made completing the fraught project one that defied the oddsmakers. Judy had, from a very early age, become addicted to prescription medication and throughout her life, various "friends" had enabled that dependency by making drugs readily available to her—a "boost" she felt she needed to get her through long production days where she had to be "perfect."

For Garland, the desire to appear on camera only when she felt she was at her best had been accepted as the price that must be paid, gladly, for her brilliance. Kelly, and especially Judy, were used to working on "Freed time," which boiled down to getting it right and making it better no matter how long it took (a legacy from Arthur Freed, the paternalistic producer who oversaw most of Gene's and Judy's movies). Conversely, Pasternak was used to wrapping up productions on a schedule you could clock with an egg timer. However, never before had Pasternak been privy to the array of musical talent that he landed for *Summer Stock*: two major stars who, with Fred Astaire, were the premiere musical talent at the studio, and a director in Walters who had worked with them all and who had an innate flair for the genre.

Looming over all of this was MGM production chief Dore Schary (never a big fan of musicals), who had little patience for the largesse granted to creatives accustomed to invoking the artistic muse, especially if it affected the financial bottom line. Schary's filmmaking credo was to churn 'em out in six to eight weeks, the sooner the better.

It has become gospel in almost every book that references *Summer Stock* to charge Garland as the sole reason for the delays that affected the film's production schedule. *C'mon, Get Happy: The Making of "Summer Stock"* will dispel that commonly held myth as well as others. In fact, there were many production delays that far superseded Garland's absences from the set, including the time needed to write, arrange, record, and film new songs that were added late in the production and the shooting of two solo numbers for Garland and Kelly that occurred weeks after the film had officially wrapped.

Although getting *Summer Stock* to the screen was not always a "get happy" experience for the principals involved, the backstory reveals strong camaraderie with practical jokes (Bracken was a chief instigator) and set visits from Garland's and Gloria DeHaven's children that underscored the deep friendships the cast shared with each other and that helped them weather the rough spots during shooting.

On the face of it, the movie is pure Joe Pasternak—a cheery, *gemütlich* affair with the kind of simple plot that wouldn't overly tax the gray matter of audiences, much less the screenwriters who concocted it—a troupe of uppity New York City actors invade a Connecticut farmstead to stage their show, which they hope is destined for Broadway. For Garland and Kelly, *Summer Stock* seemed like a backward step in their respective career trajectories, particularly for Garland who couldn't help but have a sense of déjà vu that the story of putting on a show in a barn was a throwback to the kinds of movies in which she and Mickey Rooney had starred throughout the late 1930s and early 1940s.

In 1949, when *Summer Stock* was being shot on Stage 27, Judy's star was falling, not with her legion of adoring fans, but with the hierarchy at MGM, the only studio she had ever known, while Gene's was on the ascent. Kelly was fresh off *On the Town* (1949), a landmark musical that featured several scenes filmed on location in New York City, and he was just months away from beginning work on *An American in Paris*, which would win six Academy Awards in 1951 (a record at the time for a musical), including the Oscar for Best Picture and a special award for Kelly's choreography. Seven years earlier, in 1942, it was Garland—MGM's golden child—who mentored Kelly in *For Me and My Gal*, his first movie. But in 1949, their roles had reversed and it was Kelly who provided emotional support to Garland in a film that both he and director Charles Walters considered an outdated relic from the *Andy Hardy* era of teenage opuses.

After fourteen years and more than two dozen films, eighty singles for Decca, several hundred radio shows, World War II bond and servicemen shows, an abortion, two failed marriages, being a more-or-less single mother to a three-year-old child and a less-than-satisfactory husband in Vincente Minnelli, Garland's life was cratering. She was twenty-seven. *Summer Stock* would be Judy's final movie at MGM before the studio terminated her contract. Maybe Hal Prince was right with his schizoid comment!

And yet, despite the Greek tragedy that played out sometimes daily (thankfully, offstage when the cameras weren't rolling), *Summer Stock* is a film packed with musical gems, including two of the best solo numbers that Kelly and Garland ever performed as well as a duet—a challenge tap dance in the barn—chock-full of nuance that's the very definition of *chutzpah*.

Brian Seibert, dance critic of the *New York Times*, in his authoritative history, *What the Eye Hears: A History of Tap Dancing*, which was a finalist for a National Book Critics Circle Award in 2015, regards *Summer Stock* as Kelly's finest tap dancing on film. In Seibert's estimation, Kelly's solo in an empty barn incorporating a squeaky board and an abandoned newspaper into his routine becomes an improvisational tour de force worthy of comparison to Fred Astaire's best solo numbers. "As he plays with the board's squeak and the paper's swish and rip," Seibert writes, "the predictable rhythms build in waves. The ending is just right, the way he halves and quarters the newspaper with his feet, gets interested in a headline, walks off absorbed in his reading, and happens upon the errant board for one final creak."[2] Performed to composer Harry Warren's "You Wonderful You," the number was Kelly's personal favorite of all his solo film dances; he preferred it even over his iconic title number from *Singin' in the Rain*.

The movie climaxes with Garland belting out "Get Happy," a Harold Arlen–Ted Koehler blues-tinged rouser dating back to 1930 that had been interpolated into the score much to Warren's chagrin. The song, aptly described by Hal Prince as "an appendage," was filmed weeks after production on *Summer Stock* had wrapped and was a latecomer—a kind of "Hail Mary"—that Walters thought was needed to inject more pizzazz into the movie and shore up Garland's performance with her very own showstopper.

The number, with Garland looking svelte (she had been *zaftig* throughout the film and had lost weight in the interim), and chicly decked out in a shortened tuxedo jacket, black slouch fedora, and black nylons, is a syncopated jam. Backed up by a cadre of hand-clapping eccentric male dancers (also all dressed in black), Garland struts, flourishes, and shouts like she's just been infused with the Holy Ghost at a big tent evangelist revival meeting somewhere south of the Mason-Dixon Line. The staging and her singing are electric and the song remains at the very top of the Garland canon along with "Over the Rainbow" and "The Man That Got Away." "Get Happy" turned out to be the final number Garland filmed at her alma mater, and what a finish it is!

In addition to the stellar songs and dances, *Summer Stock* features a veteran troika expert in milking laughs. Phil Silvers, who had provided wiseacre comic relief six years earlier in *Cover Girl* (1944) with Kelly, does the same in *Summer Stock*; his snarky delivery foretells a breakout television role in 1955 as the conniving Sgt. Bilko in *You'll Never Get Rich*.

A stalwart of Preston Sturges's screwball comedy stock company, Eddie Bracken (*The Miracle of Morgan's Creek*, *Hail the Conquering Hero*, both released in 1944) killed at playing milquetoasts and nerds throughout his career just as he does here. Comically nearsighted (an effect exaggerated by his round eyeglasses which, when allied to his pronounced proboscis, often made him look like a spooked owl) and with a chin so weak it seemed at times to recede into his jaw, Bracken was a natural laugh-getter who constantly reduced Garland to convulsions on the *Summer Stock* set.

Rounding out the film's comic foils is Marjorie Main playing the role of Garland's housekeeper, Esme, with the same crusty impudence that made her Ma Kettle character a hit with audiences (and might have saved Universal Studios from bankruptcy) over the course of ten Ma and Pa Kettle movies.

In 1985, when Kelly accepted the American Film Institute's Life Achievement Award, he pointed to the screen behind him and told the audience, "That's what you do up there—you dance love and you dance joy and you dance dreams."[3] He might just as well have been speaking of his screen partnership with Garland. Each brought out in the other tenderness, vulnerability, and joyous chemistry that they seldom shared with any other co-star. The affection Kelly and Garland had for each other is palpable—stretching back to *For Me and My Gal*. Perhaps because *Summer Stock* was mired in problems that cropped up each day, that solicitation—love—between them is very much on display, especially in the movie's later scenes when grudging attraction between their characters gives way to love itself. Garland was a brilliant natural actor, but even she didn't need to feign the feelings that make those scenes so heartfelt.

Perhaps more than anything, *Summer Stock* is a maddening dichotomy; a movie freighted with problems throughout the shooting schedule even before principal photography commenced and that loomed ever larger and extended even beyond Garland's absences and erratic behavior, which became more pronounced as time went on. Still, ironically, despite the pain it took to complete the film, *Summer Stock* fulfilled Pasternak's credo of a happy ending (cinematically, at least). What's more, it's a tribute to the professionalism of both cast and crew that none of the *Sturm und Drang* that informed making the movie appears on screen. And in that, *Summer Stock* exemplifies just how moviemaking was accomplished in the studio system era where every problem begged a solution and failure wasn't an option.

During our research, which involved consulting numerous archives (Internet, print, and microfiche) that any project like this understandably entails, we also tried to do something we believe is a tad novel: we buttonholed numerous contemporary dancers, singers, choreographers, musicians, and even Garland impersonators to get their take on *Summer Stock*, its stars, and any enduring legacy they think the film might have. We were pleasantly surprised at the enthusiasm many of these artists showed in wanting to contribute to our book.

As college journalists working on the *Minnesota Daily*, the University of Minnesota's student newspaper, we traveled to Los Angeles in the late 1970s and early 1980s to conduct sit-down interviews with Gene Kelly, Charles Walters, and the principal composer of the score for *Summer Stock*, Harry Warren. At each meeting, we asked wide-ranging questions about their careers, including several pointed queries about *Summer Stock*, but we had little idea then that some forty years later we'd write a book on the making of the film. Perhaps it took that amount of time for the idea to fully gestate into determined action—that and the creeping realization that the movie has often been overlooked even by movie musical fans.

C'mon, Get Happy: The Making of "Summer Stock" is our effort to remedy some of that shortsightedness and possibly encourage new viewers as well as casual fans of the film to fully embrace its many merits, and, in doing so, elevate the movie into the praiseworthy "centerpiece" (as Hal Prince would quizzically have it) that it truly deserves to be.

CHAPTER I

THE STUDIO

MGM: Dream Factory in Transition

SLATED AS PRODUCTION #1477, *SUMMER STOCK* BEGAN REHEARSALS AT MGM on Stage 27 in October 1949. World War II had ended four years previously and America was riding high as the world's first burgeoning "superpower"—one whose homeland and industry were untouched by the cataclysm that had devastated Europe and much of Asia. To many Americans, and especially the contract stars and the army of rank-and-file studio workers that enabled the major Hollywood studios to churn out hundreds of films each year, the expectation was that with the economy booming and prosperity entrenched, the future held no limits on what the industry could achieve in the way of riches. But signs foretelling a different, more ominous scenario for the movie industry as a whole and MGM in particular were looming on the horizon, and the nadir of the studio system that had prevailed since the 1920s would come sooner and land harder than anyone could have imagined.

On February 10, 1949 (nine months before *Summer Stock* went before the cameras and a year to the month before principal photography wrapped), pugnacious MGM studio chief Louis B. Mayer, the human personification of the studio's mascot, Leo the Lion, put on his best game face and presided over a star-studded luncheon to commemorate the studio's silver anniversary. The cavernous 23,000-square-foot Stage 29 was converted to a dining hall and the luncheon climaxed MGM's twenty-fifth anniversary sales convention. Film reel footage of the studio's famous roster of contract players (mostly seated in alphabetical order) captured Fred Astaire chatting with Judy Garland, Clark Gable cracking up Ava Gardner in between drags on their cigarettes, and Buster Keaton playing to the camera with the crudités—a real case of celery shtick!

In his remarks, Mayer cautioned the assembly about competitive pressures confronting the industry. "We have to economize today because of changing conditions," Mayer said, and then seemed to contradict himself when he added, "but to concentrate on cheaper pictures at a loss of quality will never solve the problems of the film industry."[1]

The biggest "competitive pressure" to which Mayer alluded was a gadget that was gaining ground and beginning to strike fear into the hearts of studio heads and movie exhibitors alike. Just the year before, in June 1948, Milton Berle had entered the newfangled world of television, and Tuesday nights would never be the same again. He became, literally, an overnight sensation and his *Texaco Star Theater* soon was responsible for selling more televisions than the collective sales effort of Philco, Admiral, and Zenith.[2] In 1949 only 2 percent of all American households had TV sets. In 1950, the year of *Summer Stock*'s release, that number had risen to 8 percent; five years later, the trickle had become a flood, with 67 percent of all American households owning television sets. Added to that, from 1940 to 1950 average weekly movie attendance in the United States dropped by twenty million, a decline that would not level off until the 1970s. It's no wonder Mayer was perturbed.[3]

The story of how and why *Summer Stock* came to the screen, then, involves the story of these turbulent market forces as well as what was happening in American society at the time and how it affected the way MGM made decisions during these tumultuous years. It's also the story of a power struggle within the studio itself.

In 1948, the biggest Hollywood film companies (MGM among them) were literally split in half by a US Supreme Court anti-trust consent decree (known as the Paramount Decree) that forced the major Hollywood studios to sell their lucrative chains of movie theaters, which had ensured guaranteed bookings for their films and a predictable revenue stream. The decree hastened the collapse of the studio system, which resulted in the release of contract players (stars) and the layoffs of thousands of employees.

Other factors in play at the time included the rise of motion picture trade unions and the accompanying unrest and violence that occurred outside the gates of Warner Bros. in 1945 due to a massive union squabble. The "Red Scare" and the Hollywood Blacklist that started in 1947 with the House Un-American Activities Committee (HUAC) hearings tarnished the image of many writers, directors, and stars and the movie business as a whole, especially with conservative moviegoers. Those troubles coincided with the industry's desire for more realism on screen. The studios' vaunted backlots that for decades substituted for worldwide locations, gave way to filmmakers who wanted to take their cameras and crews to actual locations. Realism was in; suspending disbelief for feel-good musicals like *Summer Stock* shot on the lot would soon become obsolete.

Warner Bros. may have had its gangster films and Universal its horror chillers, but MGM was the undisputed king of musical escapism. For two decades, since *The Broadway Melody of 1929* (which won the Best Picture Oscar for MGM), the studio reigned supreme with an art form invented in America. Over the years, musicals became MGM's bread and butter and conferred a unique prestige. Always among the top-grossing movies of any year, most MGM musicals made hefty profits but those margins were cut by the extra production expense of opulent staging, orchestras and soundtracks, musical scoring, extended rehearsal time needed to stage numbers, and so on. For example, Gene Kelly's groundbreaking MGM musical *On the Town*, released in December 1949, grossed $4.4 million against production expenses of $2.1 million. That same year, the studio's war movie, *Battleground*, made a whopping $11.2 million against production expenditures of just $1.6 million.

MGM would add to its musical laurels in the years ahead, but regardless of profit margins, the day of reckoning for musicals as a staple family entertainment was fast approaching. In MGM's executive suites at the Thalberg Building (named after famed "boy wonder" producer Irving Thalberg), there was more unrest; a power struggle was ensuing that would leave lasting fallout. In 1949, Mayer's time at MGM was dwindling faster than the sands in the Wicked Witch of the West's oversized hourglass. Although it would be two years before Mayer would be summarily replaced as head of the studio by his production chief, Dore Schary, his ouster as head of the studio seemed almost preordained.

A quarter-century before, Mayer practically invented the star system, discovering Greta Garbo and signing to long-term contracts Judy Garland, Gene Kelly, Clark Gable, Joan Crawford, and Elizabeth Taylor, to name just a few. Within a few short years, MGM could justifiably boast that it had under contract "more stars than there are in the heavens." Mayer did have his fair share of detractors, from business competitors to members of his star stable. "I never liked him [Mayer]," said Gene Kelly. "In the first place he lied to me, phony, yes. I thought he was a complete phony. And certainly in later years I've come to realize that he hired a lot of people who had the taste and sensitivity that he didn't have, and that certainly he was a very astute man. But as far as any aesthetics or anything like that goes, I disagree with all the old guard at Metro who lionized him, unless they're lying to me. No, I didn't care for him at all."[4]

"Mr. Mayer" took an interest in all of his contracted stars, with a particular penchant for his leading ladies. As a young starlet at MGM in the early 1940s, champion swimmer Esther Williams said that Mayer took a "keen interest" in her. "He wanted you to tell him everything," she said. "He said to me, 'Esther, I want to be a father to you.' I said, 'Mr. Mayer, I have a father.' That line of his worked on a lot of girls."[5]

Schary echoed Williams's characterization of Mayer's sham benevolence: "Mayer treated everybody kind of the same," he said. "Everybody was his son if they were men. You became disinherited if you disagreed with him. It was that simple. And all the girls were his daughters, unless he was trying to . . . I am positive he never tried anything with Judy. She was a little child and he would treat her like a little daughter. If it was an attractive, seductive dame, he'd try very hard to get in. But with Judy, no."[6]

In a scathing rebuke of what she believed to be Mayer's calculated solicitousness, Alice Vincent, writing for the *Telegraph* in the United Kingdom, compared Mayer's predatory casting couch to modern-day mogul and convicted felon Harvey Weinstein. One star in particular, wrote Vincent, was symbolic of Mayer's Weinstein-like male chauvinism: *The Wizard of Oz* (1939) and *Summer Stock* star Judy Garland. "Garland—whom Mayer referred to as his 'little hunchback'—defied the odds and weathered her childhood at MGM. By the time she was an adult she had come to loathe the endless sunshine of Hollywood, but was so indoctrinated she considered the studio home. She, too, had been victim to Mayer's wandering hands, which he would place on her left breast as he told her that she 'sang from the heart.' She wryly quipped: 'I often thought I was lucky I didn't sing from another part of my anatomy.'"[7]

According to Garland's daughter, Lorna Luft, Judy would confide these experiences to close friends but never in public. "She knew what the press could do to her," Luft said. "She was groomed by MGM, brought up by MGM. She was taught how to dress, how to walk, how to talk, how to dance and how to sing. She was made a star by the studio, but she had the talent to back it all up. At the same time, they owned you," Luft continued. "So, when she was finally let go and finally she was her own person, she was all at sea because she didn't know what to do."[8]

By the time of *Summer Stock*'s release eight months after the silver anniversary luncheon, the simmering acrimony between Mayer and Schary landed full-blown in the press. As *Variety* reported, "with Schary 'production chief' and Mayer 'studio head' it was unclear from the start exactly what the demarcation was between them on duties and authority. Originally, the idea was that Mayer would supervise overall production policy, while Schary would handle the day-to-day making of films. It soon became apparent that this wouldn't work, and that Mayer, who had for more than two decades reigned as top man in all Hollywood, resented the powers handed the much-younger Schary."[9]

Several veteran studio executives regarded the shift in power as a foreboding sign of the eventual downfall of MGM. When she heard the news, Lillian Burns Sidney, MGM director George Sidney's wife and drama coach for the studio, marched into Mayer's office and announced, "Now you've done it. You've ruined everything." She told Mayer that she was afraid Schary would eliminate all future musicals, comedies, and adventure movies and replace them with the "message" movies that he preferred. "They won't have need for anybody around here. Even you!" she told him.[10]

In addition, the politically left-leaning Schary found the arch-conservative Mayer to be an overbearing and stultifying influence. A bitter showdown prompted Nicholas Schenck (head of MGM's parent company, Loew's Inc.) to make a choice. To Mayer's shock, Schenck picked Schary. After twenty-seven years of wielding almost unquestioned power, Mayer was out.[11] In the summer of 1951, Mayer exited the studio. He died six years later of leukemia; Schary would follow him out the door four years later. In an interesting coda, Schary would produce a film about the Democratic Party narrated by John F. Kennedy that was introduced to huge acclaim at the 1956 Democratic convention in Chicago. The film has been credited as a key factor in raising Kennedy's profile and making him a force to be reckoned with as a presidential contender in 1960.[12]

The ignominious departure of both men from the studio marked the end of an era and was a far cry from MGM's glory days. When the studio was at its peak, it employed five thousand, including a makeup department that could handle 1,200 touch-ups, eyebrow plucks, lip and nose enhancements, and wig applications an hour; a telephone extension department that fielded as many long-distance calls a day as the city of Biloxi, Mississippi; and a script department that pored through 12,000 novels, plays, and short stories a year.[13]

Today, the Culver City property where MGM once stood is home to Sony Studios (the parent of Columbia Pictures) and has been pared down considerably from an area that at its height once encompassed six separate lots spread out over more than 165 acres. The MGM name still exists but as a threadbare production and distribution company that scarcely conjures its former eminence as the king of the Hollywood dream factories. In May 2021 it was reported that what was left of MGM Studios would be sold to Amazon for $8.45 billion. The deal closed in March 2022.

In a lyrical lament, former MGM songbird Kathryn Grayson decried the change. "Everything is gone now," she said wistfully, as if the Golden Age had been nothing more than a castle in the air, a chimera lost in time. "The MGM backlot is leveled. The whole studio system fell apart when Mr. Mayer left MGM. He loved quality. I hear the Sony people who now own the former MGM studio have beautiful gardens there; I wish they'd make beautiful pictures instead."[14]

CHAPTER II

THE STORY

It'll Make *Oklahoma!* Look Like a Bum

A WORD, HOKUM, USED IN A KEY SUMMER STOCK SCENE BETWEEN JUDY Garland and Gene Kelly captures the essence of the 106-minute screenplay and story by Sy Gomberg.

In his August 12, 1950, review of the film in the *Los Angeles Times*, Edwin Schallert wrote: "Writer Sy Gomberg probably had the idea of taking the backstage musical out into the rural pastures. Result: MGM found justification for a pleasant and different formula melody film in *Summer Stock*."[1] Gomberg (1918–2001) earned a Best Story Academy Award nomination a year after *Summer Stock* was released for *When Willie Comes Marching Home*, directed by John Ford and starring Dan Dailey and Corinne Calvert. The film, a World War II comedy, was based on a story Gomberg originally wrote for *Collier's* magazine—a submission that became his entrée to Hollywood.

Within days of being hired as a junior writer at MGM, the twenty-nine-year-old Gomberg put his improvisational skills to the acid test when he had to spontaneously "sell" his idea for what would become *Summer Stock* all the way up the ladder to Louis B. Mayer himself. Almost fifty years after that pitch, Gomberg, in 1996, told how on the fly he incubated the *Summer Stock* story in an article he penned for *Screenwriter Quarterly* magazine. We include what he called "The Mother of All Pitches" here in its entirety.

• • •

On a February morning in 1948, I was hired by MGM. By noon in Newark, NJ, my mother had told everybody we knew that I was now a Hollywood success and would soon be a rich millionaire. It didn't matter that I was a new $300-a-week writer without a screen credit, a contract or a secretary. What did matter was that I was at MGM.

In those golden days, MGM symbolized Hollywood's glamour. It was the biggest studio with the biggest stars and it made the biggest pictures, biggest musicals. L. B. Mayer, at 5 feet, 4 inches, was the giant who ran it. He was famous for crying at the annual studio birthday party he gave himself and being angry the rest of the year.

MGM's story department was also famous. It was run by Ken McKenna, who contracted the best-known screenwriters and college-type ($150-a-week) junior writers. But he also hired young week-to-week writers who had shown promise elsewhere. It was my short stories in the *Saturday Evening Post* and *Cosmopolitan* that got me hired. I was also lucky because weekly writers could stay on for years at $300 a week if they wrote enough good ideas to be passed on to the studio's producers. And if an idea made it even to a screenplay, it meant a contract, a $300 raise, a secretary and an invitation to L. B. Mayer's birthday party to see him cry.

A year later, I still couldn't believe I was breathing the same air as movie stars, eating at the legendary MGM writers' table, visiting musical comedy sets to watch dancers bouncing and knowing that just one good idea could mean instant success.

Actually, I had come pretty close. Four of my story ideas had gone part way up the executive ladder and Ken McKenna was so pleased he invited me to play golf. My agent said that meant I was "in like Flynn." So I bought the first new car in the history of my whole family. It was a Pontiac. But I told my mother it was a used Pontiac. I didn't want everybody in Newark, NJ to hear it was a new Cadillac and that L. B. Mayer didn't make a move without me.

Then came a call from Yip Harburg and Harold Arlen in New York. They had written the great score for *Wizard of Oz* and now had a musical hit, *Bloomer Girl*, on Broadway. They read one of my short stories, a comedy about the Revolutionary War, and asked if I'd come to New York to adapt it for a musical. I was thrilled but worried about giving up my great job at MGM for what could be a gamble. Yip said, "Come for three months, then go back to MGM." Harold said, "If we get lucky, you'll go back with a royalty *and* a piece of a Broadway hit." Now I got really thrilled. In those days, screenwriters didn't get pieces of their films—even for the biggest hits—and Yip said the royalty could be $1,500 a week.

So I went to Ken McKenna and asked if I could have three months off and I told him why. He invited me to play golf the next day, Saturday. While we were walking down the first fairway, Ken said he'd rather I didn't go to New York. I asked why and he said, "Any day now an idea of yours will make a movie and you'll get a contract, a $300 raise and have a home at MGM." I asked why I couldn't come back to a home at MGM and also get royalties from Broadway. And he said, "Because if it's not a Broadway hit, you'll come back too unhappy to write good. You'll just want to kick yourself in the ass. But if it's a hit, you won't come back for maybe a $300 raise. Your agent will ask for maybe $3,000 or he'll take you to Fox. So take a piece of advice from somebody who likes you, stay and keep us both happy."

I thought about this all day Sunday. I wanted very much to have a show on Broadway and still come back to be happy with Ken McKenna. And by Monday morning, I had it figured out. I went into his office and said I had an idea. "About what?" he asked. I said I'd sign a contract not to ask for more than a $300 raise when I came back. "Back from where?" he asked. "New York," I said and he said, "You're fired!" I couldn't believe it. So he said it again. "You're fired!"

I walked out of the office in shock. I had just gotten myself kicked out of MGM, the studio everybody dreamed of getting into; the studio whose name alone had made me famous in Newark, NJ. Now I began to feel sick. Why did I do it? Why hadn't Ken kicked me in the ass instead of firing me? Why? Why?

So, I was really hating myself when I was stopped by Joe Pasternak. Joe was a small Hungarian who mangled English but produced many of the famous MGM musicals. As it turned out, 1948 had been his most prolific year, a year in which he produced no less than six films, including *A Date with Judy* and *The Kissing Bandit*. Before coming to MGM, he had saved Universal Studios from financial ruin and was credited with saving Marlene Dietrich's career. Little did I know the impact he was soon to have on my own.

Joe was also excitable, and he grabbed me and said it just hit him from my stories that I was perfect to do the screenplay for a great idea he'd been "mauling" around for the first black and white musical with Jimmy Durante and Lena Horne in color! He was almost jumping up and down. So I told him about New York and being fired by Ken McKenna.

"Fuck on him!" he said. "If you like what's all about it my idea, you can go away forever and come back!" Joe had the power to do that, so I got excited and happy and I couldn't wait to hear the idea that could save my life and my ass. I even prayed when we went into his office. God, I prayed, let me understand him and let it be good.

Joe now told me the idea. At first I thought it was his Hungarian-English that made it the worst idea I ever heard. Then I realized it was a worst on its own. It wouldn't even save my ass in pure English. But what could I say? Joe's nose was an inch from mine and he was yelling, "What did I told you? Is it great or is it great?" My heart was in my stomach and I said, "Joe, let me tell you one."

The one I told him happened this way. The junior writer in the office next to mine couldn't get any new story ideas. So she was very sad. But as we said in Newark, she also had a "great built." So on Saturday night a week before, I had taken her to dinner to help cure this writer's block. I headed for a restaurant in Malibu that had lousy food but great rooms on the beach. On the way I told her to point to any two things and I'd show her how to connect them into a story. (I'd had pretty good luck with this before.)

So she pointed to a telephone pole and a posh apartment house. So I made up a romance about a shy telephone repairman who falls in love with a woman's voice, not knowing she's a gorgeous jewel thief with a priceless necklace other thieves are after. But when he saves her, she throws it into the ocean and they end up in love—on a moonlit beach.

The next combination, a roadside restaurant and an English sports car, became a science fiction comedy about a self-important screenwriter and a gum-chewing waitress who are snatched by space aliens researching whether Earth is worth invading. When this duo saves the planet, they also end up on a moonlit beach.

The last combination was a movie theater and a nearby billboard advertising cream cheese with an old farmer and a barn. That became a beautiful girl farmer who's trying to save a Connecticut farm and support a younger sister gone to New York to become a Broadway star but who suddenly returns with a dozen actors and a director to use "her" barn as a summer stock theater.

I was searching for another moonlit beach ending for this one when the junior writer began to cry. It seems she was in love with a New York actor who hated Hollywood. So, did I think she should give up writing and go back to New York? She cried all through dinner at a table overlooking a moonlit beach and I told her to go back.

The barn story was the one I told Joe Pasternak because a picture on the wall showed him patting a race horse on the nose. I added that the farming sister, now Jane, says "No!" to a summer stock theater in their barn. And the younger sister, now Abigail, begs because she promised it to the director and she loves him.

When I finished, Joe just looked at me. So I started to say his black and white musical in color was beginning to feel great. But he asked, "Could this show they came to do maybe be a musical, perhaps?" I said I thought I mentioned that it was definitely a musical.

That did it. Joe began to jump up and down again and said it was better "from *Oklahoma!*" and that he'd have the studio buy it as soon as I wrote the story on some paper. What story? All I had was maybe six sentences. So I said I also didn't mention that I had to leave for New York tomorrow and why couldn't he just buy what I told him?

A minute later Joe had me back in the story department telling it to Milton Beecher who was Ken McKenna's second assistant. This time I had Jane, the farming sister, saying "Okay," but that the troupe—now fifty dancers and singers—would have to work the farm for their keep. I also gave her a fiancé named Orville who got hysterical when he drove up and saw all these actors.

It was said Milton Beecher had once laughed and dust came out. But when Joe yelled, "It'll make *Oklahoma!* look like a bum," Milton smiled and said the same thing about my writing it now. But now I said I have to go to New York at 6 a.m. tomorrow. So Milton took us to Ken's first assistant, Marge Thorsen.

For her I added the New York actors trying to talk a cow into giving milk and waiting for a chicken to lay an egg and that Orville's stodgy father was now wanting Jane and Orville to end their long engagement and get married right away and send these crazy actors back to New York. Marge was allergic to animals but she loved it anyway.

So when Joe and Milton both said I couldn't write it because I had to go to New York before dawn, she took us to Ken McKenna's office. On the way we passed my agent who was just coming into the studio. His mouth dropped when he saw Joe and Milton and Marge hustling me into Ken's office. All I could do was signal him to wait.

When we came in, Ken's mouth dropped, too. He had fired me only ten minutes ago and now Joe, Milton and Marge were saying he had to hear my great story! As I was telling it to him, Joe now made chicken and cow noises to help.

This time I made Orville's father a farm equipment dealer who loans Jane a new tractor. The show's comic wrecks it and the anguished director, who's falling in love with her, has to tell her. "Tell me straight in my face," Joe now said to Ken, "is it beautiful or is it beautiful?"

To his credit, Ken said he liked it and that I was now rehired to write the screenplay when I came back from New York—for the $300 raise. But Joe was worried. My agent was outside and since I'd told the idea while I was fired, couldn't he sell it while I was putting my socks in a suitcase?

Ken turned white at the idea of MGM having to buy the story. But Joe said Darryl Zanuck would love it for Fox because he was eating vegetarian, and Ken said there had been a mistake. I wasn't fired but I'd quit to go to New York and then got the idea, right? When I said yes, he said, we'd better see Nicky Nayfack.

Nicky Nayfack was the only double executive nephew in Hollywood. His uncle, Nick Schenck, was the New York money behind MGM, and his other uncle, Joe Schenck, behind Fox. Somebody said Nicky got a big salary to look out of a window to watch for approaching glaciers. But his office was only two doors from L. B. Mayer's and he was called in to play gin when things were quiet.

For him, I added that Jane's sister now becomes temperamental because she's going to co-star with a semi-name actor who thinks they're both beautiful. I also gave Jane an earthy old housekeeper who sleeps in the barn with the girl and boy dancers to stop hanky-panky, and fires a shotgun to wake them up at dawn to do chores. Nicky loved it. He especially loved Joe's mooing and cackling. Everybody now told him how I had to go to New York and he took us into Eddie Mannix's office.

Eddie Mannix was a big Irishman who'd been the leader of a gang of young hoodlums who kept vandalizing Joe and Nick Schenck's Palisades Amusement Park in New Jersey. At that time it was the only thing they owned. So they hired him and the vandalizing stopped and they could concentrate on getting rich. Now he was MGM's vice president and the last stop before L. B. Mayer's office.

He was touched by what I made up this time: that Jane's now falling in love with the director but has to fight it because he can make Abigail's dream of becoming a star happen. So when Joe told him why we had to see L. B. right now, he picked up the phone.

My agent had followed us all the way, still not knowing anything. Now he saw Eddie Mannix and Ken McKenna hustling me into L. B. Mayer's office with Milton and Marge following and Joe and Nicky mooing behind us. The last I saw, he looked very pale.

L. B. Mayer didn't like to read. He had a storyteller named Harriet Frank who did it for him. She was telling him a story when we came in and the interruption made him angry. Even when everybody said I had this great story, it didn't help. He glared at me and said, "All right, all right! Tell it fast!"

Now I was the only one who knew I didn't have a good ending, but I knew Harriet Frank would know. So I needed a minute alone and I asked if I could have a drink. L. B. was surprised. "You drink in the morning?" I said I had a sore tooth and he told me the bar was in the far corner.

While I took the drink and tried to think, I heard the whispers about how I quit and then got this idea, that I wanted MGM to have it and not Fox, that it was miles better from *Oklahoma!* and then his whisper that this was crazy, it had never happened before and it better be good!

When I first told the idea to Joe, it took maybe ten seconds. Each telling since, including the barnyard noises and the laughs, had taken a little longer. When I told it now, it took ten minutes. But with L. B. glaring from the first minute, suddenly nobody helped with cackling or mooing or even laughing. It was just me and an ending I wasn't too sure of, and when I finished, he didn't say anything. He turned to Harriet Frank. We all did.

She looked like a thoughtful person. But as I waited, she thought for about thirty years and my whole life passed before my eyes the whole time. Then she smiled and said, "It will make a good musical, Mr. Mayer." So he stopped being angry and told me to go write it.

When everybody told him why I couldn't, he got angry again and asked how could he buy something in such a hurry that was only in my head and without even a title? So I said I would write a one-page outline and the title was *Summer Stock* and my agent was right outside.

The Broadway musical with Yip Harburg and Harold Arlen didn't work out. But that didn't bother my mother. Nobody she knew went to Broadway shows. But when *Summer Stock* opened at Radio City Music Hall, starring Judy Garland and Gene Kelly, everybody in Newark, NJ knew that L. B. Mayer didn't make a single move without me, that Judy and Gene were now my best friends and that I was trading in my "used" Pontiac for a brand new Cadillac.[2]

• • •

Sy Gomberg's recollection of "winging" the *Summer Stock* story all the way up to Louis B. Mayer appears to be based in fact, with some degree of embellishment. It's unlikely that in the seconds-long pitch to producer Pasternak, and then during a longer spiel to the head of the studio, that he was able to "nail down" virtually every detail of the plot. In fact, a six-page story treatment Gomberg wrote after he did his "song and dance" to the studio brass, presented the framework for the final film, but with plenty of details still to be ironed out, mostly likely in concert with his co-screenwriter, George Wells. There were also no stars attached to the story treatment or suggested in his outline as it was written prior to final casting.

In Gomberg's treatment, titled: "Spring Is Here," Garland's character is named Ann, not Jane, and her sister (Gloria DeHaven) is Jan, not Abigail. The part of the hapless farm supply store clerk fiancé played by Eddie Bracken is a banker named Morgan, not Orville. Marjorie Main's role as Esme is named Martha and is the family cook. When the troupe of aspiring singers, dancers, and actors set up shop on the farm and crash the stodgy and traditional community square dance, to the chagrin of the locals, Gomberg's outline describes the event as a "complete success," which in the film was deemed a disaster.

There is no mention of the comic sidekick Herb, played by Phil Silvers.

In a plot outline that never made the shooting script, Gomberg writes, "The Shakespearean actor [Hans Conried in the movie] allows a caravan of wandering gypsies to make off with most of the farm's stock." He also makes the story a love triangle battle for Abigail's affections between the leading man (Conried) and the director (Kelly).

At the story's conclusion, Gomberg has the "farm folk" enthusiastically embracing the show with some actually appearing it in and Conried's lead actor character returning to the farm (after abandoning the production) in a lesser role, having been replaced in the lead by the director (Kelly).

Gomberg's exaggeration of how *Summer Stock* seemed to spring out of his exuberant imagination as one extemporaneous ad-lib after another makes for good storytelling—he was a writer, after all. To hear him tell the genesis of the story is to bear witness to more tap dancing than Kelly did in the entire film. In fact, his entertaining recitation of the story's "build" from trying to impress a girl to sleep with him to captivating Pasternak and then winning over a skeptical Mayer is not unlike seeing a string of "topper" gags, one piled on top of the other in a great silent comedy from

Charlie Chaplin, Buster Keaton, or Harry Langdon—movies with which Gomberg would have been familiar as a child.

The ultimate truth about how *Summer Stock* was conceived, we feel, lies somewhere in between and is probably an amalgam of Gomberg's six-page treatment and his traveling dog-and-pony show to executives in the Thalberg Building, with some of the names and plot points updated in hindsight and for comic effect.

We can't be certain why Gomberg, for years, chose to relate how the story for *Summer Stock* came to be by telling anyone who asked about it the version recounted in the article he wrote for *Screenwriter Quarterly*. But perhaps an iconic line from another film, *The Man Who Shot Liberty Valance* (1962), offers a telling clue: "When the legend becomes fact, print the legend."

CHAPTER III

THE TALENT

It's up to You—Your Blood and Guts

THE VOICE: JUDY GARLAND

> This marvelous, God-given talent was put in the right spot with the wrong soul, spirit, wrong brain—wrong something that couldn't cope with it. Some part of her being was not ready for that great talent.[1]
>
> —DIRECTOR CHARLES WALTERS DESCRIBING HIS *SUMMER STOCK* STAR, JUDY GARLAND

BY THE TIME JUDY GARLAND MADE *SUMMER STOCK* IN 1950, HER YELLOW brick road and the dreams it symbolized had become filled with personal and professional potholes. As the new decade dawned, it was literally the end of the road for MGM's most bankable musical star. Perhaps never in film history has one actress embodied the hope and ambition of a single studio more than Judy Garland did starting in the mid-1930s—and at MGM, Hollywood's biggest and richest studio, no less.

Metro, thanks in no small measure to Judy's dewy Midwestern innocence and a rich contralto singing voice that belied her age, put a unique stamp on its musical films; a trademark that became the *sine qua non* to which every other studio measured itself from the 1930s to the 1950s (coincidentally, right up until around the time Judy was relieved of her duties at the studio in 1950). Billed as "the little girl with the big voice" when she toured the vaudeville circuit with her two older sisters, Judy really earned that stripe singing (and often introducing) cherished standards from the Great American Songbook during a career that featured indelible performances in more than thirty musical films.

Born Frances Ethel Gumm on June 10, 1922, to Ethel and Frank Gumm, Garland and her family moved from her birthplace in Grand Rapids, Minnesota (where her parents operated a silent movie theater) to Southern California in 1927. The Gumm Sisters groomed their act by performing at a variety of local venues with the youngest, nicknamed "Baby" or "Babe," typically commanding the most attention. Stage mother Ethel had the sisters performing at a breakneck pace, and in summer 1934, she secured a booking in Chicago, where headliner George Jessel caught the show and suggested a name change for the sisters from Gumm (too perilously close to "Glum," "bum," "crumb," and "dumb") to Garland.

Upon their return to Los Angeles and with a scrapbook full of positive notices, the sisters began making appearances in musical short films, with Judy generating the most interest from the studios, including Universal and MGM. It took at least three in-house MGM auditions from late 1934 to September 1935 before Garland *sans* her sisters signed the standard seven-year studio contract in September 1935 for $100 per week. That same year "Baby Gumm" took the first name Judy.[2]

Songwriter Burton Lane (*Finian's Rainbow, On a Clear Day You Can See Forever*) personally helped deliver Judy Garland to the world by championing her second MGM screen test. According to Garland historian John Fricke, studio chief Louis B. Mayer "had Judy tour the lot and sing for everyone."[3] In 1935, Lane had heard Judy perform with her sisters on the stage of New York's Paramount Theater and quickly arranged an audition for her. "I introduced Judy to the folks at MGM where she sang for the top studio brass for hours," Lane said. "In the crush and confusion of that memorable day, no one thanked me, including Judy.

"Flash forward six years later and I was assigned to write the score for *Babes on Broadway* (1941), co-starring Mickey Rooney and Judy. I was told by producer Arthur Freed to walk over to the sound stage and help the kids go through some of the songs. As we neared the rehearsal area, a little girl came running up and threw her arms around me. It was Judy. She apologized for not thanking me that day. 'I was so confused by all the attention,' she said. 'I can't thank you enough for what you did for me.'"[4]

Garland reported to MGM's Culver City lot for her first day of work on October 1, 1935. During her early years at the studio she was championed primarily by two people: Roger Edens, a musical composer/arranger and later associate producer who also joined the studio in 1935 and who immediately saw the potential in the studio's latest "property"; and Arthur Freed, an MGM contract composer who would soon become a full-fledged producer responsible for the studio's greatest output of successful musical films. Ironically, it would be ten months before Garland appeared in a feature film and that was in a "loan-out" to Twentieth Century-Fox for the musical trifle *Pigskin Parade* (1936), co-starring the future Tin Man of *The Wizard of Oz*, Jack Haley. In her first MGM feature, *Broadway Melody of 1938*, Garland, in a supporting role, stole the show with her heartfelt rendition of "Dear Mr. Gable: You Made Me Love You," a homage to the studio's biggest star, Clark Gable.

While she continued to toil in several other movies, MGM was busy at work preparing what was anticipated to be one of the studio's crowning achievements, the musical adaptation of L. Frank Baum's 1900 novel, *The Wonderful Wizard of Oz*. Hollywood lore has it that Louis B. Mayer was obsessed with prying Shirley Temple away from Fox to star as Dorothy Gale. Not true, says John Fricke: "The Oz property was purchased by MGM specifically as a showcase for Judy Garland. The legend that Shirley Temple was nearly cast (or preferred) as Dorothy Gale was a much-exaggerated elaboration of what was at most an unofficial and brief intra-trade discussion. The many script variations, and most importantly, the *Oz* songs, were written with Judy in mind."[5]

Arthur Freed, the uncredited associate producer on *Oz* (Mervyn LeRoy was the producer) and an accomplished songwriter in his own right, persuaded the studio to hire composer Harold Arlen and lyricist E. Y. Harburg to write the score. Freed proffered a different take on the casting story, indicating that Temple *was* seriously considered for the lead role. "I had a tough time in *The Wizard of Oz* to get her in the picture," said Freed, speaking of his desire to cast Garland as Dorothy Gale. "I got Yip Harburg and Harold Arlen to write the score. That was before Mervyn [LeRoy, the film's eventual producer] came into the picture. I wasn't the producer yet. L. B. [Mayer] had asked me and Goldwyn [Sam] who had owned this property. He never made it. They wanted Shirley Temple. I was stunned. Being a songwriter and knowing the wonderful songs that we had—Shirley could never do it. Finally, they couldn't get Shirley. But L. B. was with me. Nick Schenck [the head of MGM's parent company, Loews] said to me, 'You like Judy because you're a songwriter.' But finally, they OK'd Judy."[6]

The *Oz* score included the Academy Award–winning "Over the Rainbow." At early preview screenings of the film, studio executives thought the song "slowed down the picture." In fact, according to Fricke, the tune was briefly dropped after a second test screening. But Freed insisted that the song stay in. The studio executives relented, and Garland trilled an emblematic ballad that continues to define her career to this day.[7] *Oz* was released on Aug. 17, 1939, a year many consider to be a film pinnacle that saw the release of *Gone with the Wind, Stagecoach, Mr. Smith Goes to Washington,* and other classics. The reviews for the film were overwhelmingly positive but on its initial run it did not fully recoup its $2,777,000 production cost despite breaking attendance records throughout the country. It was only when CBS began to air *Oz* on TV beginning in 1956 that the film finally came into its own as an annual rite of passage for generations of school kids. And, to this day, *Oz*'s low-tech Kansas tornado (a muslin stocking hooked to a wind fan) still packs a more ominous wallop than any CGI-generated twister.

Although *Oz* set Garland on the road to superstardom and a lifetime of adulation, the continuous pressure of being in the limelight led to bouts of depression and the overuse of prescription drugs—the latter originally supplied by her mother when Garland was a preteen and subsequently continued by MGM executives and doctors. In addition to her commitments to MGM, Garland worked at a furious pace, making personal appearances on behalf of the studio and the war effort, recording eighty sides for Decca Records, and appearing in more than 200 network radio shows between 1935 and 1950.

"Judy was always at war with the studio," her husband Vincente Minnelli said. "She'd grown up there—had great resentments. Tough enough for a girl to pass from girlhood into womanhood, ordinarily, but when you do it in a goldfish bowl, like a studio and you're a star—it's very tough."[8]

In a revelatory article in *McCall's Magazine*, Garland recalled how the studio "helped" her survive the torrid pace of work by medicating her. "Metro thought they were raising me. They were just dreadful. They had a theory that they were all-powerful and they ruled by fear. What better way to make young people behave than scare the hell out of them every day.

"When we were in production [*Babes in Arms*, 1939] they had us working days and nights on end," she continued. "They gave us pep pills to keep us on our feet long after we were exhausted. Then they would take us to the studio hospital and knock us cold with sleeping pills—Mickey [Rooney] sprawled out on one bed and me on another. And then after four hours they'd wake us up and give us the pep pills again, so we could work another

72 hours in a row. Half the time, we were hanging from the ceiling, but it became a way of life for us. This sort of thing went on all the time I was at Metro, and it started when I was just 14 and the executives were concerned about my weight."[9] In that same article Garland wrote, "My inability to sleep was not MGM's fault. All my life I've never adjusted to sleeping at night and it began when I was a child working in theaters."[10]

Garland's staunchest supporter at MGM, producer Freed, said he had an almost "father-confessor" relationship with his young star: "I loved Judy. She came to me for drugs and I told her I can't get any. I don't know how to get them. I don't know if this was the time she had a big romance with Tyrone Power—after Rose [David Rose, her first husband, whom Garland married when she was nineteen]. Power was in the Army. One day she came in with a twenty-five-page letter she wrote to him." About her drug use, Freed said, "Everybody has a different story about when Judy got on the pills. I think she went to enough psychiatrists—they couldn't tell you."[11]

Coming off the success of *Oz*, the studio cast Judy in a series of movies opposite another MGM juggernaut, the explosive Mickey Rooney. Their partnership started with the 1937 movie *Thoroughbreds Don't Cry* and continued through nine other films. In 1944, she was cast in *Meet Me in St. Louis*, directed by Vincente Minnelli, the man who would become her second husband the following year. Garland was initially hesitant to take on the lead role of Esther Smith in the movie. "Judy didn't want to make that film, she wanted to do more sophisticated parts," said Minnelli. "She thought the teenage role of Esther Smith would set her career back twenty years. She asked Louis B. Mayer and Arthur Freed [the producer] to intercede for her but she couldn't get anywhere, so she came to the set the first day of rehearsal secure in the knowledge that she would at least make life miserable for 'this squirt director Minnelli from New York.'"[12] According to John Fricke, Minnelli's account of this story should be considered in context with her early reluctance to take on the role due to early, inferior script treatments.[13]

Although Garland may have harbored initial misgivings about starring in *St. Louis*, for Margaret O'Brien, who played Judy's kid sister Tootie, the movie was an unalloyed joy from start to finish: "Judy was just lovely to work with. People think of her as being kind of sad. She jumped rope with me and played hopscotch between takes. She was kind of a kid herself. She knew who she was. She was Judy Garland, for goodness' sake!"[14]

And who Garland was, according to Minnelli, was a protean talent the likes of which Hollywood had never seen before or since: "Not only could she cry on cue—one of the few persons: Vivien Leigh, Katharine Hepburn, among them. But you could go in, while she was being made up, and tell her 10 things that were new—you'd not know if you were getting through to her or not—but she'd go in and do every one of them perfectly. Remarkable. Quick study. And she could play a scene any one of 12 different ways."[15]

Garland's *Summer Stock* co-star, Gene Kelly, fresh off his Broadway triumph in Rodgers and Hart's *Pal Joey*, made his film debut opposite Garland in MGM's *For Me and My Gal* in 1942, two years before Garland's starring role in *Meet Me in St. Louis*. It would be the beginning of a close on- and off-screen relationship that would include Gene and Judy co-starring in two other films, *The Pirate* and *Summer Stock*. "One of the things he [Gene] always said was that Judy was invaluable and he couldn't have done it without her because he came from the stage and *For Me and My Gal* was his first film," said Kerry Kelly Novick, the only child of Kelly and his actress wife Betsy Blair. "There was a professional sense of indebtedness and she was a dear friend." At the Kelly-Blair Beverly Hills home after World War II, Garland and a regular stream of creative elites would drop in for weekend open houses that included competitive volleyball, barbeques, and impromptu performances in the Kelly living room.[16]

Despite the growing pressures of work and the accompanying stardom, Garland appeared in twenty films in the 1940s, including box-office hits *The Harvey Girls* (1946), *Easter Parade* (1948), and *In the Good Old Summertime* (1949). But dependence on prescription drugs and her fondness for alcohol was taking its toll by the latter half of the 1940s. It was about this time that another rising star at MGM, conductor, arranger, and songwriter André Previn, said he befriended Garland. Previn did some uncredited work on *The Pirate*. "I loved it," he said. "But audiences at the time didn't get the joke. I didn't like Gene in that movie. He was over-the-top. I loved the way Judy sang, but I have to say that when she read dialogue, especially when I look at it now, I always think she sounds like she's on the absolute knife's edge of hysteria. Even if she said, 'Could I have breakfast?' it made me very nervous."

Previn recalled, "She was a funny lady, very funny and she was great company. But you always knew that at any second she could go up in smoke. I took her out once. We went to see Chaplin's *City Lights* [originally released in 1931] before it was in general re-release at a little theater on La Brea Avenue. She wanted to see it, so we went. Halfway through it she said, 'Get me out of here! Get me out of here!' She was sweating and frightened and who knows why? I don't know about all of those stories about how they mistreated her at the studio—probably."[17]

As Garland's maladies grew, causing frequent production delays, she was replaced and her roles recast in several MGM productions, including *The Barkleys of Broadway* (1949) (Ginger Rogers), *Annie Get Your Gun* (1950) (Betty Hutton), and *Royal Wedding* (1951) (Jane Powell). In 1950, MGM decided to reteam Garland with Kelly and her *Easter Parade* director Charles Walters in *Summer Stock*, in an attempt to keep her career on track. "Judy emotionally was so attractive and so enticing to men because she had an inner thing that none of the rest of them had I think, before or since," said Kelly. "But you know that's the fan in me and part of the worker in me also, because having worked with her a lot, she was quick and bright and she could do more in a sentence or a look than . . . she was sort of a female Spencer Tracy."[18]

Summer Stock proved to be Judy's last film at MGM. She had appeared in twenty-eight features (including the loan-out to Twentieth Century-Fox in 1936 for *Pigskin Parade*) and several short subjects during her fifteen-year tenure at the studio. Eleven years after her unceremonious dismissal at MGM in 1950, her views on her span at Metro, and specifically on Louis B. Mayer, had softened. "He [Mayer] had moments of kindness and he followed them. I had just been thrown out of Metro, after 16 years. I was ill and I didn't have any money to go to a hospital. I went to L. B. Mayer and asked him if the studio would lend me some money. Mayer hadn't wanted to throw me out and he called Nick Schenck [the chairman of the board] in New York while I was in the office and asked if they could loan me some money. Schenck told him that they were not running a charity institution. Mayer hung up and said something strange and kind of marvelous: 'If they'll do this to you, they'll do this to me, too.' And they did, as you know. He lent me the money himself and I paid him back. [Mayer biographer] Bosley Crowther doesn't say anything about his kindness or the marvelous movies he did make. It's stylish to knock L. B. Mayer."[19]

After *Summer Stock* there would be other triumphs—Garland's 1954 Academy Award–nominated performance in *A Star is Born* and her legendary live concert appearances at the Palace and Carnegie Hall—amid corresponding lows. While unlucky in matrimony, with husband Minnelli, Garland had daughter Liza in 1946, and with her third husband Sid Luft (married in 1952), two more children, Lorna and Joey.

Although her much-heralded and now classic television variety series ended after only one season (1963–64), Garland, with a multitudinous fan base, was still in demand as an entertainer, playing dates around the world. But her personal life was as troubled as ever. After many separations, Garland divorced Luft in 1965. She quickly remarried—this time to actor Mark Herron. But that union lasted only a few months before dissolving. Garland wed former bandleader and club manager Mickey Deans in March 1969, just a few months before she died in London (where she was performing at the Talk of the Town nightclub) of an accidental overdose on June 22, 1969, at the age of forty-seven.[20]

"She needed men and I think this was the thing of her inferiority," said Arthur Freed. "I don't think her love affairs were that deep. Whether those men represented the father who left her so soon [her beloved father Frank died at age forty-nine in 1935 and his death exacted an untold emotional toll on Garland], but she needed men."[21]

In a 1967 interview, Garland talked about finding little solace in her "legendary" status and shared with the world the sorry state of the very human Judy Garland. "If I'm such a legend, then why am I so lonely? If I'm such a legend, then why do I sit at home staring at the damned telephone, hoping it's out of order, even calling the operator asking her if she's sure it's not out of order? Let me tell you, legends are all very well if you've got somebody around who loves you, some man who's not afraid to be in love with Judy Garland!

"Why should I always be rejected? Alright, so I'm Judy Garland. But I've been Judy Garland forever. Luft always knew this, and Minnelli knew it, and Mark Herron knew it, although Herron married me strictly for business reasons, for purposes of his own. He was not kind to me. But I bear them no malice. Sid Luft turned out to be a nice man, after all, and Vincente is also very nice. They've given me beautiful, talented children."[22]

While many stars from Hollywood's Golden Age have faded into the ether, Garland is a rare exception; decades after her death she continues to enjoy a large, almost cultlike worldwide fan base. Garland's *Summer Stock* director Charles Walters, who staged and appeared with Judy in her historic live Palace Theater shows in 1951, saw that devoted following close up: "She couldn't figure it out, so I don't know how the hell I can. After the show [at the Palace] she was getting dressed in a lovely evening gown to go to a big party. Somebody mentioned to us that the people were still standing out in the pie [the pie-wedge traffic island at Broadway and Seventh]. Judy said, 'I don't believe it. What do they want?' 'They just want to see you,' somebody said 'Well, shit,' said Judy. 'I'm going out the front door instead of the stage exit. If they want to see me, they're going to see me.' Well, the lobby was filled as was the pie. As we walked through the sea of humanity—not a word! She's getting into the limousine and says, 'What the hell is this, nobody's saying a goddamn word?' A silent tribute . . . I can't tell that without choking up."[23]

Saul Chaplin, who served as *Summer Stock*'s musical director and contributed to the score, worked closely with Garland and made this observation: "She led a troubled life and her troubles are in her voice. The emotion she was able to get through to an audience, she emanated a certain emotion; her vulnerability was in her voice. Put that together with a terrific sound, it's unbeatable.

"Not enough can be written about her towering talent. She was one of the greatest performers of all time. The other was Al Jolson. She made you believe every lyric. Even toward the end of her life, when her voice had lost a certain amount of quality and her vibrato had become uncontrollable, her audience found her exciting and moving. It's easy to predict that there will never be anyone like her. She was an original, and like all artists of that caliber, they come around only once."[24]

Let Gene Kelly, Garland's *Summer Stock* co-star, have the last word. "I've always thought she was the finest performer we've ever had in America. She was the quickest, brightest person I've ever worked with. In the days that I knew her, up until she began to get ill, she laughed all the time. To me, she was the best all-round performer. You couldn't say she could dance as well as a certain dancer; of course not. And maybe you prefer a certain singer to Judy, though I didn't and still don't, but all-around, when you put them together—acting, singing, dancing—she was just superb."[25]

THE HOOFER: GENE KELLY

Gene Kelly made every man believe he could dance,
and every woman *wish* that he would.[26]

DURING HOLLYWOOD'S GOLDEN AGE, THERE WERE DOZENS OF OUTSTANDING actors and actresses: Tracy, Stewart, Cagney, Cooper, Crawford, de Havilland, Hepburn, Davis. But when it came to the art of the dance, only two male names occupied that rarefied space of superstardom: Fred Astaire and Gene Kelly. And in the estimation of British theater critic and culture writer Sarah Crompton, "It is Kelly with the love of cinema itself, with his sure grasp of what the camera could do for dance, who probably had the greatest influence on film."[27]

Kirk Honeycutt, writing in the *New York Times* articulated Kelly's contribution to film dance this way: "Mr. Kelly learned to choreograph his musical numbers to be cut and edited without disturbing his audience's sense of motion and involvement. He structured his dances so his movement came toward the camera, to give them kinetic physical force. By placing vertical props on the stage for panning shots, he could increase the feeling of movement. Most of all, though, he tried to find ways of expressing character and resolving thematic or plot issues within his dances."[28]

Hollywood isn't cherished for its long memory. In fact, it's often derided as incestuous and infested with a particular brand of shark that gleefully devours those whose movies don't excel at the box office. However, even a town shot through with *schadenfreude* and as insecure and unapologetically larcenous as Hollywood can sometimes reach a meaningful consensus about real art. That happens to be the case concerning the legacy of song-and-dance man Kelly. He was and continues to be venerated everywhere in the film capital and around the world as a true original—no small achievement in a place with more than its fair share of poseurs and mere technicians.

While Fred Astaire hit the vaudeville boards with his sister Adele at the ripe old age of six, Kelly, in comparison, was a late bloomer. He was born August 23, 1912, and from an early age harbored dreams of one day playing professional baseball with his hometown Pittsburgh Pirates. The naturally athletic Kelly at age fifteen took to dance (as a way to meet girls, he would later say). In 1932, the dance studio started earlier by his mother as the Kelly School of Dance, where his younger brother Fred was also an instructor, was renamed the Gene Kelly School of the Dance.

Screen stardom was still a decade away. First, he graduated with an economics degree from the University of Pittsburgh before making his way to Broadway and scoring hits in William Saroyan's *The Time of Your Life* (1939) as Harry the Hoofer and then the manipulative title character in *Pal Joey*, the 1940 Rodgers and Hart classic. When he wasn't appearing on stage, Kelly picked up side assignments choreographing other shows in New York City. It was during Kelly's Broadway run in *Pal Joey* that he first met and was "discovered" by a teenaged Judy Garland when Garland was visiting New York during a brief vacation hiatus from MGM.

According to Garland's daughter, Lorna Luft, when her mother saw Kelly in the show, she was mesmerized by his talent. "And then when he heard my mother was there, he basically panicked and got incredibly nervous; she came backstage with a studio publicist and said: 'I want you for my next film.' Gene was totally flattered that she would make this decision before talking to the studio. Then she said: 'We're going to the Stork Club, would you like to go?' Gene told her that he couldn't afford to go. And my mother asked him what he wanted to do, and Gene said, 'Let's go pub crawling.' And they did."

Luft remembered her mother saying that together she and Kelly "ditched" her entourage, hit the bars, and got to know each other. "My mother was selfless in the sense of not bragging and she didn't like that in other people, either," Luft said. "She would never go around saying, 'Well, I discovered him.' Instead, she would say, 'Isn't he wonderful? We have so much fun together.'

"Gene was terrified on *For Me and My Gal*," Luft added, "because he had not done a film and mother told me that she guided him. She never coached—she would never use that word—when he went to her for advice."[29] Of course, Kelly and Garland could not know then that in a decade's time, their roles would be reversed and it would be Kelly shoring up an unsure Garland in *Summer Stock*.

It was from his earliest beginnings as a Broadway chorus boy and then leading man that Kelly decided he wanted to fuse the athleticism and grace of ballet with the more syncopated frenetic energy of tap and make the "hybridized" art form accessible to the masses. "As a Depression kid who went to school in very bad years, I didn't want to move or dance like a rich man," he said. "I wanted to do the dance of the proletariat, the movements of the people. I wanted to dress in a sailor suit or a pair of jeans. It was part of my social outlook."[30]

It's no surprise that in such films as *Anchors Aweigh* (1945), *On the Town* (1949), and his own ambitious homage to dance, *Invitation to the Dance* (1956), Kelly played the role of an enlisted gob. "The Navy made the best dance costume ever," he said. "The proportions, the fit, were perfect, unfussy shapes that didn't get in the way or break up the line of the body"—costumes like gabardine pants, knit vests, and full-cut shirts with spread collars (the latter resulted in Kelly's collaborating with the MGM wardrobe department on V-neck T-shirts, as well as a body shirt to keep his tails from flying out when he lifted his co-stars).[31]

"White socks are clean and they focus the eye on the feet," Kelly added. "Moccasins are cut to show the white socks. You tuck a sweater in so you can see the body move. Astaire and I always washed our hats and then trimmed the brims so that we didn't look like gangsters because we didn't play gangsters. But we did like hats. They're dancers' best props."[32] That belief can be seen in action in the simplicity of Kelly's costume in his "You Wonderful You" "squeaky board" solo number from *Summer Stock*—a yellow short-sleeved tapered collared shirt, powder blue cotton gabardine cuffed trousers, hemmed high enough to expose his white socks and two-tone loafers.

In addition to his prodigious gifts as a dancer, Kelly had that indefinable charisma (called "it" in the 1920s and "star quality" ever since) that lit up screens. With black Irish good looks that evoked silent screen heartthrobs like Ramon Novarro and Rudolph Valentino, and a hundred-kilowatt smile, Kelly radiated jauntiness.

It was while Kelly was choreographing at Billy Rose's Diamond Horseshoe that he hired an aspiring sixteen-year-old dancer from New Jersey, Betsy Blair, in 1940. The two became smitten and in 1941, shortly after Kelly had signed a Hollywood contract with producer David O. Selznick, they married. By all accounts, Kelly and Blair lived a modest life by Hollywood standards. The couple resided in a French Colonial farmhouse with red window shutters on Rodeo Drive in the Beverly Hills flatlands just south of Sunset Boulevard and tooled around town in a used Ford convertible. Their daughter Kerry was born in 1942, the year Kelly made his screen debut opposite Judy Garland in *For Me and My Gal*.

"All I know is that Betsy and I try to live our life as we think best," Kelly confided to *Modern Screen*. "We don't live for show; we don't throw great parties; we live simply and plainly according to our own tastes. We get on together because we see eye-to-eye on the fundamental things that count."[33]

The couple also shared a belief in progressive liberal politics. Kelly and Blair (who occasionally appeared in film roles) were both politically active as members of the Committee for the First Amendment, a group of A-list actors and directors who came out in support of the Hollywood Ten in 1947 (mostly screenwriters accused of the "crime" of being members or sympathizers of the Communist Party). The Ten refused to "name names" when they appeared before the House Un-American Activities Committee and eventually all served a one-year prison term for contempt of Congress. These hearings and accompanying sentences ushered in a dark period in show business history known as the Hollywood Blacklist.

Film historians and Kelly biographers Earl Hess and Pratibha Dabholkar wrote, "Kelly's politics stemmed less from political ideology and more from a basic desire to see everyone treated fairly despite their skin color, ethnicity, or social and economic distinctions."[34]

Kelly, an early social justice warrior, made the bold move in 1948 to cast the dancing Nicholas Brothers in the rousing "Be a Clown" routine from *The Pirate*. Kelly purposely integrated the gymnastic number into the film to prevent segregated theaters in the American South from cutting the sequence featuring the legendary African American dancers, a common practice in those days.

Fayard Nicholas recalled the moment when producer Arthur Freed called Kelly into his office one day and said: "'Gene, I've got the story that you can do with the Nicholas Brothers.' It was the script for *The Pirate*, but Arthur Freed [the producer] warned Kelly that any number he might do with us could be cut out when the picture played theaters in the South. Gene said: 'I don't give a damn! It'll play the same all over the world, so why do we have to just think about the South?' The movie played in the South and they never cut us."[35]

"It was the first time we did straight dancing . . . no tricks or tumbling or anything," said Harold Nicholas. "But it was interesting because the three of us synchronized our moves. Gene had seen us in New York and told us that some of the stuff we were doing was what he'd like to do."[36]

Although Kelly initially signed with Selznick, his contract was soon sold to MGM, a more logical home for his talents and a studio that in the 1940s was starting to reinvent the musical genre, mostly under the watchful eye of songwriter and producer Arthur Freed. At Freed's insistence, MGM was hiring many of the finest musical talents in front of and behind the camera (many mined from Broadway theater), including a young director named Vincente Minnelli. With the Freed-Minnelli-Garland collaboration of *Meet Me in St. Louis* in 1944, a new integrated model of story, song, and dance was perfected. "We were very serious at MGM about musicals. We thought we were progenitors of a new art form," said Kelly.[37]

In 1943, a young dancer Kelly knew from the Broadway chorus of *Pal Joey*, Stanley Donen, was recruited by MGM. The next year, Kelly, who was looking for an assistant on his loan-out to Columbia for *Cover Girl*, enlisted the services of Donen, and the two formed a productive collaboration that would last the next eleven years. After serving as Kelly's assistant, Donen received co-director credit (with Kelly) for *On the Town* in 1949. Two more films with Kelly would follow, the classic *Singin' in the Rain* and *It's Always Fair Weather* (1955).

Artistic differences between the two (chronicled in several biographies) have provided fodder for Hollywood gossip over the years; but it was truly a dream team collaboration that largely ran out of steam, with Donen embarking on a successful solo career as a director.

"Gene was ambitious, experienced, and single-minded, but probably less narrow in what he thought was good or bad in the theater and movies than I was," Donen said. "At the same time, I was extremely certain of what was good or bad. I was much less accepting or appreciative. I have enormous respect for Kelly in many ways, but we had disagreements over the way certain parts of films should be directed. Neither of us are good compromisers. Rodgers and Hart used to fight; Gilbert and Sullivan didn't speak to each other. Gene and I got along well compared to those people."[38] When asked to describe how the directorial duties were parsed between them on *Singin' in the Rain*, Donen said: "There is no way I can answer that question. Gene and I were co-directors and you can't divide that up any more than you could ask Hecht or MacArthur who wrote what in *The Front Page*."

Kelly, at least publicly, stayed above the fray and always spoke positively about his onetime collaborator. "I knew Stanley from Broadway. He was in

Pal Joey. We worked together frequently. He assisted me with choreography. After I returned to MGM [after *Cover Girl*], he asked if we could work together. We were very comfortable with one another. Usually a musical requires more cooperation and cohesion than other pictures. There is a plethora of things to do. I didn't want to handle all the chores myself. I needed somebody behind the camera who could provide insight."[39]

Like the heyday of the Hollywood musical itself, Kelly's mammoth creative contribution to the genre was relatively short-lived in years if not in influence. Not content to just appear on camera, Kelly was determined to bring screen dance to the next level. And with innovative routines in such box-office hits as *Cover Girl*, *Anchors Aweigh*, and the "Slaughter on Tenth Avenue" ballet with Vera-Ellen in *Words and Music* (1948), he did exactly that.

On the Town, which Kelly co-directed with Stanley Donen, was his all-time personal favorite musical mainly because it marked his directorial debut at MGM and the opening number, "New York, New York," and some establishing shots were filmed on location in New York City. "That was no small achievement back in 1949, especially when you consider the studio had a standing New York set that looked more authentic than parts of the real city," Kelly said.[40] After *On the Town*, Kelly was at the pinnacle of his creative powers. Two enduring masterpieces were to follow: *An American in Paris* in 1951 and *Singin' in the Rain* the following year, Sandwiched in between came *Summer Stock*, his third and final film with Judy Garland.

Singin' in the Rain, perhaps Kelly's greatest film and a benchmark by which all other musicals are measured, is a treasure trove of great numbers, but the "Moses Supposes" dance with Kelly and Donald O'Connor tapping out a rhythmic Morse Code like a couple of pneumatic drills, never fails to electrify audiences. "Donald and I rehearsed that dance for days, but most critics dismiss it as a zany Marx Brothers romp," Kelly said. "They remember the clowning around with the vocal coach that precedes the number, but not the dance itself."[41]

Kelly, in a 1994 interview with the authors, said history continued to be rewritten to the present day, including facts on his most popular film—the misinformation ranging from an erroneous birthdate in a popular biography of his life to a German journalist who reported that MGM studio chief Louis B. Mayer "foisted" Debbie Reynolds on Kelly as his co-star in *Singin' in the Rain*. "That is patently untrue," Kelly said. "Mayer wasn't even at the studio in 1952 when we shot the picture."[42]

Kelly's third and final collaboration with Donen came in 1955's *It's Always Fair Weather*, which gave André Previn his first opportunity to take full control of every musical aspect in the film, including writing the score, words, and music. "I liked Gene very much, but he wasn't as pleasant to be with as Stanley," said Previn. "As long as things went his [Kelly's] way, he was fine. But you had to do it his way. With Stanley you could argue and discuss it. There was a dance with garbage can lids and I wrote, at least for that time, some pretty wild music and Gene said, 'Jesus, Andrew, I don't like that.' And Stanley said, 'Leave him alone, it's perfect for that number,' and he talked him into it, otherwise Gene would have thrown it out like he did Michael Kidd's big solo number, 'Jack and the Beanstalk.'" Previn was referring to a solo dance performed by Kidd that was left on the cutting-room floor because it reportedly slowed the flow of the picture. "Bullshit!" said Previn. "Michael really stole that part of the picture and Gene said very calmly, 'No, not in my movie.'"[43]

Meanwhile, the "idyllic" marriage of Kelly and Blair that *Modern Screen* magazine described in 1950 was eroding, and in 1957, the couple was granted a divorce. In 1960, Kelly married his longtime dance assistant (and a featured dancer in *Summer Stock*), Jeanne Coyne, who between 1948 and 1951, had been married to Stanley Donen. The couple had two children, Bridget and Timothy. Coyne died of leukemia in 1973. Kelly married his third wife Patricia Ward in 1990. She had first met Kelly in 1985 at the Smithsonian Institution in Washington, DC, when he was the host/narrator and she the writer for a television special on Herman Melville, the author of *Moby-Dick*.

In an issue of the *New Yorker*, Pulitzer Prize–winning author John Updike, in a tribute to Kelly, cited *On the Town* as his favorite movie, too. However, he lamented the fact that Kelly rarely seemed to pair up with a female partner to good advantage, the way Fred Astaire did throughout his career.[44] "I thought Updike did a good job of summing me up," Kelly said, "but he should know that the roles I was given were way different from Fred's. The mode of dance in the 1940s and 1950s was no longer ballroom like it was with the Fred and Ginger pictures in the 1930s." In spite of such comments, ample evidence exists to dispel the notion that Kelly's best dances were solo numbers. "My few quick turns with Rita Hayworth in *Cover Girl* to those beautiful strains of 'Long Ago and Far Away' were akin to the kind of dancing Astaire did," Kelly said.[45]

For Cyd Charisse, who danced with both men, comparing Astaire and Kelly was a specious, ultimately futile exercise in empty rhetoric, like comparing an apple to an orange. "Gene was more the creative type and not shy and retiring at all," she said. "Fred created his own dances, but Gene's ambition extended far beyond the dance numbers, to directing pictures—like *Singin' in the Rain* and *It's Always Fair Weather*—two of the pictures we did together. Gene wanted to be behind the camera as well as in front of the camera. It was more of a difference in personality; they were both geniuses as far as talent went."[46]

Behind the camera, Vincente Minnelli directed the cinema's two greatest dancers, Astaire and Kelly, in their only routine together (not counting *That's Entertainment, Part II* in 1976), "The Babbitt and the Bromide" from *Ziegfeld Follies* (1946). It stands as a unique historical pairing of two legendary hoofers with vastly different styles who were in their artistic prime—a curio forever captured in the time capsule of film. "The rehearsals were maddening," Minnelli explained. "Astaire would demonstrate an idea for a step and ask Kelly what he thought of it. Kelly would say, 'fine, great, swell.' They tried to convince each other and be so polite. That dance took three weeks to rehearse, but it turned out well. Fred Astaire is lighter than air, you know, and Gene is earthier. Both are perfectionists to the nth degree. It was a fascinating thing to witness."[47]

Leslie Caron, a Kelly discovery, made her screen debut in *An American in Paris*, directed by Minnelli. Despite Kelly's aspirations as a director, he and Minnelli forged a successful collaboration. "Gene would be the one who would place me, turn me around and direct me," said Caron. "I don't remember Vincente saying much except, 'That looks good, angel.' I knew he was on the set, but he let Gene do the musical numbers." Although Caron shared the screen with both Kelly and Astaire, she wouldn't rise to the bait when asked who she preferred as a partner. "It's not an apt comparison," she said. "Some people prefer Gene, some prefer Fred. They both had a distinctly different style. For me, Gene was paternal, fraternal, and generous. He was a born father and protected and advanced the people he liked."[48]

Despite the fact that both dancers had wildly divergent styles, and the admission by Astaire in the movie *That's Entertainment!* (1974) that "More than any other star, I think, Gene Kelly became the symbol of the MGM musical of the 1950s," niggling comparisons between the two men linger to this day.

After the demise in the 1950s of the Hollywood musical as a staple form of entertainment, for the next three decades, Kelly continued to direct, act in non-musical roles and appear in television specials and as a guest-star in shows from *The Muppets* to *The Love Boat*. Recognized as a one-of-a-kind artist, he accepted well-deserved accolades, including the American Film Institute Life Achievement Award and the Kennedy Center Honors.

Kelly admitted that, overall, movie musicals were largely icons of the past. Their decline was due perhaps to audiences that just can't bring themselves to suspend disbelief anymore when an off-camera orchestra begins to swell moments before a song number. However, others saw the original MTV music videos, with their quick-cut camerawork geared to short attention spans, as the modern-day spawn of old-time musical numbers. Kelly agreed with that premise. "Film editors have become the choreographers today," he said. "Everything is 'bam!' a tight shot of a shoulder, a leg, half a pirouette, an ass. In my day, editors were simply called 'cutters'; now a whole musical can succeed or fail based on the editing."[49]

Toward the end of his life and before suffering a series of debilitating strokes, Kelly often made public appearances to adoring fans where he answered questions from the audience and screened clips from his classic dance routines. He died in his sleep on February 2, 1996. But his musicals will always be around, emblematic as they are of a peculiar brand of sunny, can-do optimism that helped define the American Century.

THE MILQUETOAST: EDDIE BRACKEN

EDDIE BRACKEN WAS BORN TO GET LAUGHS, FIRST WITH HIS FAMILY IN vaudeville, then in movies like *The Miracle of Morgan's Creek* and *Hail the Conquering Hero*, directed by the high priest of screwball comedy, Preston Sturges, and still later in a string of theater performances that continued up until his death at home in Glen Ridge, New Jersey, just across the Hudson River from Midtown Manhattan in 2002 at the age of eighty-seven. "I feel like the character and persona he created in Hollywood is one of those: 'Oh yeah, *that* guy!'" said actress Christiane Noll, who worked with Bracken in stage productions at the Paper Mill Playhouse in New Jersey near the end of the actor's life. "People who have any familiarity with Golden Age movies may not know Eddie Bracken by name, but they *know* Eddie Bracken."[50]

One look at the actor was all you needed to know that standing there in a perpetual worried squint was the perfect comic foil—diffidence personified. And if that wasn't enough, Bracken could pratfall in the best tradition of physical comedy—think a slightly taller Buster Keaton sans the "Great Stone Face" deadpan but with the concerned look of an innocent about to be overwhelmed by impending and unavoidable pandemonium. And there were few better who could wring pathos from buffoonery.

No one loved a laugh-getter better than Sturges, which is why the director cast Bracken as the lead (not his usual supporting character role) in two seminal 1940s comedies: *The Miracle of Morgan's Creek* and *Hail the Conquering Hero*, both released in 1944. And to guarantee that the laughs would be sure-fire, Sturges also enlisted William Demarest, another veteran vaudevillian better known to Baby Boomers as Uncle Charley on TV's *My Three Sons*. "Nobody knew comedy better than Sturges," Bracken said, "and no one was zanier than Bill Demarest. He was so stern most of the time that when he did a sight-gag like trying to kick Betty Hutton in the pants but falling on his ass [a running gag in *Morgan's Creek*], it was even funnier because it was so unexpected. Working with Sturges was like going to a party—games all the time."[51]

In *Summer Stock*, Bracken steals the movie from the movie's de facto comedian Phil Silvers. Although the film contains explosive dances by Gene Kelly and Judy Garland's legendary "Get Happy" number, Bracken registers memorably as Garland's wimpy fiancé, Orville Wingait, a winsome store clerk plagued with chronic sniffles from hay fever who constantly defers to his domineering alpha male dad (Ray Collins). "That was a favorite film of mine, working with Judy," Bracken said. "She never could seem to keep a straight face around me, though. She'd crack-up laughing constantly. We had so much fun as the mismatched pair."[52]

Born February 7, 1914, in New York City, Bracken grew up the youngest of three brothers in Astoria, Queens. While still in elementary school, he began appearing as "the rich kid" in the New York Kiddie Troupers, a series of silent movie shorts filmed in New York.[53] Bracken never graduated from grammar school and by the age of five was conveying himself via New York's subways to and from outlying theaters. Reminiscing about those early years, Bracken said his main advantage over college students was that he *knew* he didn't know and, therefore, would never stop trying to learn. At sixteen, Bracken hitchhiked to Hollywood (it took him eleven days, once bedding down in a small-town jail to spend the night). After ten weeks of being rejected by every major movie studio, Bracken returned to New York—this time on a bus.[54]

In 1933, Bracken was cast in the Broadway production of *The Lady Refuses*, which closed in a week. His big break came in 1936 when director/producer George Abbott cast him in *Brother Rat*, a comedy about life at the Virginia Military Institute. Three years later, Abbott once again came calling and picked Bracken to star in *Too Many Girls*, a Rodgers and Hart musical in which Bracken introduced the classic ballad, "I Didn't Know What Time It Was." A year later Bracken was cast in the movie version of the play, marking his ostensible debut in motion pictures. He had finally caught Hollywood's eye.[55] "It was all about pace," Bracken said, when describing the Abbott touch that turned so many productions into pure gold. "I think the best line he ever gave me was: 'Get on with it! Don't work with it too hard, because this may be a very bad play and we don't want the people to realize it.' So the best way to do it is to get it over with as fast as you can. I think Abbott gave me that timing."[56]

During his early days under contract to Paramount Studios, Bracken found himself in competition for parts with the studio's comic heavyweight, Bob Hope. "Which was ridiculous because we're nowhere near alike," Bracken said. "And then we did *Caught in the Draft* (1941) together, and Louella Parsons [gossip columnist] said I stole the picture, so he refused to work with me again."[57] "I had been introduced to Louella and she said to me, 'Well, now, if you keep your nose clean around here I'll help you all

I can.' I said to her, 'I don't need you, ma'am.' I didn't know who she was. And she thought that was fresh, but nevertheless enjoyable for her, because nobody had ever had the guts to talk to her that way."[58]

Doubtless his strongest and most indelible roles during that wartime era were the two successive comedies he made with Sturges. Bracken made four films with dynamo Betty Hutton, including *The Miracle of Morgan's Creek*, which is on most critics' shortlist of the greatest comedies (screwball or otherwise) ever made. "I had an awful lot of fun with her, she was a regular guy," Bracken said. "In fact, I looked upon Betty as another guy. I mean she's very feminine and there are no problems with her at all, but she was a tomboy. We would pitch pennies and wrestle and just have a ball together."[59]

In *Hail the Conquering Hero*, Sturges cast Bracken as Woodrow Truesmith, a young man filled with patriotic fervor who tries to enlist in the Marines but is rejected because of his chronic hay fever (the same allergy that would hamper his character of Orville Wingait six years later in *Summer Stock*). Due to a series of screwball misunderstandings, he's welcomed back to his hometown as a war hero. It was the kind of situation that had been exploited successfully in the silent film era by Harold Lloyd, a comedian Bracken admired.[60]

Bracken was an inveterate theater performer logging thousands of hours in Broadway productions and national touring companies. In the 1950s he was Tom Ewell's replacement in the road show version of *The Seven Year Itch*; in the 1960s he took over Art Carney's role in *The Odd Couple*. In the 1970s he joined Carol Channing on tour in *Hello, Dolly!* And in the 1980s he played the devil (Mr. Applegate), the role Ray Walston made famous in *Damn Yankees* and which Bracken's old mentor George Abbott had originally directed on Broadway. "I'm the theater's No. 1 takeover guy for everybody," he said in an interview with the Associated Press in 1966. "It's a great compliment to be asked to replace such a variety of performers." Bracken added that he didn't mind the long hours. "I'm only tired until the curtain goes up."[61]

"If I repeated every performance I did on stage without taking a day off, it would take me thirty-three years," he said in an interview given thirty years later. When asked what the secret was of his longevity, Bracken replied: "Breathing."[62]

During his incredibly long and prolific career, Bracken appeared in dozens of TV shows and in movies as recent as *National Lampoon's Vacation* in 1983, in which he portrayed Mr. Wally, the proprietor of Wally World, and 1992's *Home Alone 2: Lost in New York*. But we, like most others, prefer to see Bracken with his talent in full flower in the hands of a great director—like Sturges and, later, Charles Walters in *Summer Stock*—men who knew exactly how to showcase it.

THE INGÉNUE: GLORIA DEHAVEN

IN *SUMMER STOCK*, GLORIA DEHAVEN PLAYS JUDY GARLAND'S SPOILED younger sister Abigail, who spurns a life of toil and long days working the family farm for a chance at fame and glamour on the stage. But like her character in the film, DeHaven's dream of success as a standalone "triple threat" (an actress who could also sing and dance) was never fully realized. By 1950, DeHaven's ten-year tenure at her home studio MGM, like Garland's, was reaching a nadir. In fact, after *Summer Stock*, DeHaven would appear in only five more films in the 1950s (none of them at MGM) and not make another screen appearance until 1976's *Won Ton Ton, the Dog Who Saved Hollywood*.

Of her part in *Summer Stock* as Garland's kid sister, DeHaven had this to say: "Prior to that, we were just very good friends, but I'd never worked with her. So to film with her was . . . like a treasure for me, because she was the most incredible person. The funniest woman I'd ever been around. I mean, forget any stand-up comic or comedienne you want to talk about it; she was hysterical. Great sense of humor. [And she] could make you cry faster than anybody in the world; I mean she was an actress—superb. And just a terrific lady with a terribly mixed-up life. Everything seemed going in wrong directions."[63]

Between 1940 and *Summer Stock*, DeHaven, with her pert good looks and perky persona, was featured in a total of eighteen films; only two, including *Step Lively* in 1944 with Frank Sinatra, were loan-outs to other studios. That same year she was voted as the third most likely to become a "star of tomorrow."[64] Why then was she pigeonholed into the secondary tier of MGM contract players during that decade and eventually fall out of favor completely at the studio she had called home for a decade just when the MGM musical was reaching its zenith in sophistication and when contemporary starlets like June Allyson and Jane Powell were being groomed for leading roles and full-fledged stardom?

DeHaven's 1944 marriage to actor John Payne (thirteen years her senior) presents a clue. The union did not receive the all-important benediction of MGM patriarch Louis B. Mayer and, as a possible act of retribution, DeHaven was relegated to mostly supporting parts. What's more, when she was cast as one of the leads (the college siren) in Arthur Freed's 1947 production of *Good News* (which also marked the directorial debut of Charles Walters), DeHaven refused to accept the role and was placed on suspension. She was subsequently replaced in the part by Patricia Marshall. These acts of defiance by a young starlet who hadn't proven herself as a box-office draw didn't exactly enamor her to studio executives.

The final straw might have occurred the following year when she was cast in a lead role opposite Mickey Rooney in the ambitious flop *Summer Holiday*, a musical interpretation of the Eugene O'Neill play *Ah, Wilderness!* The movie's financial fizzle also led to the exit of studio mainstay and former box-office champ Rooney. Regardless of her checkered tenure at MGM, DeHaven would later cite *Summer Holiday* as her favorite film.

Word of marital problems between DeHaven and Payne surfaced publicly in 1948 when Hollywood gossip columnist Hedda Hopper wrote that she was "taken aback" at the news of the couple's separation. "I wish I could tell you what happened," DeHaven told Hopper. "John's made three pictures in a row and we've been having all kinds of differences."[65] Her marriage to Payne ended in divorce in 1950, the year of *Summer Stock*'s release. DeHaven would marry two more times, including a brief union with Martin Kimmel, the founder of Kimco Realty Corporation, the largest builder of strip malls in the United States, and have four children.

Despite never attaining the pinnacle of stardom, DeHaven remembered her years at MGM fondly. "You couldn't wait to go to work, and by the end of the day you didn't want to go home. You were taught by the most extraordinary people. There were doctors and dentists there for you. They furnished you with clothes, they did your hair. If you had to go out, they gave you an escort. Mickey Rooney was my escort for a while."[66]

DeHaven seemed destined for a career in show business. Born July 23, 1925, her parents, Carter and Flora DeHaven, were seasoned vaudeville performers (Gloria would portray her mother in the 1950 film *Three Little Words* starring Fred Astaire). Carter became close friends with Charlie Chaplin, which led to him serving as assistant director on *Modern Times* (1936). DeHaven and her friend Gloria Delson paid a visit to the filming location in

1934. "I visited my father on set one day with a girlfriend of mine. Chaplin spotted me. It was well-known he liked the shall-we-say 'younger women.'"[67]

"Chaplin needed two kids to play Paulette Goddard's ragamuffin sisters ... she said, 'These kids are perfect' and sent us to [the dressers]. All we had to do was wear tattered clothes, eat bananas and do big takes. I thought, if this is show business, count me in."[68]

In 1939, DeHaven's older brother Carter Jr. brought his kid sister to see his friend, bandleader Bob Crosby (Bing's brother), which eventually landed her a singing gig on the big band circuit. That was followed with a stint singing for the Jan Savitt Orchestra before she caught the attention of a Hollywood talent scout. She was soon signed to a contract at MGM and given a featured role in the 1943 musical *Best Foot Forward* starring Lucille Ball. The following year, with the full force of the MGM publicity machine behind her, she was being dubbed as the new starlet destined for movie fame. "She's lovely, versatile, a sure-fire combination for stardom. She's Gloria DeHaven, Miss Glorious!" crowed the *Toronto Sun*.[69]

The fan magazines were also effusive about this young new find. "She jumped from a bandstand to one of the leading roles in *Best Foot Forward*—and a seven-year contract!" *Movieland* magazine breathlessly exclaimed. "Her subsequent appearances in *As Thousands Cheer* (1943), *Broadway Rhythm* (1944) and *Two Girls and a Sailor* (1944) have proved that Gloria is not just another cutie with a voice and a figure. She can act, too!"[70] In MGM's *Three Little Words*, a biopic of songwriters Bert Kalmar (played by Fred Astaire) and Harry Ruby (Red Skelton), DeHaven, in a brief cameo as her mother Flora, sang a song her mother had introduced decades before and which had become in the interim a standard. "I'm only in it for about five minutes," she said. "I sang 'Who's Sorry Now,' which my mother introduced at the Palace Theater. I do that song in my club act."[71]

In 1980, DeHaven made the news, not for a film, TV or stage appearance, but because she lost about $200,000 worth of jewelry when her suite at Chicago's Blackstone Hotel was burglarized. She was in town appearing in a play with fellow MGM alum Van Johnson.[72] When prodded later in life to write her memoir, DeHaven steadfastly declined. "Oh no!" she said. "The only books that sell are kiss-and-tell. I don't want people flipping through the pages of my life."[73] For DeHaven, her film roles were public offering enough. She died on July 30, 2016, at the age of ninety-one.

THE NATURAL: MARJORIE MAIN

IN *SUMMER STOCK*, VETERAN CHARACTER ACTRESS MARJORIE MAIN PLAYS Esme, and helps Judy Garland hold down the fort, or in this case, the farm, as her trusty (albeit flinty) housekeeper. If it appears that Main likely performed this role in her sleep, she probably did. In two earlier Garland films, *Meet Me in St. Louis* and *The Harvey Girls*, she portrays characters that are essentially variations of Esme, a dutiful-yet-tough-talking confidante and sounding board. While most of her on-screen portrayals didn't stretch the acting chops for the actress with the raspy voice and tumbledown hairdo, they were foundational to the Main "brand" she established in more than eighty film roles from 1931 to 1957—friendly and reliable but with a touch of sass.

Said one producer about her critic-pleasing performances: "She saved many a bad picture and made the good ones better."[74] In an article from *Hollywood Magazine*, the writer described Main as "The one and only exponent of gravel-throated, feminine gumption in the whole film industry."[75]

Born Mary Tomlinson on a farm about twenty miles south of Indianapolis on February 24, 1890, she took to acting at an early age despite her minister father's misgivings. When exactly she changed her name and how she morphed from Mary Tomlinson to Marjorie Main is in dispute. According to one source, it was around 1913, when touring, that she adopted the name because the alliteration of the consonants in the first and last names made "it easy to remember" and would avoid embarrassing her rather prudish family.[76] Another source said that she and her husband together came up with the stage name Marjorie Main, the last name taken from author Sinclair Lewis's novel *Main Street*.[77]

It was while touring the Chautauqua Circuit (a social movement that employed performers and lecturers to bring education and culture to far-flung communities) in a Shakespearean repertory company that Main met her future husband, Dr. Stanley LeFevre Krebs, a psychologist, salesman, and lecturer twenty-six years her senior. They married in 1921 and he died of cancer in 1935 at the age of seventy-one. Main never remarried.

The actress recalled her awkward courtship of Krebs. "It was because of my voice that I felt I could get Dr. Krebs, a lecturer with our traveling Chautauqua to look in my direction if I really wanted him to. And I did want him to. I thought he was awfully nice. So one night upon leaving the show, I shouted at the doctor that I thought he was the smartest man I had ever heard talk. He turned all right. The raucous sound of my voice scared even me. I turned, too, to disappear as quickly as I could, and I fell flat on my face in a large, soupy mud puddle. The doctor and I were married shortly after."[78]

Main toured vaudeville, which included playing the Palace Theater in New York City with legendary juggler and comedian W. C. Fields in a sketch titled "The Family Ford." In 1927, what would be Main's lifetime of matronly roles was cemented early on when she was cast as Mae West's mother (although she was only three years older than West) in the stage play *The Wicked Age*. Her film debut came in 1931 in *A House Divided* starring Walter Huston, the first of several films she appeared in directed by William Wyler. The flurry of small roles that followed, many filmed in New York City, gave Main an early tutorial to performing in front of a camera.

Her biggest stage success came in 1935 when she notched 460 consecutive performances of *Dead End* on Broadway playing Humphrey Bogart's mother. She reprised the role two years later in William Wyler's film adaptation of the Sidney Kingsley stage play, which also marked the first appearance of the "Dead End Kids," who would gradually become film stars in their own right as "The Bowery Boys." Main feared she would be permanently typecast as the forlorn gangster mother and itched to show her comedic chops.

She did just that in 1939, when she appeared in George Cukor's all-female film *The Women*. From that time on, most of her roles were comedic, which was her personal preference. "It [comedy] comes kind of easy, from remembering some of the honest and quaint characters back on the farm," she said. "And I might say, a sight more natural. I just unconsciously sort of blow into things with a bluster. I always have. Why, I'm telling you, if they dressed me up to play in society, I bet I'd keep bumping into all the butlers and forever be stumbling up and down staircases. I don't have to do an awful lot of acting to appear kind of bungly."[79]

In 1940, and with the standard seven-year MGM contract in hand, the studio teamed Main with veteran actor Wallace Beery, hoping to recapture the on-screen chemistry Beery enjoyed years earlier with Marie Dressler. Between 1940 and 1949 they appeared in seven films together, most were profitable and featured Beery with significantly higher screen billing and compensation.

Hollywood columnist Hedda Hopper called MGM's move to make Main the next Marie Dressler "a mistake." "Marjorie's too great of an actress in her own right to have to follow in anyone's footsteps," Hopper wrote. "Of course, I wouldn't want to see her give up her raucous characterizations entirely. The screen would lose by that, too. But please studio and public, remember *Dead End*, and don't forget that Marjorie's got more than the ability to swat Wally Beery over the head with a boot." [80]

As was common during the studio system era, Main was contracted by MGM, but during down times, if given the opportunity, the studio would loan her out to a competitor at a higher price than they were paying her and pocket the surplus cash. In the case of Main this was fortuitous in 1947, when MGM sent her across town to Universal to co-star with Claudette Colbert and Fred MacMurray in the romantic comedy *The Egg and I*. Appearing as the stars' cornpone neighbor, in that film (and in her subsequent role of Ma Kettle opposite Percy Kilbride as Pa Kettle) Main earned her only Oscar nomination and launched the *Ma and Pa Kettle* franchise that many said helped keep Universal solvent from the late 1940s into the 1950s. At first, Main balked at committing to a series, but her home studio, MGM, saw dollar signs and continued to loan her to Universal to make the pictures, typically at a pace of one a year.

Since she was earning a fixed weekly salary from MGM, she did not share in the huge profits the series pulled in for Universal or the significantly higher paycheck co-star Kilbride received, but she would later admit that the Ma Kettle character was her favorite (and most career-defining) part and "good for a lot of laughs, and I would rather make people laugh than anything else."[81]

Brett Halsey played the Kettles' oldest son Elvin in 1954's *Ma and Pa Kettle at Home*. He remembered Main as professional, but aloof when the camera was not rolling. "When we were making the picture, she wasn't well," he said. "When we weren't shooting, she was mostly in her trailer. She had some sort of kidney problem, if I recall. When she was on the set there was always a honeywagon [portable toilet] nearby. When on the set, she was kind and nice and helpful, but we never established a personal relationship because when she wasn't working, she was trying to rest."[82]

Richard Eyer, a child actor during the 1950s, also appeared in *Ma and Pa Kettle at Home* and one later installment of the franchise. He concurred with Halsey that Main was sequestered in her sound stage trailer during much of the shoot, but the buzz around the set was "maybe she was nipping a little bit."[83] Main was known as a teetotaler, so Halsey's health-issue conjecture seems far more plausible as the reason she maintained a distance from her coworkers.

At variance with Halsey's and Eyer's memories of Main as retiring and distant, Carleton Carpenter, who appeared in *Summer Stock* with Main, remembered the actress as "a hoot" and "kind of silly." "My mother's name was Main," said Carpenter, "and Marjorie had pictures taken of me in front of her dressing room. Back in Vermont, where I was from, in the local newspaper, they printed the picture of Marjorie and me saying she *wasn't* the Main who was my mom! She was a special lady. Every time she was walking through the mud, she had this girl that would always be on hand to do her hair—so *un*-Marjorie Main. I also remember she had a big car and kept groceries in it."[84]

Hollywood Magazine described her modest lifestyle during the 1940s: "She lives in what is unquestionably the most modest apartment of any actress in Hollywood, and she keeps it up to snuff with her own two hands. She's dead set against the use of tobacco and alcohol. By arrangement with Louis B. Mayer, the boss, you'll never see her touch the stuff on the screen."[85]

Main filmed the final Kettle film, *The Kettles on Old McDonald's Farm*, in 1957, and a year later made her final appearance before a camera in a guest-starring role on the popular TV western *Wagon Train*. From that point on, Main became reclusive, shunning all film and TV offers and even most interview requests. Her last public appearance was in 1974 when Main, then eighty-four, was introduced onstage with other MGM alumni at the studio's golden anniversary charity world premiere of *That's Entertainment!* in Los Angeles. She died the following year of cancer.

"Character actors are best, I believe, when they portray characters that give them a chance to draw on their own experiences, backgrounds and observations," Main once told an interviewer for a story that eventually found its way into an historical society quarterly published in her Indianapolis hometown. "Imagine me trying to play a society woman!"[86] Throughout a long career, Main followed her own canny instincts and in doing so etched dozens of memorable performances that were as earthy as the farm folk she grew up with in the Midwestern heartland.

THE "SECOND BANANA": PHIL SILVERS

IN 1951, COMEDIAN PHIL SILVERS STARRED IN THE BROADWAY HIT *TOP Banana*. However, in his two film appearances with Gene Kelly, *Cover Girl* and *Summer Stock*, the high-domed, bespectacled comic played the ultimate second banana, providing a dollop of over-the-top burlesque-style comic relief as Kelly's sidekick. Whether it was his character of Genius in *Cover Girl* or Herb in *Summer Stock*, Silvers infused comic levity into the roles and acted as a counterbalance to the primacy Kelly had as the romantic lead in each movie.

"Gene did a lot for Phil in both *Cover Girl* and *Summer Stock*, and they were great friends from then on," remembered Silvers's first wife, Jo-Carroll Dennison. "We were at Gene's house often and had a great relationship. Phil loved Gene. He brought things out of Phil. Phil didn't know that he could dance, but in *Cover Girl* Gene taught him to be a good dancer."[87]

Born minus the "s" as Phil Silver on May 11, 1911, in Brooklyn, New York, like so many other Borscht Belt comics from that era, Silvers's penurious childhood was a mad scramble from the get-go. "I could put my socks on from either end," he joked.[88] And with seven siblings, for Silvers it was often a case of the squeakiest wheel getting the grease. With his boy soprano voice, Silvers was spotted performing at age twelve in Coney Island by vaudeville impresario Gus Edwards, who specialized in kid acts and discovered such names as Eddie Cantor, Walter Winchell, and George Jessel. Silvers signed on with *Gus Edwards' Protégés of 1923*.

By the early 1930s, with vaudeville languishing, Silvers teamed with the future Oscar winner and *Chico and the Man* television star Jack Albertson and toured with Minsky's Burlesque, which was considered a low form of variety act comedy. Silvers honed his comic persona working Minsky's chain of burlesque theaters situated primarily in big East Coast cities. "The only chance you had for individuality was your own improvisation; new facets of character or voice; bits of business," he said. Silvers's style departed from traditional burlesque because he shunned using zany, outlandish costumes and comedic gimmicks like sight gags to generate laughs. However, one emblematic trademark—his horned-rimmed eyeglasses—made its appearance and became part of Silvers's signature look, a "prop" as identifiable with the comedian as the greasepaint mustache of Groucho Marx.[89]

In 1939, Silvers won a small part in a Broadway show called *Yokel Boy*, impressing audiences and critics with a brief two-minute scene. When the lead actor ankled the show, Silvers's role was greatly expanded and the brash, hucksterish character he played went on to define the rest of his career. "That's how the role that I played for years, the aggressive, smiling, call-a-tall-man-shorty manipulator was born," he said.[90]

Judy Garland, after seeing Silvers in *Yokel Boy*, became a fan and a vocal advocate for the comedian, and soon MGM studio chief Louis B. Mayer signed Silvers to the standard seven-year contract. In Arthur Freed's 1940 production of *Strike Up the Band* starring Judy and Mickey Rooney, Silvers was given a six-minute scene opposite its two stars. Silvers reportedly stole the limelight, but Freed (doubtless not wanting to upstage his two stars) consigned the footage to the cutting-room floor.

For the next two years, Silvers was paid by the studio for remaining idle. "For the first two years they had me sit on my *keister*. Nothing. The only pictures I made were with a Brownie camera . . . pictures I could send back East to the boys at Lindy's and Toots Shor's!" he said.[91] After almost a year of waiting for a film assignment, Silvers confronted Mayer at a studio party. Mayer (not one to be upstaged himself and usually the one to make a preemptory first strike), delivered a blustery endorsement of his contract player to all within earshot. "You all seem to be thrilled by this young man. I signed him personally, after seeing him in *Yokel Boy*, but I didn't know he was so versatile," Mayer intoned. "Now, all of you had notification about him, but somehow none of you have seen fit to use him. Aren't you ashamed?"[92] The party, according to Silvers, was held on a Friday night. The following Monday, MGM dropped his option and released him.[93]

Silvers landed at Columbia Pictures and it was there in 1944 that he first teamed with Gene Kelly as best friend and sidekick in the hit musical *Cover Girl*. For Silvers it was the start of a lifelong admiration and friendship with Kelly. In fact, Silvers credited Kelly with stretching his talents beyond just delivering wisecracks, insisting that he perform as part of a trio along with co-star Rita Hayworth in the demanding song and dance "Make Way for Tomorrow."

"The number as conceived, called for an expert dancer," Silvers wrote in his memoir. "Gene, who helped many people with his enthusiasm, felt it would strengthen the story if I, the comic, danced it . . . The sequence ran for eight minutes, up and down steps, leaping onto boxes, kicking trashcans, parading. I couldn't fake it. In the end I had a great feeling of accomplishment: I felt I could do anything."[94] It would be six more years, in *Summer Stock,* before Silvers would again be able to cavort with Kelly and actually appear in a picture with his friend and champion Judy Garland.

The euphoria Silvers felt making *Cover Girl* didn't last long. Motion pictures were never particularly kind to Silvers, despite his appearing in about twenty-five films. Referring to those roles in the 1940s and 1950s as his "Blinky" years ("I was always cast as 'Blinky,' the hero's best friend"), Silvers remembered: "He always comes in and shouts, 'It's gonna be alright, we got the money,' or I'd tell Betty Grable, 'I mean it honey, he really loves you.' Of course, he'd never get the heroine. And always, they'd make me use my tag-phrase, 'Gladaseeya!'"[95]

In real life, when not chumming around with Frank Sinatra, Bing Crosby, or Gene Kelly at Kelly's famous weekend house parties, or hanging out at the Friars Club, Silvers made up for lost time and his second banana status by marrying 1942 Miss America and aspiring actress Jo-Carroll Dennison in 1944. But while filming *Summer Stock*, he became entangled in divorce proceedings with Dennison. In an interview with the authors, Dennison said their marital problems as well as the on-set challenges with Garland caused a good deal of personal strife for the comic. "I think he was stressed out," she said. "First, I left him, and second, it was difficult for him working on that film."[96] During the divorce, Dennison testified that she and Silvers lived "partly here [Los Angeles] and partly in New York where he was in a show." She added that she never saw her husband in New York because "The one evening he had off, he would spend at the Friars' Club or with friends, or at least, so he said."[97]

It was on the small screen where Silvers finally found the perfect platform for his wiseacre, street-smart persona, when writer/producer Nat Hiken developed a series tailored to Silvers's talents and one he was born to play. In 1955, *You'll Never Get Rich* (soon changed to *The Phil Silvers Show*) debuted on CBS and within a few weeks toppled "Mr. Television," Milton Berle, in the ratings. Silvers's character, Sergeant Bilko, a fast-talking schemer, fit him like a glove. Riding high on his television success, in 1956 Silvers married Evelyn Patrick and they had five daughters before the marriage ended in divorce in 1966.

Despite several efforts, Silvers was never able to recapture the Bilko magic. Ironically, in September 1963, he and his *Summer Stock* star Judy

Garland debuted separate new shows on the same weekend. In *The New Phil Silvers Show*, the comic stayed true to type, playing a shop foreman dedicated to making profits for the company, and especially himself. Silvers told columnist Hedda Hopper that he had high hopes for the new series, but by that time he had settled into fatherhood. "The only purity left in the world is children. They don't know anything but sweetness. The glory hours in my home are in the morning. They say girls are gentle—hooey! When I come home at night, they want to play hide-and-seek; in the morning they're up at dawn."[98]

Both the Garland and Silvers shows were short-lived, sending the comic into bouts of depression and physical ailments, including, years later, a debilitating stroke suffered while appearing in a successful 1972 revival on Broadway of *A Funny Thing Happened on the Way to the Forum*, for which he won a Tony Award. Like so many other comedians, Silvers had a dark side, mostly hidden from the public. His personal demons came to light in 1968 in a most public manner—a courtroom—when Silvers testified to being "caught in the whirlpool of gambling." His testimony shed light on a five-year card-cheating conspiracy at the Beverly Hills Friars Club in which (in an eerie corollary to his conniving sharpie roles) Silvers told the court he had been "bilked" out of thousands of dollars. "Gambling just engulfed me," he said. "I just gambled to gamble. I've been gambling most of my life." When pressed to state his total gambling losses, Silvers said he held on to his winnings only long enough to lose the amount he had just won. "A compulsive disease is the best way I can describe it. No greed was involved."[99]

Actress Stefanie Powers, who worked with Silvers in the 1970 Disney film *The Boatniks*, also saw the melancholy side of Silvers during shooting in Newport Beach, California. Powers, who at the time was following a macrobiotic diet based on Zen Buddhism, one that minimized animal products and emphasized locally sourced food, invited Silvers to her unit for dinner (the cast during filming was lodged in an area apartment complex).

"I figured I could cook something different for him so I called him. I said, 'Phil, this is Stefanie downstairs,' and he said 'Thank God, a voice,' and he was serious. 'Nobody calls me, nobody wants to see me.' Oh my God, when he came down it was like a confessional about how horrible his life was and that nobody loved him. The entire evening was monopolized by his confessional. There was no exchange; it was like he just needed to get it all out. He was talking about how desperate it was in life. For me, it was like being a shrink. The next morning, when we were on the set, he didn't acknowledge anything. It was like the dinner never happened."[100]

Silvers died at his Los Angeles home November 1, 1985, at the age of seventy-four. After receiving word of Silvers's passing, another television pioneer (and Silvers's one-time competitor in the ratings race), Milton Berle, eulogized him: "I'm sure somewhere up there Phil is saying to Jack Benny, Jimmy Durante and all the others, 'Hi fellas, Gladaseeya.' This top banana has joined all the other top bananas."[101]

THE FATHER FIGURE: RAY COLLINS

IN *SUMMER STOCK*, VETERAN ACTOR RAY COLLINS PLAYS JASPER WINGAIT, the domineering father to Eddie Bracken's demurring Orville. It was one of dozens of authoritative supporting roles that Collins inhabited during his career.

Born December 10, 1889, Collins made his professional stage debut at age thirteen at the Liberty Playhouse in Oakland, California, and in 1912 formed a vaudeville team with his first wife, Margaret Marriott. Collins, a prodigious worker, was rarely unemployed, working most of the 1920s on stage, including in several Broadway productions.[102] When the Great Depression hit, Collins spent most of the 1930s working in radio, picking up occasional parts in short film subjects during the first half of the decade. In 1934, he hooked up with a young wunderkind from Kenosha, Wisconsin, Orson Welles, and the trajectory of his career rose alongside Welles.

Collins joined the repertory company of Welles's *Cavalcade of America*, a weekly radio historical drama. In 1938, Welles formed the *Mercury Theater on the Air* and its sponsored continuation renamed *The Campbell Playhouse*. That same year, the broadcast of *The War of the Worlds*, an adaptation of the H. G. Wells story, aired live as part of a Halloween episode on October 30, 1938. The dramatic radio broadcast sent some listeners (who hadn't heard Welles's prologue disclaiming any real attack) into a panic as they feared a real Martian invasion was underway on the Eastern seaboard. Collins played three uncredited roles in the drama, including a newscaster who describes the destruction of New York City.[103]

In Welles's 1941 classic *Citizen Kane*, Collins made an auspicious feature film debut playing political kingpin Jim W. Gettys. He appeared in two other Welles movies, *The Magnificent Ambersons* (1942) and *Touch of Evil* (1958). During the 1940s and 1950s, Collins's reliability as a supporting actor, often playing commanding figures, was cemented in more than seventy-five films. In 1950 alone, the year *Summer Stock* was released, Collins appeared on-screen in no less than six films, including two of the *Ma and Pa Kettle* franchise, which starred another *Summer Stock* cast member, Marjorie Main.

After toiling for years on stage and screen with only a modicum of public name recognition, Collins finally registered in what would become his most remembered—and final—role. In 1957, he joined the cast of the CBS TV legal drama *Perry Mason* (starring Raymond Burr as the title character) in the part of Los Angeles homicide detective Lt. Arthur Tragg. By 1960, his health failing due to emphysema and memory difficulties, Collins's appearances in the series—in which he was almost always part of the losing prosecution effort headed by Los Angeles County District Attorney Hamilton Burger (William Talman)—were truncated, and he appeared in only nineteen episodes from 1962–65.[104]

"Years ago, when I was on the Broadway stage, I could memorize 80 pages in eight hours," Collins said in an interview during his last years. "I had a photographic memory. When I got out on the stage, I could actually—in my mind—see the lines written on top of the page, the middle or the bottom. But then radio came along, and we read most of our lines, and I got out of the habit of memorizing. I lost my natural gift. Today it's hard for me. My wife works as hard as I do, caring for me at home."[105] Collins died at age seventy-five of emphysema at St. John's Hospital in Santa Monica, California.

THE CIPHER: NITA BIEBER

THERE IS A CONUNDRUM IN THE CAST OF *SUMMER STOCK* AND HER NAME is Nita Bieber. She appears in several scenes in the movie—most vividly in a high-angle camera shot of a rehearsal sequence that lasts just seconds where, from a crouching position, she does some modernistic (for its time) squat jumps and then hits a rather tenuous landing kneeling on the floorboards of the barn. Bieber is glimpsed briefly doing some grand pliés (while reading a book) in the barnyard as Kelly's future real-life wife Jeanne Coyne pirouettes by, and with Coyne, she links arms with Kelly during "Dig-Dig-Dig Dig for Your Dinner." Finally, she whirls into a balletic split propelled by her partner (Jimmy Thompson, who would appear two years later singing "Beautiful Girl" in *Singin' in the Rain*) shortly before Kelly and Garland pair off in the "Portland Fancy" number. Her total elapsed screen time is well under a minute and throughout, Bieber is rendered mute without any lines to deliver.

Why then does she figure prominently in the opening credits, preceding Carleton Carpenter and Hans Conried who both have sizable speaking parts? Bieber is also listed in the closing credits billed as Sarah Higgins. None of the other chorus boys or girls in the theatrical troupe, including Coyne, are mentioned in either credit sequence.

Like other MGM dancers of that era (Cyd Charisse, Dee Turnell), Bieber, who died February 4, 2019, was lithe, beautiful, and photogenic. Born July 18, 1926, in Los Angeles, Bieber, after graduating from Hollywood High School, traveled as a dancer with a USO troupe. In 1946, she landed a contract with Columbia Pictures and appeared in several films, most notably *Rhythm and Weep* starring the Three Stooges. In the early 1950s, Bieber's career was interrupted when she was diagnosed with polio, but she soon returned to performing and created her own dance troupe, the Nita Bieber Dancers. The troupe appeared on local television, on the *Colgate Comedy Hour* in 1954 with Dean Martin and Jerry Lewis, and in Las Vegas, where they headlined at the El Rancho Hotel. Bieber's last film appearance before retiring was in MGM's *Kismet* (1955), starring Howard Keel and Ann Blyth.[106]

In a 2008 interview with Charles Walters's biographer, Brent Phillips, Bieber shared some memories of working with Gene Kelly on *Summer Stock*: "We kind of went back and forth. I got mad at him once," she said. "I didn't like the way he did something and he didn't like the way I did something and we were doing something together. He was a very strong-willed person; very aggressive you might say. He'd dance like a truck driver. He wanted it his way. It had to be his way."[107]

"Mom was so proud of her role in *Summer Stock*, and a film she made with the Three Stooges," remembered Bieber's daughter, Ivy Faulkner. She also said that her mother's role in the film might've been truncated because she and Garland looked a bit alike. "At least that's what mom told me," Faulkner said. According to Faulkner, her mother nursed a grievance for many years that a certain number had been cut from one of the movies in which she appeared, either *Summer Stock* or *Nancy Goes to Rio* (1950); Faulkner couldn't recollect which one it was. "They tossed it on the cutting-room floor to save running time and she was distraught about that," Faulkner said.[108]

In his review of *If You Feel Like Singing* (*Summer Stock*'s title in the United Kingdom) in the January 1951 edition of the British publication *Film Review*, writer and critic Peter Noble heralded "the show-stopping solo dance of lovely Nita Bieber, remembered for her exotic dancing in the South American number in *Nancy Goes to Rio*" (a film that was also produced at MGM by Pasternak, featured Hans Conried, and was released the same year as *Summer Stock*).

Although Bieber's short rehearsal sequence in the barn in *Summer Stock* hints at the possibility that a longer number was filmed, that is not the case. There is no record in any of the script iterations that such a dance existed or that it was ever pre-recorded and subsequently cut out of the movie. Bieber herself said that the brief rehearsal sequence was originally planned to be expanded into a full-fledged number but the idea was later dropped. The confusion stems from the fact that Noble was working from a pre-written press kit that MGM provided to newspapers, a standard practice that every studio followed when promoting their films.

A good illustration of that can be found by comparing the language in two *Summer Stock* reviews (one of them Noble's) that appeared five months and two continents apart. The duplicity cannot be dismissed as coincidence, because both writers obviously cribbed from the same press kit. Both reviews also refer to a dance Carleton Carpenter does that, like the Bieber number, is fictitious.

Salt Lake Telegram ("Judy Garland and Gene Kelly Go All Out in Summer Stock," August 29, 1950)

> . . . Judy Garland, who can make you cry one minute and laugh the next, is delightful as the distraught lady of the soil who at first considers the flock of thespians invading her farm more trouble than a squealing litter of pigs but who eventually finds the love of the theater getting into her blood, too.
>
> . . . And additional applause goes **to the gangling Carleton Carpenter, who makes the most of a spectacular combination square dance and jive routine, and Nita Bieber, remembered for her exotic dancing in *Nancy Goes to Rio*.**

FILM REVIEW (United Kingdom, January 1951)

> . . . Judy Garland is at the top of her form **as the distraught lady farmer who at first considers the flock of actors descending on her land more terrible than a squealing litter of pigs.**
>
> . . . You will also enjoy **the gangling Carleton Carpenter, whose sensational square dance and jive routine is one of the best numbers in the film.**

MGM's press book for *Summer Stock* was a potpourri of clip art, pre-written stories ("prepared reviews"), and paragraph factoids ready-made for lazy reporters to riff off of when writing their own stories of the movie. The kit contained an explanatory headline that defined the offering as "Advertising, Publicity and Exploitation"—and *exploitation* is the operative and telling word here. When they appeared in *Summer Stock*, both Carpenter and Bieber were fresh, young faces at the beginning of their careers. They had just signed long-term contracts with MGM and it benefitted the studio to generate as much publicity "buzz" as possible around them regardless if the facts sometimes strayed dramatically from the truth on the ground.

Upon Noble's death in 2011, the British newspaper *The Independent* characterized him as "king of the name droppers and last of the great gossip writers. The ever-smiling, always charming Noble never had a bad word for anyone in show business." And therein might be found the key to Bieber's illusory dance in *Summer Stock* (as well as Carpenter's nonexistent hepcat jive number alluded to in both reviews, and doubtless others). Noble's assertion of a show-stopping number (when it was actually a snippet) might've mirrored the encomiums he liberally spread as a hail-fellow-well-met to the actors with whom he crossed paths—in essence, Bieber's "showstopper" was a well-meaning but fabulist exaggeration calculated to flatter courtesy of an overreliance on the hyperbolic, canned press kit jargon provided by MGM. It's the most plausible explanation of the cipher that is Nita Bieber's appearance in *Summer Stock.*

THE INNOCENT: CARLETON CARPENTER

HE WAS THAT TALL (6' 3"), GANGLY GUY WHO LOOMED IN DOZENS OF films, television shows, commercials, and stage productions, usually suffused in a state of naïveté as extreme as his height. Carleton Carpenter was signed by MGM in 1950 and in that year appeared in four films (one uncredited) including *Summer Stock,* where he played Artie, the stagehand/foil to the comic shenanigans of Phil Silvers. But Carpenter is probably best remembered for two musical numbers (in *Three Little Words* and *Two Weeks with Love*) that he performed with Debbie Reynolds, films that bookended *Summer Stock* (one coming before and one after). In *Three Little Words,* Carpenter played the timorous and squirming object of Reynolds's amorous advances as she tied him up in romantic knots while lip-synching to Helen Kane's iconic vocal on "I Wanna Be Loved by You."

In the second film, *Two Weeks with Love,* Carpenter and Reynolds paired up again for a rapid-fire, tongue-twisting patter number called "Aba Daba Honeymoon." Their duet became an instant hit (the song itself was an old chestnut composed in 1914), and according to Carpenter, the biggest single from any studio soundtrack up until that time. In fact, it reached #3 on the *Billboard* chart in 1951. The song was inserted into the film quite by accident, or, as Carpenter recalled, was a case of perfect timing. "Debbie and I were scheduled to perform a couple of numbers together, but in the rehearsal hall there was a huge pile of sheet music. I pulled out this sheet with monkeys on the cover and played it for Debbie. I was hatching a scheme in my head."[109] Cut to a couple days later in that same rehearsal hall when Carpenter saw the film's producer, Jack Cummings, enter the room. Carpenter immediately called Reynolds, gave the sheet music to the rehearsal pianist and they began performing the number at a Gatling gun pace. Cummings immediately took notice, said Carpenter: "He told us that the number would be great for the two of us and we shot it."[110]

The adage about Hollywood stardom, "So many are called, but few succeed," was unfortunately the case with Carpenter. His likable screen presence, despite a co-starring role with a lion in the 1952 film *Fearless Fagen*, never burgeoned into a robust film career; he appeared in just ten films throughout the 1950s.

Carpenter was born in Bennington, Vermont, on July 10, 1926. Before making his first foray into stage work, followed by early live television and then films, he enlisted in the US Navy as a Seabee and was part of the 38th Battalion that built the airstrip on Tinian Island in the Pacific, where the Enola Gay took off on its atomic bombing mission of Hiroshima. After serving in the military, "Carp," as he was known to his friends, started his show business career in 1944. "I arrived in New York City in the winter of 1944 and within 24 hours had my first Broadway role in a play called *Bright Boy*. The character was written as a tall, lanky blonde who wanted to be an actor. Talk about perfect casting."[111]

That show was followed by *Three to Make Ready* starring Ray Bolger, *John Murray Anderson's Almanac* with Hermione Gingold and the 1957 premiere of *Hotel Paradiso* with Bert Lahr and Angela Lansbury in her Broadway debut. Carpenter also toured as Cornelius with the Mary Martin company of *Hello, Dolly!* and served a stint entertaining troops in Vietnam at the height of the war. His final Broadway credit was the 1992 production of *Crazy for You*, which he also toured across the country. His last New York performance was in the 2006 City Center Encores revival of *70 Girls 70*.[112]

Carpenter performed on numerous radio and TV shows beginning as early as 1946, when he was a regular on the NBC show *Campus Hoopla*. He made his film debut in Louis de Rochemont's controversial 1949 film *Lost Boundaries*, about a Black family that passes as white.[113]

During the studio system era, in order to foster a wholesome image of its stars, studio publicists often "fixed up" actors who were gay or bisexual with starlets or up-and-coming actors so they could be photographed about town living the straight life. Carpenter was no exception, although he balked at being described as a gay actor. "I slept with as many women as I did men, I guess. I really didn't keep count," he said. When an interviewer asked Carpenter if his bisexual lifestyle hurt his career, he responded, "Never crossed my mind."[114]

In addition to acting and penning a 2017 memoir, *The Absolute Joy of Work*, Carpenter wrote a few tunes, including "Christmas Eve," which was recorded by Billy Eckstine, as well as a series of mystery novels. He passed away January 31, 2022, at the age of ninety-five in Warwick, New York.

THE WORKER: HANS CONRIED

ONE OF THE STRENGTHS OF *SUMMER STOCK* IS ITS SOLID BENCH OF SUPporting actors. Some, like Marjorie Main and Gloria DeHaven, were MGM contract players; others, like Eddie Bracken, Phil Silvers, Ray Collins, and Hans Conried, were freelancers cast in the film and not tethered exclusively to one studio (although some years earlier Silvers had been under contract to MGM). In *Summer Stock*, character actor Conried plays the imperious stage prima donna Harrison I. Keath, who dismisses Joe Ross's show as merely a "little barnyard entertainment." Although his role is small (his vocals were dubbed during the "Mem'ry Island" rehearsal scene and his lines were scant), Conried handles his part with the assurance of a veteran pilot making his umpteenth landing. In the rehearsal scene with Kelly, Conried was given a chance to stretch his acting muscles a bit. Unfortunately, when it came time for him to sing a snippet of "Mem'ry Island," another actor's voice was dubbed in (quite obviously). For comparison's sake, during a later scene shot outdoors, if you listen intently, you can hear Conried rehearsing in the background in his real singing voice.[115]

Dubbed or not, suffice to say that for a production beset with problems, Conried, the ultimate professional, came in and did what was required—no drama. In fact, in an odd coda to his performance in *Summer Stock*, at the end of 1950, Conried worked with Garland again in a special *Lux Radio Theater* Christmas presentation of *The Wizard of Oz*. Conried was cast as the farmhand Hunk who would become the Scarecrow (Ray Bolger in the 1939 film) in Dorothy's dream. In a replay of what happened in *Summer Stock*, Conried was the only member of the radio cast whose singing voice was dubbed.[116]

The actor often found himself portraying characters far older than his actual age. Conried's stodgy stage veteran Keath is a prime example. He was just thirty-two when he filmed the role but appears far older and more mature, which was necessary to his characterization as the "New York name" (marquee attraction) in Joe Ross's summer stock stage production. In fact, by 1950, *Summer Stock* was just another "stock" job for Conried, who, according to his daughter Trilby Conried, was laser-focused on working continuously and obsessed about bringing home a regular paycheck to support his family.[117] No doubt his numerous roles on stage, radio, film, television, and voiceover work in animated cartoons, assured the indefatigable Conried a comfortable living.

"He was a strong believer in the union, so any union job that came along he took," said Trilby, the oldest of his four children. "He was in some very good films and some that were cringeworthy for him. He was just pleased to be a working actor and supporting his family."[118] In the case of *Summer Stock*, like so many of his film roles, Trilby said her father probably didn't seek the part, but rather auditioned and was just happy to get the work.[119]

"For some producers, I was only a German spy; only a Nazi spy," Conried told an interviewer in 1973. "For some, I was only a fuddy-duddy little old man. Sometimes I was only an offensive floorwalker or an affected English butler. For one, I was a New York gangster. But each saw me differently. Happily, there were enough producers who saw me in sufficiently different fields and aspects that I kept working for all of them. I made over 100 motion pictures, you know, but that was another industry that no longer exists for the character actor."[120]

In Conried's day, a character actor's role was to make the top-billed stars look good and make the director's job easier. "As a character actor, you came in and they knew that you were a capable actor," he said. "You had been cast for the part. They knew you knew your lines, and they expected you to play the part. And it wasn't important because their concern was with the star."[121] *Summer Stock*, as Conried said, was just one of about 100 films that he appeared in. Most, he admitted, were "inconsequential." He does have the dubious distinction of playing the title role in one of filmdom's all-time cult clunkers—1953's *The Five Thousand Fingers of Doctor T*, the one and only film ever scripted by Theodor Geisel, better known to the world as Dr. Seuss. "I had the best role I've ever had in my life and it was a resounding flop. It never played more than five days anywhere in the United States," Conried said.[122]

If Conried oscillated between radio, film, television, and stage roles with seemingly little effort, his contributions as a dependable character actor were not lost on writer Don Page, who wrote in the *Los Angeles Times*: "The term 'great' has significantly lost its significance. Naturally, there are exceptions, and one in particular is Hans Conried. He is not only a superb actor, but a 'great performer.' I use the term without reservation."[123]

"Many parts I played were very modest parts—little comedy vignettes, what they now call cameos," he said. "The word cameo indicates a very prominent actor who is working for virtually no money; in those days they paid you a lot, but it was a small part."[124] The closest Conried came to a defining role was as the recurring character of Uncle Tonoose on the 1950s–1960s Danny Thomas sitcom *Make Room for Daddy*. Conried was versatile; a master of dialects, he projected an urbane persona in many of his roles (including *Summer Stock*), and "gained a reputation as a man of spontaneous and articulate wit with just a tinge of the sardonic." His versatility also brought him leading roles in two Broadway musicals, Cole Porter's *Can-Can* and, later, a revival of *Irene* opposite Debbie Reynolds.[125]

Born in Baltimore on April 15, 1917, Conried was raised in New York City, where he acquired his knack for dialects from the ethnically diverse melting pot of immigrants that defined the city in those days. He studied at Columbia University and set his sights on more serious roles, including Shakespeare, finding that his voice was his meal ticket. Soon after, Conried began a long career in radio and later worked in all facets of show business, including summer stock and dinner theater performances (a late-career home for many stars from the Golden Age).

While Conried's fellow *Summer Stock* cast member Ray Collins was a member of Orson Welles's legendary 1930s *Mercury Theater of the Air* radio shows (which included the famous *War of the Worlds* broadcast), Conried became a regular on Welles's later radio show, *The Orson Welles Show* in 1941–42. When television supplanted radio, Jack Paar, who served with Conried in the Army during World War II, invited him to be a regular guest on Paar's *Tonight Show*.

From the 1950s to the 1970s, Conried became a guest star fixture on dozens of television shows, including *I Love Lucy, The Many Loves of Dobie Gillis, Mister Ed, The Beverly Hillbillies, Hogan's Heroes, The Monkees, The Love Boat*, and *Laverne & Shirley*. Perhaps his most memorable guest spot was as the disoriented World War I aviator Wrongway Feldman in *Gilligan's Island*. He's also remembered for his voiceover work, notably Snidely Whiplash in the "Dudley Do-Right of the Mounties" segments of the *Rocky & Bullwinkle Show* cartoons and "Wally Walrus" on *The Woody Woodpecker Show*.

One of Hollywood's busiest actors for more than forty years, Conried was always circumspect about his career as a working actor, "When I tell you that I've been an actor, active for thirty-eight years, doing something—either a voiceover or a cartoon or a picture or talking at a college or playing in a dinner theater, doing a pageant, directing, acting, something—I have been very lucky. I am very conscious of that and my gratitude is enormous to whatever gods are responsible for the good fortune."[126] Plagued by a history of heart problems, including a stroke in 1974, Conried died of a heart attack on January 5, 1982, at the age of sixty-six.

THE PRODUCER: JOE PASTERNAK

> Pasternak didn't do anything memorable, but he was practical-commercial. We are an industry. There's nothing wrong with that, when you know you're commercial and there aren't any illusions of doing something else.[127]
>
> —DIRECTOR BILLY WILDER

"BOY MEETS GIRL. BOY LOSES GIRL. BOY SINGS A SONG AND GETS GIRL. The plots were that simple," opined Frank Sinatra in the 1974 film *That's Entertainment!*, a compilation of MGM studio's finest musical moments. Sinatra was summing up what, to a great extent, was the ballast (thin as the narratives might be) that kept many of those films from floating away like loosed circus balloons.

The man responsible for delivering more than his fair share of those airy frolics, including *Summer Stock*, to a public eager to escape (if only for 100 minutes or so) the hardships of the Great Depression and later the horrors of World War II, was producer Joe Pasternak. "My father's mantra was 'forget your troubles,' despite enduring his own share of personal hardships," said his son, Jeff Pasternak. "In many ways, the lyrics to the song 'Get Happy' [performed by Judy Garland in *Summer Stock*] embodies much of the storylines in his film work."[128]

According to the producer himself, around 100 of his movies starting with *Zwei Menschen* (*Two People*) shot in Berlin in 1930 and ending with *The Sweet Ride* made for Twentieth Century-Fox in 1968, earned $450 million (about $3.7 billion in 2022 dollars), for the two studios (Universal, MGM) in which he worked over the course of his long career in the movie business.[129]

Born József Paszternák on September 19, 1901, in the Hungarian town of Szilagy-Smolyo, Pasternak, whose boyhood dream, he once said, "was to have my own bathroom," never answered to Joseph or the more European pronunciation of his name. To his friends, family, colleagues and the public at large, he was just plain old Joe. About that bit of down-to-earth informality, he exclaimed in a 1980 interview, "I did it, before Jimmy Carter did!"[130]

At his producing zenith, Pasternak had a receding hairline that evened out around the middle of his skull and in doing so accentuated his domed, dirigible forehead. He also spoke in a Euro-Hungarian accent thick as goulash and had a proclivity for uttering malaprops. Famed *New York Post* syndicated gossip columnist Earl Wilson was so amused at Pasternak's mangling of the English language that he quoted the producer in his "Best Laughs of 1958" column when he wrote of Pasternak telling one actor, "Take this script home and *maul* it over."[131]

According to Saul Chaplin, who contributed songs to *Summer Stock*, Pasternak was a sweet man with a Louis Armstrong speaking voice. In his Hollywood memoir, Chaplin likened Pasternak's impenetrable accent to something that George Jessel once said about Spyros Skouras (the former president of Twentieth Century-Fox), who spoke with an equally incomprehensible Greek accent: "'He's been in this country over thirty years, but when he speaks, he sounds like he's going to arrive next Wednesday.'

"I heard him [Pasternak] say the following sentence in describing a scene that took place in a barn," Chaplin wrote: "'When the girls are in the *hay loaf* (hayloft), they wear their *gunga dins* (blue jeans); then in the evening they change into their *carolines* (crinolines), but the problem is that the scene needs a better *transaction* (transition) from the last one.' And that was just one sentence. That quality that Arthur Freed, Pasternak and Jack Cummings [other MGM producers] shared was enthusiasm."[132]

As a producer in Hollywood, Pasternak discovered or popularized such stars as Deanna Durbin, Esther Williams, Margaret O'Brien, Van Johnson, Kathryn Grayson, and Mario Lanza, and inserted into his films classical musical artists such as Leopold Stokowski (*One Hundred Men and a Girl*, 1937),

Lauritz Melchior (*Thrill of a Romance*, 1945), and José Iturbi (*Anchors Aweigh*) by way of protracted musical numbers, thus delivering some "highbrow culture" to the bourgeois masses that comprised most of the audiences for his movies.

Pasternak never lost his star-making desire. As late in his career as 1960, he introduced singer Connie Francis and Paula Prentiss to the screen and launched the teen beach movie craze with *Where the Boys Are*. The actress born Paula Ragusa said Pasternak gave her the screen name Prentiss: "He liked alliteration and chose the name from a movie with Ann Sheridan called *Nora Prentiss* [1947]."[133] When the title song to the film recorded by Francis became a chart-topper throughout the world and didn't receive an Oscar nod, the ordinarily placid Pasternak, according to Francis, snapped, "A song that does the most for a motion picture's supposed to be the *basic* [basis]. 'Where the Boys Are' was number one in fifteen countries in six languages even before the movie was released. They even love it in *Cancers* [Kansas]."[134]

Although, as Francis observed, Pasternak could become indignant when he felt his films were being ill-served, he harbored no pretense about his own contribution as a producer. In his 1956 memoir *Easy the Hard Way*, Pasternak described his role as: "A kind of super-foreman who makes sure that all the parts are properly machined and finished and that they fit nicely. I don't know how to write a script, score a picture, design costumes, act, direct, light a set, record a song, or apply makeup. I try to get these things done well." In eschewing the nuts-and-bolts technical aspects of filmmaking, Pasternak touched upon his own area of savvy—one that he shared with other veteran producers of the studio system era like Arthur Freed—an inchoate longing to create beautiful things. "It's instinct, a feeling, a theatrical hunch that comes alive inside of you," Pasternak said. "You feel it's right and if you were pressed, you really couldn't say why. You just know."[135]

When Gene Kelly accepted the American Film Institute Life Achievement Award in 1985, he acknowledged the unsung heroes of his musical films, including his *Summer Stock* producer. "I'd like to say one quick word about the people the public has never seen, not just the photographers and crew and the art directors and the costume designers, but the [Vincente] Minnellis, the [Stanley] Donens and Pasternaks . . ." In addition to *Summer Stock*, Kelly starred in two other Pasternak productions at Metro: *Thousands Cheer* in 1943 and *Anchors Aweigh*.[136]

Pasternak, who emigrated to the United States in 1921, started from the ground up in the motion picture industry, mopping floors and washing dishes in the commissary at Paramount's Astoria, New York, studios before becoming a waiter, actor, fourth assistant director, and finally an assistant to director Allan Dwan in 1923. Beginning in 1928, he worked for eight years in Europe making films for Universal Pictures, first in Berlin, then in Vienna, and finally in Budapest. With the Nazi scourge looming large in the mid-thirties, Pasternak, a Jew, knew it was time to leave his native Hungary and return to America. In fact, he took pride in the fact that Hitler had erased his screen credit from all his pictures exhibiting in Germany. Pasternak pleaded with his father, sister, and other family members to leave Hungary but it was futile; he returned to the States alone, knowing that he would never see his family again.

From May 15 to July 9, 1944, the Hungarian gendarmerie, under the guidance of German SS officials, deported around 440,000 Jews from Hungary. Most were directed to Auschwitz-Birkenau, where, upon arrival and after selection, SS functionaries killed the majority of them in gas chambers.[137] Thirty-one Hungarians with the last name of Pasternak (Joe's family certainly among them) were murdered at Auschwitz during that time.[138] "He [Pasternak's father], my sister Helen, her husband, their six young children, and some 40 relatives of mine, as well as my old teacher, Schwarz, were taken by the Germans during the war and destroyed in their murder camps," Pasternak said. "I'm sure my father's last words, as were those of another great Jew, a plea for forgiveness of his tormentors. He was that kind of man."[139]

In his memoir, Pasternak wrote about a recurring daydream he had of traveling by train across Germany where he was seated in the same dining car as Hitler, Hermann Göring, Paul Joseph Goebbels, and Ernst Rohm, co-founder of the Nazi militia who was murdered on Hitler's orders in 1934 during a purge called "The Night of the Long Knives." "If I had known then what I know now, how much agony and pain I might have spared the world with a well-placed grenade or machine gun! I know it is murder even as I daydream, but the loathing is so deep within me that I'm even prepared to do murder."[140]

While Pasternak rarely talked about the emotional toll the fate of his family had in informing his resolve to make "happy" motion pictures, Connie Francis, who became close to the producer and was a frequent guest in his home after the making of *Where the Boys Are,* said: "He cried when we talked about the Holocaust and he cried when JFK was assassinated. He became very emotional and he was not usually an emotional man."[141]

On the brink of bankruptcy in the mid-1930s, Universal Studios was Pasternak's ticket back to Hollywood. The studio began its return to profitability in 1936 when Pasternak produced *Three Smart Girls* starring fifteen-year-old Deanna Durbin. Pasternak didn't discover the lyric soprano songbird who excelled at playing innocent sweethearts, but he did the discoverer one better; he found a formula to popularize her in ten hits and make her one of the studio's biggest stars between 1936 and 1941. However, around that time, Pasternak did notice a lanky, good-looking actor visiting one of his Durbin movie sets and immediately cast Robert Stack in the picture's lead role. The 1938 film, *First Love,* marked Stack's film debut and he became famous for planting the first screen kiss on the starlet. "I was only with her on screen . . . unfortunately," the actor mused.[142]

As a parting gift to Universal, before leaving the studio, Pasternak is credited with resurrecting the career of Marlene Dietrich (after a protracted string of flops that caused her to be labeled as "box office poison") by casting the sultry actress as the saloon singer Frenchy opposite James Stewart in *Destry Rides Again* (1939). Pasternak offered Dietrich half the salary she had received for most of the decade, but the role—and her rendition of Frank Loesser's "See What the Boys in the Back Room Will Have," a winking parody of her vampish screen image—made her once again a force to be reckoned with in Tinseltown.

In 1941, several studios showed an interest in acquiring Pasternak's services, but the "Cadillac" of the dream factories, MGM, won out and signed him to what was reported to be a five-year, $3,500 a week salary. His brand of films were a natural fit for the wholesome verities preached by MGM's studio head and *pater familias,* Louis B. Mayer.

The studio immediately assigned its newest singing acquisition, coloratura soprano Kathryn Grayson, to the Pasternak unit. She soon became MGM's reigning thrush in musicals and operettas of the 1940s and 1950s, starring along the way in no less than seven Pasternak productions. Under what she said was Mayer's benevolent and encompassing gaze, Grayson literally grew up at MGM, coddled and protected by the all-powerful studio system. She came to fervently believe she was special because everyone in MGM's "extended family" was special.[143]

At Metro, Pasternak established himself as one of the three leading producers of Hollywood musicals, along with Arthur Freed and Jack Cummings (Mayer's son-in-law). Judy Garland, Gene Kelly, and Fred Astaire were the engines in the 1940s and 1950s that provided MGM the star power to dominate the musical genre. All three primarily worked for producer Freed and his vaunted unit. Freed was a songwriter ("I Cried for You," "Singin' in the Rain," "Broadway Melody") turned producer whose primary strength was assembling the best artists—often mined from hit Broadway shows—in the musical field.

According to a report in *The Independent*, a London tabloid, "Pasternak was always in a lesser lead because he had a propensity for schmaltzy, even trite situations . . . If Pasternak's musicals never begin to rival those by Freed, there are pleasing ingredients in them, partly because he was able to borrow Freed's talented arrangers and choreographers and to benefit from the sheer confidence MGM had in the form."[144]

At Metro, Pasternak's prolific output (borrowed or not) included such hits as *Anchors Aweigh*, *In the Good Old Summertime*, *The Great Caruso* (1951), and a rare serious picture, the Ruth Etting biopic *Love Me or Leave Me* (1955) starring Doris Day and James Cagney, which told the story of Etting's ill-fated life with her controlling husband, a gangster nicknamed "Moe the Gimp" Snyder. But even Pasternak wasn't impervious to the occasional dud. In 1947 he produced *The Kissing Bandit*, an unmitigated bomb (critically and at the box office) for stars Sinatra and Grayson. "Darryl Zanuck [a producer and later studio head at Twentieth Century-Fox] had his *Wilson* [a 1944 biopic of President Woodrow Wilson that reportedly lost $2 million at the box office]. I had *The Kissing Bandit*," Pasternak joked about his rare misfire.[145]

Aqua-musical star Esther Williams appeared in several Pasternak productions at MGM, including *On an Island with You* (1948), *Texas Carnival* (1951), and *Easy to Love* (1954). Through them all, multiple pregnancies notwithstanding, she managed to stay true to her size nine bathing suit. She did say, however, the pregnancies invariably created havoc with the shooting schedule of her films and irked Pasternak no end. "They had to rearrange entire shooting schedules so I could get into the swimming suits and be photographable because we didn't finish those pictures until after five or six months," she said. "I remember calling Joe and telling him, 'Joey, I'm sorry. I know we've had this conversation before, but I'm pregnant.' And he said, 'God damn it, why do you keep doing this to me?' And I said, 'It's not being done to you Joe, it's being done to *me*!' And he replied, 'I know, I know, but if you don't tell that husband of yours to knock it off, he'll be barred from the lot.' And I said, 'Joe, it doesn't happen on the lot!'"[146]

Pasternak was married to the actress Dorothy Darrell from 1941 until his death and had three sons. "He left everything at the studio," said son Jeff. "By the time he did come home, he'd perhaps pour a martini, play a little gin rummy with a friend like José Iturbi, listen to the horse races, and then go to bed. As a father, he was rarely effusive and played his cards close to his vest."[147] The Hungarian expatriate with an accent thick as goulash liked to cook the real thing made with hotdogs. In 1966, he published a book of his favorite old-world recipes, *Cooking with Love and Paprika*. "I so fondly recall those unforgettable weekends we spent at his home in Bel Air telling stories for hours, barbecuing and eating his fabulous Hungarian-Jewish food," said Francis.[148]

Pasternak's last producing credit came in 1968 with the surfer/biker exploitation film *The Sweet Ride*, which, ironically, was not a happy-ending musical but a box-office flop that tried to capture the angst and turmoil young people were experiencing in the wake of an unpopular war and the assassinations of Bobby Kennedy and Martin Luther King Jr. At this time, Pasternak's health had also begun to ebb with a diagnosis of Parkinson's disease that would slowly chip away at his good-natured spirit and eventually take his life. With *The Sweet Ride*, his son said, "He wanted to be hip, wanted to change, but he really didn't know how." Shooting a nightclub scene for the film, Pasternak even asked his son for a suggestion on a rock band to use. Jeff recommended an up-and-coming group called the Doors. He settled instead for a group called Moby Grape, because, Jeff said, they wanted $5,000 less than the Doors, who were just on the cusp of making it big.

Toward the end of his life (Pasternak died September 13, 1991, at the age of eighty-nine, six days before his ninetieth birthday) with his speech greatly impaired by Parkinson's, the producer betrayed some regret when he told his son: "'If I could do it all over again, I would do things differently.' He wanted me to know that. Who knew exactly what he was referring to, but it was a big thing for him to admit. I once asked him, 'Dad, why don't you make a more serious movie?' He never really had an answer. He just wanted people walking out of the theater feeling good because so much joy was taken away from him. When I bought a Volkswagen, he was furious! He always carried a heavy heart due to the Holocaust."[149]

Francis affectionately called Pasternak "Uncle Joe" (the only one, she said who called him that) and once asked the producer if he ever wanted to make a message film. "If you want to send a message, go to Western Union. I want people to leave the theater happy," he replied.[150] In a career that spanned five decades and played out over two continents, Pasternak accomplished just that. *Summer Stock*, in all its effervescence, innocence, and good humor (characteristics that belied its troubled backstory), stands as a prime example of the producer's abiding credo that people in general and filmgoers in particular should (like he did shouldering his own melancholy burdens) just get on with it and get happy.

THE HELMER: CHARLES WALTERS

WHEN ONE THINKS OF DIRECTORS OF THE GREAT MGM MUSICALS, THE names Vincente Minnelli, Gene Kelly, and Stanley Donen are usually top of mind. The often overlooked "backbenchers," worthy of praise in their own right, are George Sidney and the director of *Summer Stock*, Charles Walters. His second-tier status didn't seem to bother Chuck (the informal sobriquet Walters's parents dubbed him with at birth)[151] and the name he insisted everyone call him.

Always workmanlike and professional, perhaps a reason for Walters never being included in the same conversation as Minnelli (a master of saturated Technicolor and painstakingly detailed scenic design) or the Kelly-Donen co-directing collaboration with two groundbreaking musicals (*On the Town* and *Singin' in the Rain*) to their credit was that he didn't have an overt signature directing style and knew his place in the pecking order of the studio assembly-line system. Even Sidney had a knack for adapting hit Broadway shows like *Annie Get Your Gun*, *Show Boat*, and *Kiss Me Kate* into cinematic successes. Still, like Kelly, a dancer himself, Walters knew musicals.

"You're supposed to be backstage," he once told an interviewer. "You can't star yourself—that is the danger. You've got to feature the stars, and you've got to know them better than they know themselves."[152]

According to Walters's biographer Brent Phillips, Walters disliked cutting and only cut when he needed to: "That is so apparent in 'You Wonderful You' from *Summer Stock* which I always say is eight minutes of film with the entire song filmed in one fluid take. The way he would dance with his camera is reminiscent of Busby Berkeley. As a dance director, Chuck had been on Berkeley's sets and was able to watch how he perfectly captured dance where you didn't have to wait for an editor to piece it all together."[153]

Walters, who passed away from mesothelioma on August 13, 1982, was a native Californian born Charles Walter in Pasadena on November 17, 1911. The surname, adding the "s," didn't occur until he embarked on his professional career in the 1930s.[154] Fresh out of high school and with no formal dance training, he journeyed to New York City in quest of stardom. During the 1930s and early 1940s, Walters enjoyed success on the musical comedy stage as both a performer and choreographer. He appeared as the juvenile lead in such shows as *Jubilee* (1935), where he introduced the Cole Porter standard "Begin the Beguine," and *DuBarry Was a Lady* (1939), in which he appeared with Betty Grable.

But Walters's most closely held ambition was to someday return home to California and replace journeyman hoofer George Murphy, whom he considered to be a poor dancer, in film roles. That goal was partially realized in 1943 when Walters was asked to choreograph a number for the film version of *DuBarry*. Although he never replaced Murphy, Walters did land a long-term contract at MGM and would work under the auspices of MGM's top musical producers, including Arthur Freed, Joe Pasternak (*Summer Stock*), and Jack Cummings. He started at MGM with a four-week guarantee at $500 a week to do a number for Gene Kelly and remained at the studio for the next twenty-two years.[155]

"*DuBarry* was the last show I was in as a performer and my first Freed film," Walters said. "It's being in the right place at the right time. My manager-agent-best friend [John Darrow] and I were living together in my house and he also handled Gene Kelly. Kelly had just done *For Me and My Gal*. He called our agent and said, 'Is Bob Alton [a choreographer] available? I cannot stand Seymour Felix [another choreographer]. I just can't work with this guy again. And he's scheduled to do my next picture, *DuBarry*, with Lucille Ball.' Well, my agent told Kelly that he just signed Felix for *Ziegfeld Follies*. And Kelly said, 'Geez, is Charlie Walters around?' Gene's the only person in the world who ever called me Charlie. So Kelly asked me to do this number for him and I was signed up for four weeks. Well, Kelly liked the number I did so they took another number away from Felix, gave me that; took another number away, and I ended up doing the picture. They liked the picture so they put me under long-term contract. I was there twenty-two years, fifty-two weeks a year."[156]

Walters was initially signed to choreograph one number, to the Cole Porter song "Do I Love You?" "That was the number I was signed to stage. For some strange reason I asked for a script. 'What do you need a script for, you're just going to do solo staging for Kelly?' they asked. Having been in the Broadway show, I might have been curious what they did with it and if Kelly was playing my part or another part . . . that might have been it! I never thought of that.

"Anyway, it happened that Kelly had a scene in Lucy's [Lucille Ball] dressing room before the number, and then he left the dressing room and jumped on stage. I thought, gee, wouldn't it be nice if we could start the number in her room with a look of encouragement from her and continue the number out of the dressing room and up on stage. Now he's got a motivation to be up and gay and bright. So I told the producer—Arthur Freed—my idea and he just looked at me. I thought, oh Jesus, I really bombed! Well, he said, 'Chuck, that's the way directors think. That's very good. I like it.'

"Later on at MGM we were running dailies of 'Madame Crematon' [a Garland number Walters staged for *Ziegfeld Follies*, released in 1946], and Freed, who was always very non sequitur, said nothing. I looked at him to see what he thought and he said, 'I bought a new property today, *Good News*.' It was like somebody had put a firecracker under me. He said: 'Chuck, that might be a good first picture for you.' Arthur was the kind of man who never forgot. The seed was planted in his mind that someday I would be a director."[157]

Freed didn't forget, and when it was time to adapt the popular college stage musical *Good News* to the screen in 1947, he tapped Walters to helm the picture. "I was very big in dramatics, if you can imagine, at Anaheim High School," Walters said. "The senior class play was to be my choice. We'd never done a musical and *Good News* was very popular at the time. So I said, let's do *Good News*. We got the high school orchestra and then we found out that we couldn't afford the rights. So we used the same storyline, but different popular music."[158]

Walters graduated to full directorial status in 1947 when he helmed *Good News*. For the next nineteen years he maintained a remarkably high standard directing such musicals and light comedies as *Easter Parade, Summer Stock, The Barkleys of Broadway* (1949), *Lili* (1953), *The Tender Trap* (1955), *High Society* (1956), *Please Don't Eat the Daisies* (1960), *Billy Rose's Jumbo* (1962), and *The Unsinkable Molly Brown* (1964). In addition, Walters contributed another invaluable attribute to the films he directed, one that brought him favor in the MGM executive suite—he worked efficiently and brought most of his films in on time and under budget, including his first three directorial efforts: *Good News, Easter Parade*, and *The Barkleys of Broadway*.

"I had been a dance director for four years and it was only the last year that I was able to cut and shoot my own numbers," he said. "Before that time, I would stage a number, and the director would take it and shoot it his way. When I finally got to shoot my own numbers, I would film them so they couldn't be chopped. I found that I was automatically staging for cutting. Then, when I got into directing, I would shoot only what I wanted, so all the cutter could do was cut off the leader and glue them together. I wanted to protect what I visualized."[159]

As a choreographer, Walters brought a kind of elan or sophistication to his numbers. But, characteristically, he was more succinct (and dismissive) in describing his dance style: "Pure bastard."[160] Always self-effacing, there was scarcely a better team player on a movie than Walters. For example, his more well-known contemporary at MGM, Vincente Minnelli, picked up the Best Director Oscar for his work on *Gigi*, but Walters was tasked with reshooting several scenes, a little-known fact that the director revealed to the authors during a 1980 interview.

"How did you know I did things on *Gigi*? I never said anything. I never let the cat out of the bag. Wow! I did all the retakes and shot a lot of the numbers like 'The Night They Invented Champagne' and Louis Jourdan doing 'Gigi.' As a matter of fact, I redid the scene where he comes in to propose to her. I also reshot 'She's Not Thinking of Me.' I couldn't think of how to tag it, how to get Louis Jourdan so annoyed at Eva Gabor without her having done anything to him. That's why I had him pour champagne down her front in frustration which was a big laugh. *Gigi* was one of the toughest things I've ever done because I had to blend the studio footage into the Paris backgrounds. Lerner and Loewe [the film's composers] wanted to send me a flowered horseshoe, but they were afraid it would get back to Vincente, which wouldn't be very nice."[161]

Walters, the ultimate company man, knew that the studio system was star-driven and must be catered to. And there is no better example of that in action than his relationship with Judy Garland, perhaps MGM's biggest asset. By the time Walters was assigned to helm *Summer Stock* in 1949, he had already established a long working relationship and friendship with Garland. During her frequent bouts of emotional upheaval, Garland was most comfortable working with friends she could trust and who offered the constant reassurance she craved. In the case of *Summer Stock*, Walters and Kelly certainly fit the bill.

According to Garland's daughter Lorna Luft, "Chuck was always an incredibly generous and lovely guy that she [Garland] really had a good and great friendship with, and he *really* was her friend. It wasn't that he was just another director. In the films that they worked on, he was funny and he had a great sense of humor and he protected her. That was the thing about the directors that my mother really loved: the protection value."[162]

The Garland-Walters collaboration started in late 1942 when he worked simultaneously with her on *Girl Crazy* and then shortly thereafter as a choreographer and dancer (uncredited) on *Presenting Lily Mars*, partnering with Garland in *Mars*'s lavish finale. Walters was first introduced to Garland by producer Joe Pasternak, who was looking to reshoot the *Mars* finale. Prior to their meeting, Walters had a preconceived notion that he wouldn't jell with Garland. "I didn't even sit through *Little Nellie Kelly* [a 1940 Garland film]," he said. "I went home. I didn't like Judy. She was like a bold Meglin Kiddie [a troupe of child performers popular in the 1930s that counted Shirley Temple among their alumni]. Too strong—like a professional child actor—and it bugged me. I found no sensitivity; no simplicity; no warmth."[163]

That initial reaction quickly changed when Walters started working with her. "She was to meet me and if Judy dug me, I would restage a new finale and dance with her," Walters said. "I met her on the set and fell madly in love with her. When I met Judy her personality was overwhelming. 'Hey, you can sure move,' she told me. She was warm, spontaneous as if we were friends all her life."[164] After completing the dance routine, Garland told the new contract employee, "'Hey, welcome out here! You're a helluva dancer!

I hope we can make you happy.' It was her first sophisticated number. She just didn't want to be little Judy Garland, the little campfire girl with little Mickey Rooney, the nice Andy Hardy boy."[165]

Immediately after *Mars,* Walters continued working on another Garland vehicle, *Girl Crazy* (1943), where he again served as an uncredited dance director and Garland's on-screen partner to Gershwin's lilting "Embraceable You." It was an on-set visit by studio chief Louis B. Mayer and the film's producer Arthur Freed that would change the trajectory of Walters's career. "Mayer said to Freed, 'why don't you sign him as a dancer?' Arthur responded, 'I think he'll be more valuable to us this way [as a choreographer], and, if we need him, he can always dance.'"[166]

That value was on full display in 1944 when Walters was again tasked to stage dance numbers for another Garland vehicle, *Meet Me in St. Louis,* directed by her future husband, Vincente Minnelli. Walters recalled: "Oh, that was a lovely experience. The only funny thing about that was I thought Ralph Blane and Hugh Martin had written an original score. I thought, what the hell is this 'Skip to My Lou?' I couldn't get any handle on how to stage it. One evening I had my parents over for dinner, and I told them there was one number in the picture I didn't know what the hell to do with. Well, they pounced on it and started singing 'Skip to My Lou.' That song was around when they were kids. So, my square, untheatrical parents helped me choreograph the number."[167]

Walters's and Garland's seamless rapport was on full display in the 1948 classic *Easter Parade,* which teamed Garland with Fred Astaire (who came out of retirement and replaced Gene Kelly, who had suffered a broken ankle). Fresh off that blockbuster success, MGM again wanted to reteam Astaire with Garland, but it was not to be. On July 19, 1948, due to her frequent absences, MGM placed Garland on suspension without pay. She was soon replaced on the picture by Ginger Rogers in her tenth and final pairing with Astaire. Working with his idol Astaire fulfilled all of Walters's childhood aspirations.

"Once I found out that Astaire was going to be in it [*Easter Parade*], my knees got weak because he was my hero," Walters remembered. "So when you say sophistication—I loved the way he danced, the way he walked, his entire style. I never copied a step, but just his whole attitude was wonderful. I think a lot of that rubbed off on me." Chuck's assessment of Garland as a dancer: "good faker." And Rogers? "She could do the steps, but she was such a good actress you didn't care. Judy was a perfect mimic. The 'Madame Crematon' number [in *Ziegfeld Follies*], that was mine. I found the easiest way to work with her was to do it for her then she'd do it."[168]

What made the intricately complicated Garland tick? For Walters, who knew her better than almost anyone, the answer (if there is one) can be found in a comparable life: "Sometimes you have to get to other people for that. For instance, Marilyn Monroe's hang-up: she was nothing but a sex symbol without talent, according to her. Judy: a talent without sex appeal. She would have sacrificed the talent to be Lana Turner or Marilyn Monroe. [Judy was] the essential romantic. I've always felt there was guilt in her that she hadn't earned her talent—she never spent a nickel on her voice or her acting or her dancing."[169] Ironically, Walters said the same thing when he referred to his own skill set, according to Walters's biographer Phillips.[170]

Given that insight, when working with Garland, Walters employed a little trick that invariably brought out the best in her performances. "The interesting thing about Judy was that she was so insecure, except to get up and sing," he said. "For instance, we were doing a number that she was scared to death of. I don't know how I thought of it, but one day I said, 'Judy who's your favorite dancer?' And she said Renee DeMarco, who was part of a famous dance team. I told her, 'From now on, whenever we rehearse, you're Renee DeMarco.' From then on she was just perfect. Now if you remember 'Get Happy' [from *Summer Stock*], I told her to be Lena Horne. This got Judy away from 'me dancing' and she *felt* Lena. It worked beautifully."[171]

After *Summer Stock*, Garland was released from her MGM contract. Walters, as a favor to his friend, staged her triumphant live shows at New York's legendary Palace Theater the very next year in 1951 and then her other show also at the Palace in 1956. "I staged both of Judy's Palace shows," he said. "It was my idea to give them more than just a personal appearance, like: 'Here I am, little Judy Garland.' We had a wealth of musical material to draw upon and Judy loved the idea of having production numbers."[172]

The 1960s sounded the death knell for original Hollywood musicals and Walters suffered the same fate that befell many of his MGM colleagues. Projects seemed to evaporate over time and then came to an abrupt halt, except for scattered directorial chores on a few television shows, some with his old friend Lucille Ball. Walters blamed the demise of the musical on money: "It just got too expensive."[173]

Looking back at the twenty-one features he directed, Walters was candid when disclosing to the authors his favorite and least favorite films: "I decided the other day that I think *Jumbo* is my favorite because I had done so many intimate and small comedies and musicals. To get a chance at a 'biggie' was a thrill. My least favorite was *The Belle of New York* [a 1952 musical that starred Fred Astaire and Vera-Ellen]. I hate it. I just hate it. It was like putting a gun to your head every day. I couldn't stand Vera-Ellen. I would talk to her about a scene and she'd be doing pliés. That's the kind of concentration you got."[174]

During the last few years of his life, Walters was invigorated by teaching students at the University of Southern California a course called "Film Style Analysis—The Work of Director Charles Walters." His students discovered Walters's puckish playfulness when on the first day of class he'd enter the room and ask the aspiring film students where the Charles Walters class meets and then reveal that he, in fact, was Charles Walters. Writing in the USC student newspaper, reporter Mary Whiteley said: "This strategy typifies the sense of fun Walters brought to class, which encouraged students to stay overtime and let them experience firsthand the atmosphere in which his films were created."[175]

Practical jokes notwithstanding, there was one lesson Chuck made sure he imparted to the students in all his classes. "When I started there was no such thing as a school or a book. It had to be on a gut level," he told them. "For openers, I tell the kids learn all you can then throw the book over your shoulder and go from your guts. There is only so much you can learn; then it's up to you—your blood and guts."[176]

THE TUNESMITH: HARRY WARREN

FOR SONGWRITER HARRY WARREN AND HIS LYRICIST COLLABORATOR MACK Gordon, the score for *Summer Stock* didn't produce any major hits, and it would prove to be their swan song as a team after a successful run in the early 1940s working together at Twentieth Century-Fox. In fact, after *Summer Stock*, Warren scored only three more MGM musicals: *Texas Carnival*, *The Belle of New York*, and *Skirts Ahoy!* (1952). As such, Warren portended the end of the heyday of musical films at the same time his own tenure at MGM ended. The studio had been a dream destination for Warren since his earliest days in Hollywood.

"It was as if the songwriting trade had suddenly ceased to be in demand," he said. "It wasn't too bad for me, because I still had offers over the next few years to write songs for pictures, but a lot of the writers were out of work. If it hadn't been for royalties from old songs, they would have been in trouble. It seemed to me a tragedy that the Metro musicals had to come to an end because they were good bits of entertainment and they employed the best people in the business. It was a marvelous community of musicians, arrangers, composers, conductors, singers, and coaches. A great atmosphere."[177]

Warren wrote over 800 songs between 1918 and 1981, publishing more than 500 of them, including the melody for "Chattanooga Choo Choo" which won the first gold record ever awarded. But despite a trunk overflowing with riches, among even ardent fans of the movie musical, the name Harry Warren remains a puzzling enigma, a kind of musical chameleon that some pundits have dismissed as being without a signature like those of his songwriting contemporaries such as George Gershwin, Cole Porter, or Irving Berlin. "Oh, I think I have a style," Warren told an interviewer in 1977. "A lot of people tell me that, but I don't know. They used to say to me that I had a good bass line, but that bass line I got from the church when I was an altar boy and sang in the choir."[178]

In 1933, along with lyricist Al Dubin, Warren wrote the score for the film that would revolutionize the Hollywood musical, *42nd Street*. In 1980, producer David Merrick and director-choreographer Gower Champion combined forces to recreate the simplistic backstage plot for the Broadway stage, which subsequently enjoyed unparalleled success at the Winter Garden Theater. The show's popularity was due in large part to such Warren standards as "Lullaby of Broadway," "Shuffle Off to Buffalo," "We're in the Money," and, of course, the title song. Unfortunately, the newfound popularity of his songs, perhaps, had come too little and too late to counterbalance a cantankerous personality that was the result of professional resentments nurtured over many years. Harry Warren, you see, was a world-class curmudgeon. "I guess I wasn't newsworthy," he said. "In the first place, the average person that you see advertised a lot wants to have his name known. He's got what they call *chutzpah*, which I've never had. I'm very shy. I don't like to play piano in front of a fellow that plays well. It gives me an inferiority complex."[179]

On a 1958 episode of the television show *This Is Your Life*, the spotlight focused on just such a reluctant Warren. Host Ralph Edwards asked his *Summer Stock* collaborator Mack Gordon if it was true that Warren had to be prodded to eventually hire a personal publicist. Said Gordon: "Yes, we did. And when the publicity man got Harry's name in the papers, Harry bawled him out. He said it was embarrassing to see stories about himself. And he let the guy go."[180]

In his later years Warren mostly worked independently from a detached bungalow located at the back of his Beverly Hills estate. It was in this sunny aerie that Warren listened to music, watched TV, and played the piano. His three Best Song Oscars sat on a window ledge, rays glinting off the heads and shoulders of the statues and radiating miniature sundogs on the walls opposite. Warren was nominated for the Academy Award for Best Song eleven times during his career and won for "Lullaby of Broadway," "You'll Never Know," and "On the Atchison, Topeka and the Santa Fe." Stacked on bookshelves were videocassettes of all of Warren's movies. The bungalow also acted as a kind of refuge for Warren. According to Nick Perito, a close friend of Warren's who served as Perry Como's longtime conductor/arranger, it was the only place Warren could escape the "Teutonic" henpecking of his wife Josephine, whom he had married in 1917.

"She could never identify with Harry's Italian ethnicity [she was German], and it bothered him," Perito told us. "He really preferred the company of boys such as myself and other composers like Gene DePaul and Johnny Mercer."[181] Warren's "loner" penchant for privacy may be the prime militating factor that has consigned him to the second tier of artists (at least as far as renown is concerned) who composed standards that make up the Great American Songbook.

"Harry was a very low-key individual and I don't know why he's so obscure in the public's mind," said singer Alice Faye, who was a prime interpreter of Warren's tunes. In 1943, she introduced the Oscar-winning standard "You'll Never Know" in the musical *Hello, Frisco, Hello*. It became her signature song and the sheet music alone sold over one million copies. "I was fortunate to be at the right studio [Twentieth Century-Fox] to sing his music. I'll always remember him and I can't say that about all the people with whom I've worked."[182]

Warren had the distinction from 1935 to 1950 of having had more Top Ten songs on the radio program *Your Hit Parade* than any other composer, including Irving Berlin, Cole Porter, and Richard Rodgers. His list of hits is endless: everything from sultry Academy Award–winning ballads ("You'll Never Know"), to up-tempo dance numbers ("I Only Have Eyes for You," "Chattanooga Choo Choo"), to goofy novelty songs ("Jeepers Creepers"). Other hits include "September in the Rain," "Serenade in Blue," "On the Atchison, Topeka, and the Santa Fe," and Dean Martin's signature Neapolitan crowd-pleaser "That's Amore," to name just a few. His last hit came from the title tune of the 1957 Cary Grant–Deborah Kerr tear-jerker, *An Affair to Remember*.

And Warren's contribution to the Hollywood musical goes much further than *42nd Street*. His music can be heard in more than sixty films made between 1933 and 1961. As the first major American songwriter to write primarily for the movies, Warren has been given the encomium "Mr. Hollywood Musical," and rightfully so. He was the only composer who conquered all four major Hollywood studios—Warner Bros., Twentieth Century-Fox, Metro-Goldwyn-Mayer, and Paramount. Indeed, Warren's music (if not the man himself) has become part of the American pop cultural fabric and stands as a seamless melodic link to major events of the twentieth century, notably the Great Depression and World War II.

"I never took part in any Hollywood nightlife in those days, I was too busy working," Warren said. "My wife used to bawl me out all the time because we couldn't go anyplace. I don't know any other songwriter that worked as much as I did. I worked for something like twenty-four years in the studios."[183]

"Harry Warren was an absolute giant," said singer Mel Tormé. "He's one of the great songwriter gods to me. I'd lump him with [Jerome] Kern, [Richard] Rodgers and [Lorenz] Hart, Gershwin, Porter, and Berlin. Warren stands head and shoulders with each of them." Tormé compared Warren to Ira Gershwin, whose fame was eclipsed by his older, more celebrated brother George: "Warren was the alter ego of Ira, who stayed in the background. There was a colorless aspect to Harry that transcended him getting the kind of due he deserves."[184]

Born Salvatore Antonio Guaragna on Christmas Eve 1893, in Brooklyn, New York, Warren (the youngest of eleven children) recollected starting to play the piano around age ten but said he never had a single lesson and he took pains to discount his rare, untutored gift: "I think you're just endowed that way, born that way. I think it's a god-given gift. That's the only excuse I can give you."[185]

"You're either a writer or you're not," Warren expounded. "You're either born with it or you're not born with it; you can't learn it. I don't care how much music you know. You can study from now to doomsday and that wouldn't make you a songwriter. You might be a musician, but it's something different—writing songs. That's why a lot of these screen composers get mixed up because they don't write lyrically, they write instrumentally."

To hear Warren tell it, before he achieved success in 1922 with his first published song, "Rose of the Rio Grande," he did just about everything including playing the snare drum in a band, acting in silent films, and even working in a circus. Warren's first real musical triumphs came at Warner Bros., where he and Al Dubin wrote most of the music for the Busby Berkeley extravaganzas. Of the four studios in which he toiled, Warren said Warner Bros. provided the worst working atmosphere. "The studio executives knew nothing about musicals. How could they? They didn't have any experience in music. Some people are still around attempting to make musicals but know nothing about it."[186]

A career pinnacle was achieved in 1944 when Warren signed a long-term contract with MGM, the acknowledged masters of movie musicals. "My favorite musicals—best work—were all at Metro but it never showed," he said. "I didn't like the other pictures at all. I didn't like the scripts. There was nothing to them. I like a story script where you can write something to it. At Metro, nobody bothered you. When I worked for Arthur Freed, you didn't even know you were working."[187]

But there is a bittersweet coda to Warren's songwriting career at MGM. Two of his best musical scores at Metro—*The Barkleys of Broadway*, noted as Fred Astaire and Ginger Rogers's last screen pairing, and *Summer*

Stock—were sullied by the interpolation of other composers' music into Warren's complete scores, something that is anathema to any songwriter. It was a wound Warren was still smarting from thirty years later. "Arthur Freed, the producer of *Barkleys*, played a dirty trick on me on that picture," Warren said. "He inserted George and Ira Gershwin's 'They Can't Take That Away from Me' for Fred and Ginger's reunion dance when they should have reprised my 'You'd Be Hard to Replace.' I was so mad at him I couldn't see straight. The same thing happened on *Summer Stock*. Producer Joe Pasternak who was nothing more than a singing waiter,* added 'Get Happy' by [Harold] Arlen and [Ted] Koehler for Judy. After I write a whole picture, they inject someone else's song; it's not fair. But, hey, they don't give a damn."[188]

Warren often referenced the seldom seen and much neglected 1948 MGM film *Summer Holiday*—the musical version of Eugene O'Neill's play *Ah Wilderness!*—as his favorite score. "I was very fond of that film. I think it's the best thing I ever did at Metro. The script to *Ah Wilderness!* lent itself so nicely to music. It just flowed. You could write music to every word. I think it will be rediscovered," Warren said. "As for a favorite tune, I can't answer that right now. It's like asking a guy which of his ten kids he prefers most. They are all my kids."[189]

Although Warren never gained a large measure of personal fame (like Irving Berlin) from his songs, the awards he won (three coveted Oscars) didn't impress him; in fact, he seemed to have unjustified contempt for them. "I only went to receive the first one for 'Lullaby of Broadway.' Now I use them as doorstops. I'm not proud of them," he sniffed. "I was in Palm Springs when I won my third and I told Harold Arlen 'You're two Oscars behind me.' I quit the Academy."[190]

By the end of the 1950s, film musicals were on the wane, as were requests for Warren's services. "They retired me. I never got a call from a studio anymore," Warren said. "They said I made too much money. They never even asked me how much I wanted."[191] Harry Warren assiduously avoided the show business limelight, preferring to occasionally tinker at the keyboard if a melody came to mind. He said his greatest pleasure came from listening to the symphonic music of Puccini, Verdi, Rachmaninoff, and Tchaikovsky. "They tell me that my music has a kind of a Puccini coloring. I'm a great admirer of Puccini but I never tried to copy him, but sometimes

*In his early life, Pasternak did indeed work as a busboy and waiter, but there's no proof that he was a "singing waiter."

it comes out that way. I think the fact that, from a child up, I absorbed so much music. In fact, I used to know all the marches; I knew all the waltzes. I absorbed all this music and it comes out in a different way, that's all. I have an inherent love for music—I still have it."[192]

Despite the fact that he is responsible for some of the catchiest, most insistent tunes in the American musical canon, true appreciation of Warren's songs may never be fully realized. Perhaps Bing Crosby summed up the Warren legacy best when he said, "The record throughout the years of Harry's film contributions is most impressive. No one in the field has done better, and the world's musical library has been permanently enriched because of his work."[193]

But most of the praise, effusive as it was when it came, fell on deaf ears. When he did pass away September 22, 1981, several musical notes were etched on Warren's tombstone from a song he wrote and they are as ironic an epitaph as you're ever likely to see from a man who's been called the greatest forgotten songwriter that ever lived. The notes are from "You'll Never Know."

THE WORDSMITH: MACK GORDON

SONGWRITER HARRY WARREN, THE LEAD COMPOSER ON *SUMMER STOCK,* rose to prominence in the early 1930s, collaborating with the corpulent, cigar-chomping lyricist Al Dubin on a string of hit Warner Bros. musicals that helped soothe the Depression-depressed masses. When Warren departed Warners for Twentieth Century-Fox in 1939, he picked up a new collaborator, Mack Gordon, another portly lyricist (one who could give a walrus pause) and who, like Dubin, also favored stogies. Their first joint venture, the score to the 1940 Shirley Temple film *Young People*, produced no hit tunes and ended the iconic child star's long and successful run at Fox. But for Warren and Gordon, it was just the beginning of a pairing that would produce many song hits before ending with *Summer Stock*, after which they dissolved the partnership.

Their five-year collaboration (1940–45) at Fox birthed one Oscar winner, "You'll Never Know." They contributed to a string of musicals, many featuring big band leaders Glenn Miller, Sammy Kaye, and Harry James and starring such Fox stars as Alice Faye, Betty Grable, Carmen Miranda, John Payne, and Dick Haymes. During World War II, Warren and Gordon introduced hits that came to define the big band era of swing music, including "Chattanooga Choo Choo," memorably danced by the Nicholas Brothers and Dorothy Dandridge in *Sun Valley Serenade* (1941) as well as "It Happened in Sun Valley," "I've Got a Gal in Kalamazoo," "Serenade in Blue," and "I Had the Craziest Dream," among others.

Prior to teaming with Warren, Gordon enjoyed a successful partnership with British composer Harry Revel beginning in 1929 that lasted through much of the next decade, working as studio songwriters at Paramount and then Twentieth Century-Fox. In total, Gordon contributed lyrics to about ninety feature films between 1929 and 1956. Gordon's most popular hits with Revel were "I Can't Begin to Tell You," "My Heart Tells Me," "Did You Ever See a Dream Walking?," and "Good Night, My Love." Gordon would go on to receive a total of nine Academy Award nominations for best song, four with Warren, two with James Monaco, two with Josef Myrow, and one with Alfred Newman.[194]

When the Revel-Gordon partnership ended in 1939, Gordon himself asked studio boss Darryl F. Zanuck if he could recruit Warren, who had just terminated his long and successful tenure with Al Dubin at Warner Bros. Zanuck gave the new team his benediction.[195] The duo's first assignment with Shirley Temple didn't hit a popular chord with audiences, but the pairing led to Warren and Gordon becoming arguably the most successful songwriting team of the war years.

"It took a while to get adjusted to Mack, because he was just about the opposite in temperament and lifestyle to me," said Warren. "He was a socializer, and he enjoyed the Hollywood life, going to parties with the producers and the stars. That didn't appeal to me at all. Working with him was similar to working with Dubin in that the ideas and most of the titles were his, and both of them would work from a lead sheet and come back with a complete set of lyrics."[196]

Gordon was born Morris Gittler in Warsaw, Poland, June 21, 1904, soon settling with his family in New York City. Changing his name to Mack Gordon, he migrated early to show business, singing in minstrel shows, then becoming an actor, comedian, and vaudeville performer.[197] "My father was a huge ham," said Roger Gordon, his son from his second marriage to the former actress Elizabeth Cook Gordon. "He was larger than life in more ways than one. He was a big tipper, very gregarious, and made his presence known wherever he was."[198]

Like many composers from Tin Pan Alley, Gordon's musical gifts were primarily self-taught with little formal training or education. Known as a killer song demonstrator with an almost angelic tenor voice, Gordon was never shy about trying out a lyric to anyone within earshot. Said partner Warren: "He talked all the time. He kept shouting out lines to you. He'd even do them for the barber while getting a shave. He'd go to Hillcrest Country Club and he's playing cards and he'd say, 'I just wrote this line. Let's hear what you think about it.' He was trying to get an opinion whether it was good or not. I guess he didn't trust himself."[199]

Gordon was married twice, and both times the divorces became contentious and ended up in the newspapers. In 1936, his first wife, Rose Gittler (Gordon's real last name), testified that he disputed her right to share in his "glory" as a songwriter and kept her away from his friends. "He said he was ashamed to take me out and frequently called me a dummy."[200] The divorce was finalized with his wife retaining custody of their two children. When his second marriage to Elizabeth Gordon hit the skids and again the newspapers in 1948; the couple squabbled in court about the value of thirty-four bottles of perfume, finally settling on a $1,250 monthly settlement for Mrs. Gordon and custody of their then six-year-old son Roger Mack Gordon.[201]

Roger Gordon said his father had a voracious appetite for life, food and "guy pursuits," most notably gambling. "I remember we went to a little hot dog stand on Pico Boulevard [in Los Angeles]. He ordered two tamales, two chili dogs, and a hamburger and that was before lunch! Even the guy at the hot dog stand noted how my father could really put it away." According to Roger, his father, while on gambling binges in Las Vegas, could sit at the card table for up to three days without eating. But he also remembered some special father-son moments. "He was a fun guy to hang around with. We would go to the Hollywood Stars baseball games or he'd take me to the wrestling matches at the Olympic Auditorium to see Gorgeous George, or we'd just go to the beach."[202]

In the early 1950s, Gordon, via diet pills, made a conscious effort to lose weight and according to Roger, dropped more than 100 pounds. The slimmed-down Gordon and his pleasant tenor voice can be seen and heard in a 1955 episode of *The George Burns & Gracie Allen Show* where he sings his hit tune "I Can't Begin to Tell You" to an awestruck Gracie.

After his tenure with Warren ended, Gordon attempted to embark on a different career, producing the 1946 musical *Three Little Girls in Blue* starring June Haver, Vivian Blaine, Vera-Ellen, and Celeste Holm in her movie debut. Working with songwriter Josef Myrow, the pair produced the hit "You Make Me Feel So Young," later popularized by Frank Sinatra. According to his son Roger, Gordon lost interest in producing after that film, because he found the job "overwhelming."[203]

Gordon's final score (with Josef Myrow) was for the 1956 RKO musical-comedy *Bundle of Joy* starring Hollywood's "it" couple at the time, Debbie Reynolds and Eddie Fisher. Gordon was living in New York City when he passed away February 28, 1959, at the age of fifty-four from a heart attack and bleeding ulcer. "He always had stomach problems and some heart difficulties," said Roger Gordon. "He didn't take care of himself, never exercised a day in his life or paid attention to his diet. He ate all the deli food you could imagine and that will kill you as it did him."

Although the Gordon-Warren partnership at Fox had ended with *Billy Rose's Diamond Horseshoe* in 1945, Warren brought back his former partner one last time to collaborate on the score for *Summer Stock*. "Mack Gordon was a good lyric writer, but he wasn't as intelligent as the other fellows [Al Dubin, Johnny Mercer]," Warren said, plainspoken as always. "But he had a great song sense."[204]

CHAPTER IV

THE PRODUCTION

How Dare This Look Like We're Having Any Fun!

THE STARS AND DIRECTOR OF *SUMMER STOCK* HAD SOME VALID MISGIVINGS about the thin story line being reminiscent of the kind of Mickey Rooney/Judy Garland "Let's put a show on in the barn!" films of a decade earlier. And they weren't far off the mark in their concern, because producer Joe Pasternak first conceived the movie as a screen reunion for Garland and Rooney. However, after they appeared together in *Words and Music* in 1948, MGM released Rooney from its payroll. Subsequently, another reteaming—that of Garland with Gene Kelly—seemed like a more winning formula. According to Garland historian John Fricke, "Gene Kelly was infinitely better box-office insurance than Mickey, and Kelly agreed to do the old-fashioned picture as a favor to Judy."[1]

Summer Stock, which takes its title from a type of live theater performance, is a warm and enduring homage to passionate thespians who just want to strut their stuff before an appreciative audience. As theater, summer stock originated in the late nineteenth century and refers to amateur or professional actors—typically in a repertory setting—that perform musical and nonmusical plays during the summer months, often reusing stock scenery and costumes scrounged from other productions. Summer stock venues can range from outdoor amphitheaters, tents, or in the case of the movie *Summer Stock*, a barn.

The term *summer stock* is not often used today but the performance mode is still practiced throughout the United States in spaces such as the American Players Theater in Spring Green, Wisconsin. Summer stock, like the Hollywood musical at large, is thoroughly American and was a recognizable term to movie audiences in the 1950s. In fact, the term is so American that the title of the film was changed to *If You Feel Like Singing,*

Sing (the song that Garland trills to open the film) so as not to confound audiences in the United Kingdom when the movie was released there.

As a slice of homespun Americana, *Summer Stock* was an ideal film to usher in the 1950s—the optimistic postwar decade that saw suburban sprawl, "two cars in every garage," and nuclear family units that would soon be mesmerized by wholesome TV fare like *Leave It to Beaver* and *Father Knows Best*.

The opening credits—as the names of cast and crew are superimposed over a rural mailbox with its red carrier signal flag—set the mood and telegraph to audiences the rustic Technicolor entertainment to follow. Even the music, a medley of "Hoe Down"/"(Howdy Neighbor) Happy Harvest"/"If You Feel Like Singing, Sing" over the main title, is orchestrated like a hootenanny with a preamble of countrified fiddling that gives way to the lush accompaniment of other instruments that was a distinctive hallmark of MGM's musical arrangements.

FARM FRESH

THE PLOT THAT PLAYED OUT ON SCREENS IN 1950 OPENS ON JANE FALBURY (Garland), a Connecticut farm owner who has worked hard to keep her family farm productive, but three years of bad harvests have left her mired in debt. Despite her financial crisis, Jane continues to pay for the expensive education of her sister Abigail (Gloria DeHaven), who is studying acting in New York City. After her hired hands, Frank and Zeb, quit, taking jobs in Hartford, Jane realizes that she must procure an expensive tractor to help her with the heavy work on the farm. However, because she doesn't have enough money to pay for a new tractor, Jane tries to get a loan through her fiancé, Orville Wingait (Eddie Bracken), whose father, Jasper Wingait (Ray Collins), owns a general store in town and is a leader in the community.

Jasper initially balks at Jane's extravagant request, but because he knows that his son is in love with her, he tells Jane that she can have the tractor as an early wedding present. Jane feels honor-bound to pay for the tractor herself and refuses to accept Jasper's terms, but he gifts her a new tractor anyway.

Jane returns to her farm only to discover that it has been overrun by a troupe of actors that Abigail has brought in from New York to rehearse a musical in the family's barn. Furious with Abigail for not having asked her about this huge imposition, Jane tells the troupe they must leave. Joe D. Ross (Kelly), who is Abigail's boyfriend and the director of the show, is also angry with Abigail for not having asked Jane's permission to use the barn. Abigail guilts Jane into agreeing to let Ross and his troupe use the barn for their show. Jane insists, however, that if they are to stay, they must perform some of the daily farm chores. The troupe grudgingly agrees to the arrangement and Jane immediately gives them lessons on how to maintain a working farm, resulting in plenty of comic shtick from the clueless city-dwellers.

One day, while helping her housekeeper Esme (Main) wash the dishes, Jane improvises a little tap dance she saw Joe perform (unaware that he is watching her). She becomes embarrassed when she notices Joe, but he compliments her dancing and tells her that she has real talent. As word spreads through town that an acting troupe from New York is staying at Jane's farm, Jasper becomes concerned about the sudden influx of show business people in the quiet community. Jane is summoned to town to explain the situation. Meanwhile, Herb Blake (Silvers), a member of the troupe, accidentally crashes Jane's new tractor into a tree. When Jane returns to the farm and learns about the accident, she orders the troupe to leave and demands that Abigail stay on the farm, reminding her younger sister that half the farm debts are hers, too!

Jane later reverses her decision when Joe sells his car to help pay for a new tractor. Joe continues to encourage Jane's interest in the theater and Jane and Joe begin to realize their attraction to each other. When Abigail and Harrison I. Keath (Hans Conried), the show's leading man, suddenly leave to star in a play in New York, Joe decides to take over the male lead and asks Jane to take Abigail's part. Orville sternly objects to Jane's involvement with the troupe, and when Jasper learns that Jane is in the show, he threatens to use his influence to stop it. Jane responds by threatening to call off her engagement to Orville. At the end of the first performance of the show, Abigail returns to the farm assuming that Jane will relinquish her role. Jane refuses to give up the part, having fallen in love with show business . . . and Joe.[2]

THE CASTING ROLLER COASTER

ALTHOUGH MICKEY ROONEY'S NAME WAS BANDIED ABOUT FOR THE MALE lead in *Summer Stock*, that casting choice never gained steam. Kelly was also seen as a more empathetic ally to Garland who could help her make it through the rough patches of filming. None of it, however, negated the hard fact that Kelly had grave misgivings about the story line.

According to one of Kelly's biographers, "Gene was upset by the thought of retreating to tired, overused material after the trailblazing *On the Town*" [which had not yet been released].[3] Kelly had enjoyed a successful collaboration with producer Joe Pasternak making the box-office hit *Anchors Aweigh* in 1945, for which he had been nominated for an Oscar as best actor, and "had no wish to make waves with a powerful producer at Metro who was close to Mayer, but he resolved now to be firm and decline the role. He tried to talk Pasternak away from choosing him for *Summer Stock* but, for the producer, casting Gene made good sense."[4]

Any misgivings Kelly had about embarking on a third film with Garland were dashed by his loyalty and friendship to the troubled star who helped him seven years earlier when, as a neophyte movie actor, he was learning the filmmaking ropes in *For Me and My Gal*. His commitment to Garland and *Summer Stock* was also perhaps commingled with some guilt: he said he was "brokenhearted" when he was forced to pull out of *Easter Parade* with Garland due to a fractured ankle. "They sent me this so-called script and they had some fellows come in—and I don't like to dwell on this because it was all so bad—and play some songs," Kelly said about first encountering the *Summer Stock* screenplay. "The songs were tawdry and the script was, well, it was *Babes on Broadway* [1941] or *Babes in Arms* [1939]. I said I can't do this shit, I really can't."

Kelly talked himself into the part of Joe Ross, adding that despite his qualms, he willingly took on the assignment when he understood the complexities of Garland's emotional frailties and was told by her doctor that "she needs someone in whom she trusts implicitly."[5] "Chuck Walters was directing the picture, so naturally he was worried silly even though he had the sophistication and the grace to realize that what he was working on was a piece of crap," Kelly groused. "I, on the other hand, was in a more luxurious position of just being the leading man."[6]

And Kelly wasn't the only one with concerns about the script; Garland had them, too. Although the story line of *Summer Stock* may seem like a do-over, it was the first starring vehicle for Garland in several years that took place in a contemporary setting and featured her as a strong, independent woman. Going back to 1946, every Garland film in succession had been a period piece set in an earlier era: *The Harvey Girls* (the Old West), *The Pirate* (the Caribbean of the early 1800s), *Easter Parade* (New York City during the era of President William Howard Taft), and *In the Good Old Summertime* (turn-of-the-century Chicago).

"Judy knew that with Gene as her co-star, the picture would be stylish and pleasant," wrote Judy's then-husband Vincente Minnelli in his memoir. "A story about putting a show in the barn and its conventionality depressed her. We discussed her approach to the picture. 'If I can just get one great number across, I won't mind the story too much,' she said."[7]

Garland would get her wish with "Get Happy."

HOUSE PARTY AT 725 N. RODEO DRIVE

IN 1949, KELLY AND HIS WIFE, ACTRESS BETSY BLAIR, WERE FAMOUS FOR "open-house" parties that occurred most weekends at their Beverly Hills home and that began in 1943, shortly after Kelly and Blair rented a house on Alta Drive. The parties were suspended when Kelly served in the Navy and resumed from 1946–50 at the new Kelly home at 725 North Rodeo Drive. The get-togethers included a who's who of celebrities who would drop by and featured competitive games, potluck meals, and sing-alongs at the piano, where everyone would congregate and perform. "Judy was there all the time, practically every weekend," remembered Kelly's daughter Kerry.[8] "It was never a steady group, it was whoever was available at the time and it was amorphous, but then we began to have a steady gang," said Kelly. "Our house was the bistro and we all met there for games and performances. We'd all get up and perform as if it were an Irish wake."[9]

Kelly added that the gatherings would often morph into intense political discussions. The much-publicized House Un-American Activities Committee hearings for the "Hollywood Ten," under chair Congressman J. Pernell Thomas, commenced in 1947 and the film community would be rocked for years from the "Red Scare" and the subsequent blacklist that destroyed the careers, and in many cases lives, of hundreds working in Hollywood, including Kelly's wife Betsy Blair. "It was a left-wing group," Kelly said, describing the people who frequented his open houses. "But at any rate, Judy learned a lot about a lot of things that she hadn't known."[10]

Kelly's daughter Kerry recollected that Garland always considered the house parties to be a kind of safe haven for her, surrounded as she was by supportive friends. But at one such gathering, she had appeared "puffy and overweight" and when coaxed to sing, she went at it so disjointedly, her vibrato out of control, that—always the best judge of her own performance—she broke off and started to cry, then fled the house. That night Gene reportedly told Blair that Judy's career was history.[11]

Although Garland was attached to *Summer Stock* from the earliest announcement in the Hollywood trade press dating back to December 1948, by February 8, 1950, her name had been inexplicably dropped and only Kelly remained consistently attached to the film. In remarks that day made at an MGM sales meeting, production head Dore Schary gave his nationwide sales team a *Summer Stock* preview:

> Summer Stock—that deals with the straw-hat circuit—is to be produced by Joe Pasternak. It has all the bubble and bounce of a teenager free-for-all. It is tuneful, it's smart and it's fresh. It will be loaded with Metro talent, and the original score is to be written by Harry Warren and Mack Gordon, who have probably written as many hits as any team of popular songwriters. We are not sure of the cast on this one yet, but we do know that Kelly—Gene Kelly—will be in it along with a host of others.[12]

In Schary's minutes from his executive business meeting the next month, March 23, 1949, the question of the film's female lead remained in flux, with June Allyson attached to the project as the headliner and Gloria DeHaven slotted to play her sister. It wasn't until June 14, 1949 (when Judy was in Boston receiving treatment for prescription drug addiction), that Louella Parsons announced in her column that Garland would return to MGM to star in *Summer Stock*. When Pasternak appeared to have dropped Garland from the cast, it raised the ire of studio chief Mayer. "He [Mayer] was not satisfied with his underling's doomsday catalog of her [Garland's] recent disasters, which had cost Metro hundreds of thousands of dollars in reshooting costs. 'I know all that,' snapped Mayer. 'Judy Garland has made this studio a fortune in the good days. And the last thing we can do is give her one more chance.'"[13]

Over the course of the summer of 1949, other cast members for the film fell into place. Some were erroneously announced, most likely from an MGM publicity department that was continuously trying to wheedle the names of new contract players into print. For example, one Hollywood columnist, Edith Gwynn, wrote that the dancing (and married) team of Marge and Gower Champion was to be added to the cast.[14] On September 10, 1949, the *Los Angeles Times* reported that Argentine actor, singer, and Olympic swimmer Fernando Lamas had signed a long-term studio contract and would make his film debut in *Summer Stock*.[15]

None of that wishful thinking ever materialized. The next month, Hedda Hopper, in her column, correctly reported that character actor Eddie Bracken was joining the cast of *Summer Stock*.[16] On September 6, Hopper used her column to drop the names of two additional cast members—Marjorie Main and Moscow-born opera diva Marina Koshetz. It's no surprise that at one point Koshetz's name was attached to *Summer Stock*, although it's hard to envision what role a high opera singer would have played in the film. Pasternak had a soft spot for classical performers and had often cast high-brow entertainers in his musicals. Although Koshetz didn't appear in *Summer Stock*, she did appear in five Pasternak productions as did Danish-American tenor Lauritz Melchior and concert pianist José Iturbi.

In October 1949, a month prior to the start of filming, the final cast took shape with the naming of newcomer Carleton Carpenter and veteran comic Phil Silvers, fresh off his Broadway success in *Top Banana*. Silvers's casting was noted in the press: "One of the brightest reunions heralded in a longtime is Gene Kelly and Phil Silvers in *Summer Stock*, the Joe Pasternak feature, since they were so good together in *Cover Girl*."[17] Other actors who joined the cast, such as Hans Conried and Ray Collins, didn't warrant special mention in the press.

THE FILMS THAT GOT AWAY

IN ORDER TO FULLY COMPREHEND THE CHALLENGES THAT FACED GETTING *Summer Stock* through pre-production and onto the screen, it's important to take into consideration Judy Garland's mental state and the stresses she was under during that period in her life—an immense weight that affected two movies she was scheduled to star in and was subsequently dismissed from before the cameras rolled on *Summer Stock*. The first, *The Barkleys of Broadway*, was directed by Charles Walters and was intended to reteam Garland with her *Easter Parade* co-star Fred Astaire after their successful pairing in that film.

As *Barkleys* was ramping up pre-production in June 1948, ponder the litany of problems that Garland had to deal with: The preceding eighteen months had subjected her to the ongoing deterioration of her marriage to Vincente Minnelli; periodic but increased periods of prescription medication dependence and abuse; the extensive problems of filming (and then reshooting portions of) *The Pirate*; the strain of completing *Easter Parade* on schedule and under budget; at least two stays in sanitariums for nervous collapse and withdrawal; and the stressful knowledge that several major productions were awaiting her at the studio.[18] In addition to these factors, Garland was parenting a toddler, daughter Liza, born March 12, 1946. Overlaying all this was the omnipresent fact that Garland owed the studio two films a year for which she was well paid. Her reported 1948 salary was $310,483.[19] Adjusted for inflation, that amount would equal nearly $3.7 million in 2022 dollars.

Garland gamely reported to work on *Barkleys* "frail, fragile and medication-propelled."[20] She made it through ten days of rehearsals and wardrobe fittings from June 14–July 1, 1948, missing three days due to illness, but was unable to work for the next two weeks. On July 17, producer Arthur Freed dropped her from the film and replaced her with Astaire's former screen partner, Ginger Rogers, heralding their first film together in a decade.

Perhaps the biggest film prize that escaped her was the coveted title role in the screen adaptation of the Broadway hit *Annie Get Your Gun*, with music and lyrics by Irving Berlin. It was a dream part that seemed a predestined perfect fit for Garland's talents. As the film was about to go into production in the spring of 1949 with Busby Berkeley as director, Garland's personal problems continued to mount. She and Minnelli officially separated on

March 30, 1949. For a fragile Garland, Berkeley, known for his on-set tirades and endless rehearsals, couldn't have been a worse choice as director. By the time Freed acknowledged his hiring error (Berkeley was replaced with Garland's more sympathetic ally, Charles Walters), it was too late. The production was shut down on May 10 and Garland put on suspension.

The loss of the role was a huge blow to Garland's self-esteem; when she learned of her dismissal, she invited Walters to retreat with her to her dressing room for a drink. "Laughing hysterically, but not crying, Garland said, 'I'm not only fired from this—I'm out of Metro!' I let her get stoned. 'Have another, honey, it's the only answer,'" Walters told Garland biographer Gerold Frank. "She's crying and laughing," Walters continued about his and Judy's dressing room heart-to-heart. "'I don't believe it. After the money I made for those pricks! These dirty bastards! These lousy sons-of-bitches! Goddamn them!' I said, 'let it rip, let it all out. Let it go!'"[21]

According to John Fricke, at this low ebb, Garland didn't lay all the blame on the heartlessness of Metro's executives. "I don't blame the studio for suspending me," she said. "I've been a bad girl for not getting to work on time. Studios are run to make money. They can't take chances with careless people like me."[22] Garland was replaced in the part of Annie Oakley by Betty Hutton, on loan-out from Paramount Studios, and Walters was replaced as director by George Sidney.

Walters's abrupt dismissal from *Annie* and subsequent replacement by Sidney came as a surprise to the director, who learned about the development after reading it in Hedda Hopper's syndicated column. Walters phoned Hopper to learn the source of this "news." "'Oh my God,' she said. 'You didn't know? I'm sorry, it's true. I got it from L. B. [Mayer].' So there you are. And that's how I didn't direct *Annie*," said Walters.[23]

"Judy was made to order for it [*Annie Get Your Gun*], but she didn't know what the hell she was doing," said Freed. "I was going to do *The Band Wagon* with her, *The Barkleys of Broadway*. I had wonderful scripts, but she just couldn't function. Not a question of showing up on time; it was a simple fact that she couldn't function. That was the total of it."[24]

Hollywood during the studio system era was a fraternal company town knit together with confluences and trajectories among stars, directors, and producers continuously in play, which often duplicated themselves from film to film. In a queer case of cinematic déjà vu, after exiting *Annie*, Berkeley was briefly assigned to direct *Summer Stock* for producer Pasternak.

However, sometime during pre-production, Charles Walters again replaced Berkeley as director; but this time he stayed on to complete the film, as did Garland.[25]

BOSTON BOUND

SHORTLY AFTER THE *ANNIE GET YOUR GUN* DEBACLE, ON MAY 29, 1949, AN emotionally and physically spent Garland voluntarily entered the Peter Bent Brigham Hospital in Boston in an effort to eliminate her dependency on prescription medications and enable a return to Hollywood cleaned up and ready to face the cameras again. It would be the first of two extended stays (the first beginning May 29, the second a two-week stay in August 1949). After her return from Boston, she would report to work on *Summer Stock*. Garland was accompanied to Massachusetts by Carleton Alsop, who had taken on the duties of Garland's daily "personal manager" and who was married to the actress Sylvia Sidney. Garland called Alsop (often likened to an urbane character sprung from a Somerset Maugham story) "Pa," and he was always at the ready to deliver a nasty jibe or riposte (something Garland loved) when the occasion called for it. In Boston, Garland was a patient of Dr. George W. Thorn, a distinguished internist and physician-in-chief, but she was placed in the day-to-day care of Dr. Augustus Rose.[26]

MGM did pay Judy's hospital bills—some $40,000 for her Boston stay. Records show that Metro loaned her $9,000 on June 28 while she was at Peter Bent Brigham. The loan had two provisos: that she would pay it back when she returned to work, but on the condition that the studio would not put her before the cameras until she came back with a letter from Dr. Thorn stating that he "reasonably believed" she was able, ready, and willing to work.[27] Vincente Minnelli (separated from Garland during her time in Boston) said Louis B. Mayer tried seeking on a number of occasions to schedule professional treatment for his troubled star, but his efforts never seemed to come to fruition. "L. B. was always concerned when Judy was ill and would bring psychiatrists to the house," Minnelli said. "She did go east to a clinic while we were still married, and I went there a couple of times to see her and eventually bring her home."[28]

At the time Garland was admitted to Brigham, she was, wrote Gerold Frank, in a low mood. She couldn't sleep or work, suffered migraine headaches, and couldn't control her temper and would fly into tantrums at the slightest provocation.[29] Garland had seen more than a dozen psychiatrists up to that point and was rightfully cynical of Dr. Rose's belief that her stay in Boston would cure her of her dependencies. Soon, Judy was on a strict regimen to regulate her sleeping cycle and her meals. All the time, Alsop was her primary "Man Friday," making sure Dr. Rose's regimen was closely followed. Garland also received encouragement from her friends, including Frank Sinatra, who regularly called and eventually was allowed to visit. Even Louis B. Mayer, who started his show business career in the Boston area, came to see her.

On June 10, Garland's twenty-seventh birthday, daughter Liza, with her governess, arrived at Boston's South Station, where her mother picked her up and posed for photos with the press. After the fourth week, Dr. Rose declared Garland completely pill-free and her sleeping and eating habits normalized. She was transferred to outpatient status and moved to the Ritz-Carleton Hotel, all the while under the watchful eye of Alsop.[30] "In Boston, whenever I could get her well enough to go, I'd take her to a [Boston Red Sox] ballgame," said Alsop. "All the ballplayers stopped playing ball and wanted her to autograph baseballs. They had said, 'Come and join us for a bite.' I couldn't allow it because I never knew when she'd go to pieces. I'd have to get her back to the hospital quick. I'd keep a driver waiting."[31] Gene Kelly, who was then at work on *On the Town*, knew little about Garland's stay in Boston. "The only common ground I had with her tenure in Boston was that she found out I idolized Ted Williams and thought he was the greatest ballplayer that ever lived," he said. "She had gotten to learn about Ted during her stay and that's really all I know because I never pried; never asked her any questions."[32]

After Garland returned from a July 4th holiday in Cape Cod (spent with Alsop, Liza, Sylvia Sidney, and Sidney's son from a previous marriage), Dr. Rose made the determination that perhaps she was ready to return to Hollywood and resume her career as a movie star. Before leaving Boston, Garland paid a return visit to Children's Hospital, where she had previously gone for a series of tests, primarily some electronic brain scans, and while there befriended a group of disabled young fans who were patients at the hospital. Garland made several visits to the hospital, bonding with the children and feeling the reciprocal love the children had for her. It was arguably the best medicine she received during her time in Boston. On her final visit, while making the rounds to say goodbye to the children, she bent over to hug and kiss the last child, who had remained silent up to this time. Suddenly the child jumped up on her knees and said, "Judy!"[33]

Reflecting on that experience years later, Garland said, "I guess it was one of the great moments in my life when she spoke like that. I felt I had . . ." She paused, searching for words. "I just didn't give a damn how many pictures I'd been fired from, or how much humiliation . . . I had done a human being some good! I felt on top of the world."[34] With the Boston sojourn over, it was time for Judy to return to the Dream Factory and embark on what would become her twenty-eighth and final feature film at MGM, *Summer Stock*.

A review of Schary's meeting minutes in the months leading up to production shows that the *Summer Stock* start date was initially scheduled for July 5, 1949, when June Allyson was briefly slated to co-star with Kelly, who had just wrapped filming on what would become a landmark musical, *On the Town*. The start date was later pushed back to October 15, then October 22, November 7, and finally November 21. According to Schary's minutes, MGM executive Benny Thau was tasked with naming the director and Chuck Walters received the assignment on August 23. It's uncertain whether the start date was pushed back due to normal production delays or to accommodate Garland because of uncertainties regarding her readiness. Walters, as already noted, expressed serious misgivings about the triteness of the script, but, as a loyal company man, he was determined to make lemonade from lemons. "Walters strove to make *Summer Stock* an honest depiction of rural theater, conveying the backstage chaos, the amateur temperament, and curious mix of fear and anticipation that beset opening night," wrote Walters's biographer, Brent Phillips. "The slight story at least explored the need for self-fulfillment, particularly in Garland's character, and her evolution from subservience to star attraction provided the emotional core."[35]

When Garland returned to Los Angeles from her stay in Boston, she was accompanied by Dr. Rose, who was tasked with transitioning the fragile star back to work. He frequently accompanied her to the set. "Carleton [Alsop] kept repeating he felt she was returning too soon, but he was paid little attention," wrote Minnelli in his memoir. "Dr. Thorn thought it was all right."[36] According to Minnelli, the only medication Garland was taking was a series of glucose injections prescribed by her physician for energy and stamina.[37]

As rehearsals began the first week of October, the real palliatives for Garland were not glucose injections but the bracketing support she would receive from Kelly, Walters, Bracken, DeHaven, and Silvers. *Summer Stock* may have come up wanting as a screen story, but the collective care of friends who understood her problems was a balm, or at least it was hoped to be. Still, with the studio abuzz about Garland's return (it had been nearly a year since her last film, *In the Good Old Summertime*), the pressures were tremendous. Walters couldn't help but approach the job with a good deal of trepidation. "The bets around the studio lot were that we wouldn't finish the film," he said. "So that's an encouraging note in which to go to work every morning."[38]

The news the first week of October 1949 saw Mao Zedong proclaim to the world the formation of the People's Republic of China; the first Black-owned radio station, WERD, open in Atlanta, Georgia; the United Nations headquarters building dedicated in New York City; and Iva Toguri D'Aquino (known as Tokyo Rose) imprisoned for treason for wartime propaganda radio broadcasts (she received a presidential pardon from Gerald Ford in 1977). Also that first week in autumn, *Summer Stock* began rehearsals at MGM on Stage 27, the second largest soundstage on the lot. Filming would begin the following month. Although most films used more than one stage, Stage 27, because of its size, played host to a fair share of Metro musicals. In 1948, some of *Words and Music*, which featured Kelly in his groundbreaking "Slaughter on Tenth Avenue" ballet, was filmed there; and for Garland, Stage 27 certainly evoked memories of *The Wizard of Oz* in 1939 and its "Munchkinland" set with the Yellow Brick Road snaking from that stage across the studio's Main Street to Stage 15 (the biggest on the MGM lot).[39]

That fall, Joe Pasternak was joined in the process of production at MGM by his two colleagues, Arthur Freed and Jack Cummings. Each man had a musical in development. Cummings was producing *Three Little Words*, a biopic of songwriters Bert Kalmar and Harry Ruby, starring Fred Astaire and Red Skelton. And Freed (just a few days after *Summer Stock* started rehearsals) began shooting *Annie Get Your Gun* starring Betty Hutton in the eponymous role of sharpshooter Annie Oakley. Hutton had been a rushed replacement for Garland.

The lot was humming.

A CASE OF COLD FEET

KELLY AND GARLAND WEREN'T THE ONLY ONES INVOLVED IN *SUMMER Stock* who were concerned about the hoary script. Less than one month before rehearsals were to begin, director Walters was in a state of high agitation and expressed misgivings about the film, specifically the story line. In an audacious move, Walters went over the head of his immediate boss (Pasternak) and arranged an in-person meeting with Dore Schary in Schary's Thalberg Building executive suite. Walters probably felt emboldened to bypass Pasternak and go straight to the top of the MGM hierarchy because he stood in good stead with the studio brass. He had just come off directing three consecutive box-office hits for producer Arthur Freed: *Good News* (which marked Walters's directorial debut), *Easter Parade*, and *The Barkleys of Broadway*, which was originally intended as a follow-up to the Astaire-Garland pairing in *Easter Parade* but became instead the tenth and last Astaire–Ginger Rogers film after Garland dropped out.

To better prepare Schary prior to their meeting, Walters put his concerns about *Summer Stock* down on paper in a typewritten letter. In his deprecating missive dated September 12, 1949, Walters (misspelling Schary's first name) wrote:

> Dear Dory:
>
> Understand we are to have a meeting with you on "Summer Stock" this Wednesday or Thursday. Realizing how little time you have for personal "chats," am writing this note to let you know my feelings re: "Summer Stock" prior to our story conference. I do not want Joe [producer Pasternak] to feel I'm going over his head so please keep this confidential. Joe seems so excited and enthused over the whole venture that it is very difficult to approach him with the major faults I find in his "baby."
>
> First of all, the story is trite, and obvious, and has no deviation from the straight, formularized pattern which I feel we have seen under the shroud of other titles many, too many, times.
>
> Second, it's a shame to waste the talents of Judy Garland in a straight ingénue role. She is a female Charlie Chaplin for my dough, who can make you laugh and cry simultaneously—the perfect "Patsy" who, nine reels later, fits Prince Charming's glass slipper.

Third, "Summer Stock" is a great title and the actual workings of a stock company—the roughing it, physical labor of painting scenery, making, borrowing, or begging costumes and props, has never been, to my knowledge, depicted in its true form. I have outlines for a story that not only would give full value to our title "Summer Stock" but be an ideal characterization for Judy; that of a stage-struck farm girl, who joins the local stock company, only to become the Patsy who paints, and hauls scenery, props, etc. and gets, momentarily, no nearer the stage than the moving of scenery and working the act curtain. I would like to give you that story outline in full.

Fourth, if we must use the present story, we need a Sid Sheldon or Freddie Finklehoff[e] to make the scenes, dialogue and situations interesting, amusing and believable; and make a few detours off that beaten-up beaten path.

Sincerely, Charles Walters[40]

The two screenwriters Walters referenced in his letter, Sidney Sheldon and Fred Finklehoffe, had extensive experience working with both Walters and Garland. Sheldon was one of the credited screenwriters on *Easter Parade* and Finklehoffe had worked on *For Me and My Gal, Meet Me in St. Louis*, and other Garland films, several co-starring Mickey Rooney. While what transpired during the closed-door meeting between Walters and Schary is unknown, Walters's desire to bring in some additional screenwriting muscle and reposition the story with Garland playing the starstruck patsy/rube to the show-wise city slickers, was never developed and Sy Gomberg and George Wells remained the credited writers of *Summer Stock*. Gomberg's treatment/synopsis for *Summer Stock* became a scheduled production reality in December 1948 when MGM officially announced that it took an option on his original story.

Although Gomberg and Wells collaborated on two films, they could hardly be described as a writing team akin to Betty Comden and Adolph Green, who scribed some of the screenplays for the Freed unit. In all likelihood, said Gomberg's daughter Katherine Blake, the studio had both writers under contract and randomly paired them to fine-tune the final shooting script for *Summer Stock*. Blake couldn't recall her father and Wells ever seeing each other socially outside of the work hours they spent together.[42]

ENTER GEORGE WELLS

When the decision was made to assign a writer to work with Gomberg to adapt the story into a workable screenplay, Joe Pasternak tapped George Wells, a studio contract writer who was building a reputation for crafting winning light comedies and musicals. In 1949–50, Gomberg and Wells would collaborate on two screenplays for Pasternak, *The Toast of New Orleans* and *Summer Stock*. Born in New York City, Wells was the son of Billy K. Wells, a vaudevillian who advanced to writing sketches for the *George White Scandals* and *Harry Delmar's Revels* on Broadway. After graduating from New York University, George followed his father as a scribe and wrote for the *Jack Pearl Show* on radio and *Lux Radio Theater*.[41]

Wells signed on to MGM in 1943 and was under contract to the studio until his retirement in 1970. His first credited work was the Red Skelton vehicle *The Show-Off* in 1946. The next year, he wrote the screenplay for another Skelton film, *Merton of the Movies*. Working for the studio's other top musical producers, Arthur Freed and Jack Cummings, Wells found firm footing writing screenplays for *Take Me Out to the Ballgame* (1949), *Three Little Words*, *Excuse My Dust* (1951), *Texas Carnival*, and *Lovely to Look At* (1952). In 1952–53, Wells did double-duty writing the screenplays for and producing two Esther Williams aqua-musicals, *Dangerous When Wet* and *Jupiter's Darling*, the latter a box-office flop that proved to be Williams's final film at MGM and Wells's last producing credit.

Switching it up (film genres, to be exact), Wells grabbed the brass ring in 1957 and won Oscar gold for his screenplay of the romantic comedy *Designing Woman*, starring Gregory Peck and Lauren Bacall. That same year he also penned the hit comedy *Don't Go Near the Water* that starred Glenn Ford and Gia Scala. Wells stayed on at MGM to write a number of films, including *Party Girl* (1958), *Ask Any Girl* (1959), *Where the Boys Are* (1960), *The Horizontal Lieutenant* (1962), and *The Impossible Years* (1968). After twenty-seven years with the studio, Wells finally left Metro in 1971. He died in 2000 at the age of ninety-one.

THE SCRIPT EVOLVES

CHARLES WALTERS WAS JUSTIFIED IN HIS CONCERNS ABOUT THE QUALITY of the *Summer Stock* screenplay. An earlier version of the script called a "temporary clean script" was sent to puritanical "Censor Czar" Joseph Breen at the Motion Picture Association of America (MPAA) on May 12, 1949. "All Hollywood shrank when, lurking behind a crucifix, he sucked the life from hundreds of studio films," wrote film historian Sam Staggs about the all-powerful Breen, who was head of the Production Code Administration (PCA), the chief morals enforcement agency in Hollywood. According to Staggs, "Breen not only enforced the Code in the most literal and restrictive terms, but also functioned as a de facto agent of the arch-conservative Roman Catholic hierarchy in the United States."[43]

That said, even a Pasternak "feel-good" musical like *Summer Stock* didn't escape the scrutiny of Breen and his watchdogs. On May 17, 1949, in a letter to L. B. Mayer, Breen enumerated his concerns after his perusal of the *Summer Stock* script:

> We wish to call your attention to a few minor details: At the outset, we direct your particular attention to the need for the greatest possible care in the selection and photographing of the dresses and costumes of your women. The Production Code makes it mandatory that the intimate parts of the body—specifically, the breasts of women—be fully covered at all times. Any compromise with this regulation will compel us to withhold approval of your picture. In accordance with Code requirements, it will be necessary that you consult with Mr. Mel Morse of the American Humane Association as to all scenes in which animals are used. Mr. Morse may be reached at Stanley 7-3976.
>
> Page 2: We assume it is not your intention to show any of action of Judith "slipping out of her nightgown into a dress."
>
> Page 16: Abigail's costume must cover her person properly.
>
> Page 23: Please make certain that in the various dance routines, none of the dance movements are sex-suggestive or otherwise objectionable.

Page 31: Again, care will be needed with the costuming of the three girls.

Page 35: In the various kissing scenes please make certain that none of the kisses are lustful, prolonged or open-mouthed.

Page 52: Again, we call your attention to the care which will be needed with the costuming of Abigail when she "leaps from her bed, shucking the bed jacket."

Page 94: The "slap on the rump" is unacceptable.

You understand, of course, that our final judgment will be based on the finished picture.[44]

JOSEPH I. BREEN AND THE PCA

It seems reasonable that a musical like *Summer Stock* would easily pass muster with Breen and his colleagues at the MPAA, and for the most part, it did. Still, that didn't mean the movie industry's chief overseer of suitable content didn't have to approve every word spoken, song sung, scene filmed, and costume worn in the film. Born October 15, 1888, "an Irish-Catholic with a background in journalism and public relations, Joseph Ignatius Breen was accused by some of being an anti-Semite because he blamed the Jews who largely controlled Hollywood studios for the sex, violence, and perceived decadence in films."[45]

Breen's ascension to the position of morals enforcer in the film industry began in 1931 when Will Hays, president of the Motion Picture Producers and Distributors of America, first enlisted him to squelch threatened movie boycotts by religious groups unless the industry cleaned up its act and started producing more wholesome, family-friendly entertainment. In 1934, Breen was named to head the PCA. His job was to help the film industry self-censor in order to avoid government intrusion and costly boycotts by groups such as the Catholic Legion of Decency, which was always on the lookout for morally offensive content from Hollywood studios.

"Breen set himself up as America's moral conscience, and by 1934, under threat of boycotts of films led by religious groups, he set up a stronger code," wrote Robert Kolker in *The Cultures of American Film*. "The PCA vetted every script headed to or being considered for production by the studios. It carried out ongoing negotiations with the studios about what could and could not be shown, and, at times, it supervised the editing of films."[46] In addition, the Code strictly controlled sexual and political content and the degree of dress or undress that could be seen on-screen. "Breen could be both blunt and accommodating—on his terms—in dealing with filmmakers," Kolker said.[47]

Breen briefly stepped down as the head of Code enforcement in 1941 to become general manager of RKO Pictures. That tenure lasted about a year, whereupon he returned to his old job as "Censor Czar." Ten years after Breen resumed his post, in the early 1950s, the PCA's iron grip on the industry began to weaken. "One of the reasons the PCA grew more cooperative over time was declining pressure from industry foes," wrote Richard B. Jewell in his book *The Golden Age of Cinema: Hollywood 1929–1945*. "Another was sensitivity to protests from professors, artists, advocates of free speech and filmmakers who charged that Breen and his acolytes were anti-intellectual philistines impeding the development of the cinema as a mature art form."[48]

In 1954, Breen ended his dominion as head of Code enforcement, the same year his former boss, Will Hays, died. During his twenty years as director of the PCA, it's estimated that Breen's office edited more than 3,000 scripts each year. He died December 5, 1965.

THE SEPTEMBER 19 SCRIPT

LOOKING AT HANS CONRIED'S SHOOTING SCRIPT OF *SUMMER STOCK* dated September 19, 1949,[49] just one week after Charles Walters wrote his letter of concern to Dore Schary, it was apparent that extensive revisions were necessary. Whether Walters worked with Sy Gomberg and George Wells exclusively or included Gene Kelly and Joe Pasternak in the revision discussions is impossible to tell. What is known is that the script went through several significant modifications and trims before the cameras started to roll about two months later. Conried's working script provides a fascinating window into an organic creative process as the script was cut, sculpted, and reshaped into what we now see on screen.

For starters, Gomberg and Wells's screenplay was overly long (not taking into full account the musical numbers that would need to be filmed) and it contained significantly more slapstick than is evident in the film. Considering that Phil Silvers's character of Herb is sixth-billed in *Summer Stock*, he is given an inordinate amount of lines and other business in the September 19 version of the script. Regardless, in this early iteration virtually no character was immune from taking a pratfall or being on the butt end of some other form of visual humor. When the September 19 screenplay is compared to later versions of the script, the jokiness has been significantly toned down (primarily at Walters's insistence), and Silvers's foolery is drastically diminished.

In an early scene, when Esme awakens the troupe of players sleeping in the barn with a blast from her shotgun so they can begin their chores, the scene is described as pandemonium with . . . "sheets falling down, kids leaping for the rafters; somersaulting out of bed; Herb falling out of a window; Joe doing a nip-up (a gymnastic handspring from a supine position that Kelly employed in other films most notably the 'Be a Clown' number from *The Pirate* with the Nicholas Brothers); one kid rolling off the hayloft, hanging on the edge, his legs dangling into space, etc., etc." In the film, the comedy in this scene has been substantially scaled back. After Esme's shotgun blast wakeup call, the troupe members in the hayloft leap awake, startled, with Joe and Herb holding each other in a fearful embrace. Indeed, at several points in the screenplay a "trigger happy" Esme brandishes her shotgun, which is named "Ben." In the film, she uses the nameless gun only this once.

In the scene when the two young boys discover Judith's (she's not named Jane in the September 19 script) wrecked tractor and run to the barn to ask her if they can play with the parts, Joe chases after them. "He leaps after them, trips over the axle, lands on his face. Struggling to his feet, he streaks out the door in hot pursuit." In the film, Joe chases the kids but without the pratfall. The footrace ends with Joe muzzling one of the kids aside and twirling Jane onto the dance floor where "The Portland Fancy" number soon commences.

When Joe finally finds Herb (who wrecked the tractor) hiding in the bushes, Herb "whirls and streaks across the barnyard, Joe hot on his trail.

Trying to make a fast turnaround in the pigpen, Herb grabs the gate stanchion—recently—repaired, for leverage. It jerks loose, the corner of the pen collapses again—releasing the horde of pigs." In the film, Joe discovers Herb hiding in some shrubbery, chases and catches him and then, partially obscured inside a shed, kicks or slugs him with Herb letting out a piercing yowl. No pigs are released.

From page to screen, here are more significant characters and scenes in the September 19 script cut and/or changed in the final shooting script. There is no opening number with Jane in the shower singing (in the film, "If You Feel Like Singing, Sing"). Instead, the opening scene is a preamble of shots before the first notes of a song:

> A flock of chickens join the rooster, clucking rhythmically. A bird whistles a shrill phrase. Cows plod in from pasture, mooing in harmony. Pigs in the pen "oink" musically. Plow horses gallop heavily across the meadow, their hooves drum-beating the tempo. In a huge four-postered bed a huddled figure lies sleeping. This is Judith Falbury, 22 and lovely. The bird's song, plus a dancing sunbeam, awaken her. She sits up suddenly, listening, then jumps out of bed and runs to the window. She wears a long flannel nightgown—her hair in braids. She opens the window wider, breathes in the fragrance, joins joyously in the song. Then, still singing, she dances as she dunks her face in a wash basin, brushes her teeth, slips out of the nightgown and into a dress . . .

When Judith drives to Wingait Falls in pursuit of a tractor, the script introduces a character named Lem, described as the "town do-nothing" with a "harmonica against his chest, a sleepy look in his eye."

> ***Lem:*** *Nice day, ain't it, Miss Judith?*
> ***Judith:*** *I don't know yet.*

After Judith leaves Wingait's store, tractor joyfully in her possession—and as the lead-in to the song "Happy Harvest"—Judith again encounters Lem loitering in front of the Wingait storefront, this time playing his harmonica. Judith now responds to his earlier question with:

> ***Judith:*** *It's a wonderful day, Lem.*

Lem also crops up later as one of the musicians playing his harmonica in the barn dance sequence while "eyeing Sarah's legs swinging from the loft." As the music changes from polka to swing and members of Joe's troupe jump off the hayloft to the dance floor below, "Lem swoops up Sarah [Nita Bieber]."

Upon first meeting Joe, the script has him "grabbing, swinging, and planting a firm kiss on Judith." In the film, the two characters share just one passionate kiss, much later, immediately following the "You Wonderful You" number.

When Judith consents to letting the troupe of players stay on the farm, a euphoric Joe spouts a line cribbed straight out of *Yankee Doodle Dandy* (1942) and George M. Cohan: "Miss Falbury, my father thanks you, my mother thanks you, the theater thanks you and I thank you," he says. In the film, his response is less labored and theatrical and more genuine.

As the troupe launches into "Dig-Dig-Dig Dig for Your Dinner," the script has Abigail joining in the number and "wild, passionate movement" from Sarah. In the film, Abigail is off camera up in her room and Sarah's movement in the number could not even remotely be termed wild or passionate (no matter what the press kit might've fibbed otherwise!).

In this script version, Herb has a penchant for quoting Shakespeare in several scenes. These lines were cut and substituted with snarky, wiseacre dialogue more identifiable with Silvers's persona at the time and throughout the rest of his career. Some examples of Herb quoting The Bard of Avon:

> ***Herb:*** *The actors are at hand—and by their show,*
> *You shall know all that you are about to know!*
> *Midsummer Night's Dream, act five, scene one.*

Later, when Herb pesters Joe to act in the show:

> ***Herb:*** *I know you're not going to let me act!*
> *I've been practicing!*
> *To be or not to be, that is the question!*
> *Whether 'tis nobler . . .*
> ***Joe:*** *Shut up, shut up!*
> *If I find a part, I'll let you know!*
> *Until then, you're just the stage manager!*

When Joe finds Herb hiding in the bushes after demolishing the tractor:

Herb: *Joe! Joe! Joe!*
This is Herb—your old friend. Joe, listen.
"The quality of mercy is not strained." Joe, "Merchant of Venice," Joe!
Act four, scene one. Joe. No! No!

An unlikely Esme even one-ups Herb in his Shakespeare recitations as they're clearing dishes off the dinner table:

Herb: *(with dignity, licking his fingers) "'Tis a poor cook that cannot lick his own fingers!"*
Romeo and Juliet—act four, scene four.
Esme: *Be thou familiar, but by no means vulgar.*
Hamlet—act one, scene two.

On two occasions in the script, Herb is sleep-talking and muttering the names of some famous MGM stars (Lana Turner, Greer Garson, and Ava Gardner):

Herb: *No—no—no—Lana—no.*
Greer stop—now please—Greer.
Ava—you know better—
(Joe muffles the mumbling by covering Herb's face with a horse's straw hat, then exits.)

In the barn dance scene, the script references "two old maids at the side of the platform acknowledge the patter of applause." It introduces one of these senior women as Amy Fliggerton, who proceeds to ramble on about the historical significance of the polka and how townsfolk centuries ago had to watch out for the "ever-present menace of wolves" when attending nighttime dances. In the film, the lines and characters don't appear.

Prior to their launching into the "You Wonderful You" number, Joe gives Judith a crash course in show business history, including the meaning of the words *hokum* and *ham*. In the film, the scene was amended with Joe telling Jane that it's the smell of greasepaint that's easy to wipe off your face but hard to get out of your blood:

Joe: *Oh, you can wipe it off your face, all right*
But all the ham fat in the world won't get it out of your blood.
Judith: *Ham fat?*
Joe: *That's what the old timers used—instead of cold cream.*
So they began calling them hams—
That's me—a ham. And I like it.

When Abigail abandons the show to return to New York and join Keath, Joe must scramble for her replacement. Instead of Joe and Herb "convincing" Judith to replace her younger sister, Judith willingly volunteers to take on the part. In the film, Jane's tag-teamed by a relentless Joe and Herb, who browbeat her into accepting the lead role.

Perhaps the longest section of the script that was excised (about three and a half pages worth) in any of the script versions is one that appeared in the September 19 script. It's a segment where Orville hatches a plan to have townspeople boycott Joe's show. In a rather bizarre pastiche of the real-life Paul Revere ride, Esme and Herb scour the countryside recruiting farm children to be in the show, which would presumably save Joe's show (called *Fall in Love*) by drawing to the barn a large audience of their parents:

Herb: *(frantically) Joe, listen! They're going to stop the show!*
Joe: *Who?*
Esme: *The Wingaits! I just heard Orville on the party line—tellin' folks to stay away from the openin'! Looks like nobody's comin'!*
Herb: *(to Joe) It's murder! We'll die in an empty house! You can't play a show to six producers!*
Joe: *(grimly) A boycott, huh? All right, let him try!*
He turns suddenly to Susan, [another character cut from the script]
You want to be in this show?
Susan: *(stunned) Me? Sure!*
Joe: *Okay, stand over there!*
(he pushes her to one side, points to the other farm kids)
You! You! You! All of You! You want to be actors? Come on!

(The kids cheer, piling into the barn.)

Herb: *Joe, what are you doing?*

Joe: *Did you ever hear of a parent who didn't think his kid had talent! Put their names on the program! Spread the word! Tell everybody for 20 miles who's in this show! They'll fight to get in!*

Herb: *(saluting) Depend on me, Joe! I'll spread the word. I'll spread the alarm—through every Middlesex village and farm!*

(he grabs Susan, kisses her, rushes out)

Paul Revere rides again!

(Esme, at fever pitch, salutes also and scrambles after him.)

(COUNTRY ROAD—NIGHT—HERB AND ESME)

(galloping madly along on a beaten-up nag, waving a flaming torch. Herb's hat is pinned into a cocked shape—the printing on his T-shirt: "Camp Shanks—Infantry.")

Herb and Esme: *(yelling) The actors are coming! The actors are coming!*

(The horse swerves off the road, pounds up the steps of a farmhouse. A door opens and Herb thrusts a leaflet at a startled farmer.)

Herb: *Opening tomorrow night! Fall in Love at the Falbury Farm!*

Esme: *Fall in Love at the Falbury Farm*

(they are gone in a cloud of dust)

First Farmer: *(hoarsely) Bertha! Lunatics!*

(A woman appears behind him, scared stiff.)

(HERB AND ESME—GALLOPING)

Esme: *(yelling) Come one, come all!*

Herb: *Run, don't walk to the box office.*

(FARMER AND BERTHA—IN DOORWAY)

First Farmer: *(reading leaflet) Our Polly! She's in that play!*

Bertha: *(with pride) I always said Polly was clever!*

(HERB—KNOCKING ON SECOND FARMHOUSE DOOR)

Esme: *(on horse) Hurry, hurry, hurry! See the big show!*

(the door is opened by a woman; Herb throws in tickets and a leaflet)

Herb: *Twenty girls, twenty! And one of them is yours!*
(He flings himself back on the horse, the woman staring after him.)

(HERB AND ESME—RIDING)
(hanging as the horse heads for a fence.)

Herb: *Music! Dancing! Singing! Comedy! Whoops!*
(they catch themselves just in time)
Tragedy!

(SERIES OF FLASH SHOTS—INTERCUT)
(WITH SHOTS OF Herb and Esme galloping along roads and over fields.)

Husband and wife—reading news. ***Husband:*** *Our little girl!*
Husband and wife, ***Wife:*** *(tearfully) Remember how she recited when she was only six?*
Kid (about six), racing upstairs in his nightshirt. ***Kid:*** *Lena's in a show! Lena's in a show!*
Grandmother: *(reminiscently) I was in a show once! Darn good, too!*

(HERB AND ESME—GALLOPING DOWN MAIN STREET)

Herb: *(scattering leaflets) To arms, to arms, to the Falbury Farm! One if by land, two if by sea!*

(PEOPLE)
(picking up leaflets)

(HERB AND ESME—POUNDING ON DOOR OF A SUBSTANTIAL HOUSE)

Esme: *(bellowing) Down with the boycotts! Up with freedom!*
(The door opens, she hands out a pamphlet. Then Herb sees the Wingaits standing in the doorway.
Herb: *(stifles a scream) Redcoats!*

(They jump on a horse.)

In this version of the screenplay, *Summer Stock* ends with the show-within-a-movie featuring a reprise of several numbers performed earlier in the film. This was before Harry Warren, Jack Brooks, and Saul Chaplin were engaged to write three new songs and long before the inclusion of the Harold Arlen-Ted Koehler song "Get Happy." In this version of the script, the final musical montage begins with a reprise of "Dig-Dig-Dig Dig for Your Dinner," featuring Judith and Joe, then Herb, and then farm kids who take over during the second chorus as they develop a routine "showing people in various walks of life 'digging for their dinner.'"

The film closes with a radical role reversal: Abigail will run Falbury Farm while Judith embarks on a life in show business with Joe. The closing scene reads:

> *Farm people, in wagons and trucks, are also singing. Joe dances Judith out of the house and swings her onto the front seat with a kiss. Herb dances Sarah into the other station wagon and runs back to kiss Esme—who is singing tearfully as she waves goodbye. Farm people kiss their children, who dash to find seats in the third station wagon. Zeb and Frank appear in the barn door, to sing and wave goodbye. As the station wagons start out of the farmyard, Abigail appears on the porch, in a farm dress—with the Wingaits on either side of her. Abigail points happily to an engagement ring on her finger (Orville has just proposed) as she joins the song. The Wingaits beam at each other and harmonize. One by one the station wagons leave. Herb drives the first with Sarah. Artie pilots the second, Joe drives the third, an ecstatic Judith by his side.*
>
> *FADE OUT. THE END*

In the next iteration of the script, dated October 17, 1949, Walters, in his copy, redlined the entire Paul Revere scene and the name of the Judith character was changed to Jane, among other modifications.

THE OCTOBER 24 SCRIPT

IN YET ANOTHER REVISED SCRIPT DATED OCTOBER 24, 1949, JUST SHY OF one month before cameras rolled, the screenplay remained in transition but is much closer to what was filmed. Jane opens the movie singing in the shower. The town "do-nothing," Lem, is out. Herb no longer spouts Shakespeare and Kelly's character is now Joe D. Rosse. The "e" will be dropped in the character credit line.

A humorous exchange between the two sisters, Jane and Abigail, is also cut from this script:

Jane: *(to Abigail) Just for your information, I'm not an old maid!*
I've been engaged to Orville four years,
And we're going to be married just as soon as—
As soon as he passes his allergy tests!

When Joe chides Abigail for not working hard enough in rehearsal, he explains his reasoning to Jane:

Joe: *But they're (actors) not ordinary or normal—*
They're talented.
A little show of temperament's a very good thing.

In the film, the dialogue in this scene is reworked to focus on how Joe needs to toughen up Abigail and not as a generalized truth about actors being abnormal yet talented.

Also cut is the entire car caravan end scene with Abigail on the porch pointing at her engagement ring. The script finishes with a reprise of "If You Feel Like Singing, Sing" with Jane and Joe embracing as the film fades out (a freeze-frame after their embrace is how the film ends but to a reprise of "(Howdy Neighbor) Happy Harvest." After seeing a rough cut of the movie, Breen's office and the MPAA granted its benediction, a certificate of approval for *Summer Stock* on May 15, 1950.

Although Walters and company improved the script by trimming it down and excising much of the hamminess, the dialogue in *Summer Stock* still echoes a simpler America in which values largely mirrored what could be heard on radio and later seen in a weekly episode of TV's *Ozzie and*

Harriet. To contemporary audiences, the film's songs and dances still pack a wallop, but some of the lines, like the following exchange between Abigail and Orville, invariably elicit snickers:

> ***Abigail:*** *Orville, a woman doesn't want apologies.*
> *She wants romance, excitement—she wants to be swept off her feet!*
> ***Orville:*** *That's only in big cities.*
> ***Abigail:*** *Oh no, it isn't.*
> *A woman doesn't want to be asked, she wants to be told.*
> *You have to be strong—forceful!*

Hindsight, as they say, is always 20/20, so perhaps it's best to view musicals like *Summer Stock* through the more magnanimous prism of perspective informed by the era in which a film is made—and, like Esme and Herb in their barnstorming gallop, just sit back and enjoy the ride.

ROLL CAMERA . . . ACTION!

ON NOVEMBER 21, 1949, THE DAY THE CAMERAS STARTED TO ROLL, WALTERS received congratulatory "pep talk" notes from his mentor Freed and production chief Schary. Wishing good luck, Freed bolstered Walters's confidence by saying that he was certain Walters would add his characteristic good taste and inventiveness to the picture as well as assuring him that everyone in the "unit" (the Freed unit) were "all rooting and waiting for you to come back." Freed was nothing if not a benevolent *paterfamilias* to all the leading lights of his unit, even when they worked on projects outside his supervision.[50] For his part, Schary, in his memo to Walters, acknowledged the "hard work" he had already put in on *Summer Stock* and was appreciative of his "sincere and unselfish interest in it."[51]

With Garland's diet and sleep patterns regulated thanks to her stays in Boston, a different problem presented when she reported to work; the actress who had been alarmingly gaunt in her previous films now appeared too stout, and farm attire (bib overalls) did nothing to flatter Garland's diminutive frame. "She slimmed down as filming progressed but her difficulties were still much with her," Minnelli said.[52] *Summer Stock* costumer

Walter Plunkett remembered: "We tried to make her as thin as possible, but we weren't miracle workers and we didn't succeed."[53]

During pre-production, Garland had missed six days in the first twenty; She received a warning letter from the studio on October 31, 1949, and immediately requested off *Summer Stock* and a release from her contract. Mayer reportedly talked her out of both.[54] But what happened behind the gates of the Culver City studio rarely stayed a secret for long with busybodies ever ready to leak the smallest bit of gossip to the Hollywood press. Within twenty-four hours of MGM's warning letter, the *Los Angeles Times* announced: "Poundage Nearly Costs Judy Garland a Role." The story went on to say that "film actress Judy Garland almost lost her role in *Summer Stock* yesterday for being overweight, but Metro-Goldwyn-Mayer executives finally decided she could shed the poundage before shooting starts."

According to the media account, the MGM brass held a noontime meeting to discuss Garland's removal from the film and even a possible suspension as she reportedly defied company orders to shed six to eight pounds. Garland's absence at a Saturday rehearsal that purportedly kept a large cast waiting was also mentioned as a possible motive for the suspension threat. A spokesman denied that report, but admitted that Garland called in sick one day the previous week due to "a cold."[55]

A couple of months later, Garland's on-set troubles again made the newspapers when columnist Hedda Hopper reported on January 12, 1950, that the star missed a "few days" of filming due to illness. Hopper, in her column, jumped to Garland's defense, writing to play down any rumors: "I checked with other members of the cast, and they told me that Judy couldn't have been more cooperative during the entire picture. A series of strenuous dance routines has to be draining her energies. She contracted laryngitis and a virus infection. On Saturday she was too sick to work. She reported to the set Monday, got into makeup, and was then ordered home by the doctor. The film has but eight more days of shooting, and Judy will finish as soon as her doctor permits."[56]

Despite Garland's chronic tardiness (which predated *Summer Stock*), her stature and value to the studio was well recognized and she was granted accommodations that were not offered to most other stars. "Our shooting day was from 9 a.m.," said Arthur Freed who produced many of Garland's biggest hits at MGM. "That meant a girl had to come into makeup around

7 a.m. If a difficult makeup, it could be 6 a.m. I went to Eddie Mannix, the studio manager, and I talked to L. B.—I said, 'I'd like to start Judy at 10 a.m. Let her get a little extra sleep.' They OK'd it. And 10 a.m. meant 11 a.m."[57]

It was Carleton Alsop (not her husband, Minnelli) who was often charged with dispensing the "tough love" to Garland, and as her manager, he also ran interference with the studio executives. Alsop recalled:

> Those 2–3 a.m. sessions, sitting on the staircase in her pajamas, saying, "Pa, I can't face a camera this morning," and Vincente hopping nervously about not knowing what to do about it. He doesn't call a doctor; he calls me to come up there. Now, you know there is something wrong about that to start with.
>
> So I'd be gentle with her at the moment and harsh with the studio. And then I'd give it to her: "All right, now, you believed all that shit I told the studio. But you must remember that they're paying you $150,000 for this picture, and you're supposed to go to work to earn it. That means getting up in the morning! That means makeup, hairdressing, etc! Now I'm not here to discuss the charm of Mr. Mannix or Benny Thau or anything about Mr. Mayer. You have a job, a contract; they're paying you a lot of money. The lies I tell them—because I don't know how much you're putting on is fake and how much is real; if it's real, you should have a doctor, not me, if your husband can't take care of you, don't you think so? Now, Goddamnit, go back to bed and go to sleep or get your ass up and go to work!"[58]

On the set, the baton was passed to Walters and key members of the cast to keep Garland motivated and upbeat. Said Walters: "I would go to the dailies and think, how dare this look like a happy picture. We were going through absolute torture. And Gene was right in there helping. He was marvelous. He'd placate her and hold her hand and say, 'Anything I can do today?' I'd say, 'Please just knock on wood that she's here.' But I just couldn't believe that this looked happy, but it did. It looked like we were having a good time."[59]

After years of working with Garland, Walters, along the way, had learned little tricks that would motivate her to deliver stunning performances. He recalled an episode during the *Summer Stock* shoot where he and his star retreated at midday for a little "pick-me-up" that resulted in a reprimand from Mayer:

> We had a little saloon cafe just off the lot, and Judy would say, "Let's go over to the Retake Room." She said, "Now, look, Buster, I' m going to have a beer. I'm having a beer if you want me to work this afternoon." I said, "Sure, you can have a beer, as long as you eat and we get back to work." I'd have a martini and she'd have a beer. One day at lunch, I'm called to Mr. Mayer's office. The entire upper echelon is lined along one wall, and at the far end of the room at this gigantic desk is Mr. Mayer. The first thing that throws you is the double doors. "Mr. Mayer will see you now." So I open the door and boom! There you are in this room, enormous, with a fireplace and the desk. So he gets up from the desk and he said, "I don't know you, Mr. Walters, personally, but I feel it is important I speak to you. It has come to my attention that you are encouraging Judy Garland's drinking." Well, of course I got myself together and I said, "Mr. Mayer, if you want Judy to work in the afternoon, she's going to have a beer, come hell or high water or she's heading for the hills, as she very pointedly puts it to me. Now which do you want?" "Well, I uh . . ." was his response. That's when I met Mr. Mayer. And I'd been there . . . my God, how long had I been there? I was a dance director for four years. I'd been there eight years and this was my introduction to him. "Fuck you, Buster!"[60]

As filming progressed, Walters continued to make special accommodations for Garland depending on her particular state of readiness on any given day. "One day all she had to do was to go up the stairs and walk around," said Walters. "She couldn't. She staggered. We put up scenery so she could hang on that as she walked up. She couldn't make it in high heels so we put her in flat heels and changed camera angles. She told me, 'You're the kindest, the most understanding.' We thought we'd never get through the picture."[61] Another tactic Walters employed to maintain Garland's equilibrium was to just let her vent. "One day she said, 'Listen buster, if you think I'm going to act today, you can go fuck yourself. I'm heading for the hills.' I said, 'Ok, if you wait until I finish my coffee, I'll go with you because I feel just as much making you act as you feel like acting.'

It took the wind out of her sails. I'd play it very cool. I'm doing the acting. The ulcer is inside. 'George [a grip on the shoot], bring Judy some coffee.' She's muttering to herself, 'What the fuck am I supposed to do today . . .' I knew I just had to wait it out."[62]

Directors know that a certain amount of handholding is practically written into their job description, but Garland biographer Gerold Frank felt that Walters's role as armchair shrink went above and beyond the call of duty. Navigating Garland through the shoot, Frank wrote, required "Support, support, support! Encouragement, encouragement, encouragement! When she went before the camera to lip-sync a pre-recorded song, Walters would keep up a steady barrage of praise and adjurations like a coach, a cheerleader. 'Yah, honey! Keep going, honey! Keep your chin up!' She loved it. She blossomed under such treatment."[63]

KID GLOVES

IN A KEY SCENE IN *SUMMER STOCK*, JANE SCOLDS JOE FOR BEING TOO harsh with Abigail during rehearsals. Joe promises that going forward he will handle Abigail with "kid gloves." For his own part, Kelly took the advice of Garland's character to heart and, off-camera, treated his co-star with those same deferential kid gloves. "I would say that I had always tried to help Judy not in the sense of paying her back for whatever help she gave me on our first picture together [*For Me and My Gal*], but because I thought it was a privilege to be able to routine a number for her," Kelly said. "It was a privilege to be able to say, 'Judy, if you do it this way, the sound will be better because of the movement of your body.' Whatever I could contribute . . . it was a privilege to help her out."[64]

Garland wasn't the only one Kelly supported while he was filming *Summer Stock*. He also interceded on his wife Betsy Blair's behalf when she was trying to convince Mayer to cast her in a film, *Kind Lady* (1951), starring Ethel Barrymore and Maurice Evans. Kelly and Blair were well-known Hollywood liberals and their political ideology clashed with Louis B. Mayer's ardent conservatism. At the time, much of Hollywood was mired under the cloud of the Red Scare and the blacklisting of industry folk (both in front of and behind the camera) who were suspected of having been affiliated with the Communist Party, or at the very least had shown tacit sympathy for

Communism as fellow travelers. Kelly, an A-lister by any measure, was mostly impervious to the blacklist; not so Blair, who was a minor contract player and far more outspoken in her support of left-wing politics. In the June 1950 issue of *Red Channels* (a pamphlet that named names of entertainment industry workers purported to be Communists), Blair had been listed as a "subversive."

In order to win the part in *Kind Lady*, Blair had to literally enter the lion's den, the inner sanctum of the Thalberg Building, and convince Mayer that despite her politics and political affiliations, he should grant her permission to appear in the film. The meeting took place while Kelly was on Stage 27 shooting *Summer Stock*. In her memoir, Blair recounts the day of the meeting when she purposely dressed for the occasion in a conservative power suit. "I chose to wear a 'new look' navy suit, fitted jacket and flared skirt, flat patent leather pumps and white kid gloves," she wrote. "My hair was clean and shining, my makeup discreet. I was twenty-five."

According to Blair, the one-way conversation (Mayer did all the talking) went on for quite some time, with the studio boss sounding more patriot drumbeats than "The Star-Spangled Banner" and lecturing her on how fortunate she was to live in the land of the free and home of the brave. Finally, the conversation ended when Mayer's secretary appeared. "'Mr. Kelly is in the outer office,'" she said. "When I hadn't appeared on his sound stage by three o'clock, Gene came up to rescue me. Mr. Mayer got up, escorted me out to Gene, put one arm around each of us, and said, 'You've got a lovely girl here—and she's as American as you and me.' As we walked down the hall, Gene grinned at me and said, 'You with your white kid gloves—you must have given an Academy Award performance in there.'"[65] The couple enjoyed a good laugh at Mayer's expense and Blair was cast in *Kind Lady*. However, when her name appeared in *Red Channels*, she became a victim of the blacklist and did not work again for four years, until 1955, when she was cast in *Marty* (1955). She won that coveted role, but only after her husband again interceded on her behalf.

BRACKEN'S WORLD

IN ADDITION TO THE TWIN TOWERS OF STRENGTH OF WALTERS AND KELLY, another person positively therapeutic for Garland during the filming of *Summer Stock* was co-star Eddie Bracken, who developed a close relationship with her. Their on-set shenanigans and incessant gags broke the tension and were a bonus for cast and crew alike. "Now we get into the scene and Eddie is so funny," said Walters. "She looks at him and breaks up. We cannot get the scene because she's breaking up. Then it gets to the hysterical point—she couldn't even look at him. She'd control herself. 'I'm all right, I'm all right now.' I'd say, 'roll it,' and she'd look at him and fall on the floor. That was a bitch of a day. One day in the life of Judy Garland."[66]

Bracken remembered:

> I wanted to work with Judy because we were good friends and the character of Orville was well-written. We had so much fun that we couldn't stop laughing. She was my patsy. When we did the proposal scene with Ray Collins, we did twenty-two takes of that. We could not continue because Judy was in hysterics holding her stomach. She could not look at me and I was trying not to be funny. The next day she came in and they separated us in rehearsals. Then she would look at my forehead. We got it on the first take the next day, but she developed pleurisy from trying to hold back laughter from the night before and then at that point she was out for about three or four days.
>
> I'm a pick-pocket. And I told some people I can take a bra off a woman without her noticing it. I can do all that stuff. Judy and I were having a ball in front of 400 people. I asked her to dance with me. I showed her a few steps, and then in front of 400 people I removed Judy's bra without her supposedly knowing. But Judy and I had it all planned. She put on a phony bra, one that's really easy to take off, and I pulled it out and held it in back of me and people thought that I had actually removed her bra. Judy said, "Oh, my goodness!" and tried to cover up, ran off, and the 400 people thought I was a living genius.[67]

During downtime on the shoot (whether due to Garland's absences or other delays), Bracken, who was on a weekly salary, took it all in stride and said he made the most of the situation. "When she [Garland] was gone, you'd just go to the studio and wait for her," he said. "What would we do during that time? Well, you'd just play around and have an awful lot of fun. On the lot at that time, Dick Powell was doing a movie, he was directing one, so I saw him a lot. And most of the people who worked there I knew well."[68]

As *Summer Stock* filming continued to plod on, Bracken was confronted with his own looming deadline, a contractual obligation to return to Broadway. When Dore Schary visited the set, Bracken asked him about Garland's absences. Schary's unsympathetic response was, "There's nothing wrong with her, she's just being obstinate." Bracken was unconvinced and asked Schary if he could call her. "Go right ahead," he said.

The conversation, as recounted by Bracken, went this way:

> "Judy, I know you're ill and I know you're in bed and I know you're going through holy hell. But I've got to get back to Broadway, there's a thing that I have to do. Could you do me the favor, could you get enough strength to come into the studio to do this last scene with me so that I can get the hell out of here?" And she says, "Well, yeah, I can do that." I said, "Wonderful. Can you do it tomorrow morning?" And she said, "Yes, fine." I said, "That's great, Judy. I'll see you tomorrow morning. I love you." I hung up and said, "She'll be in tomorrow morning." That's how she finished *Summer Stock*. Because she would rather do a favor for somebody like me, whoever called her like that, than she would Dore Schary or anybody at the studio. They were using the wrong tactics. They were making demands and saying she had to do this, she had to do that, and she told them what to do with themselves. But when you do it that way, she's an old vaudevillian; naturally, she'd do it for another actor.[69]

Bracken's recall is slightly off-kilter (like he was!). Dick Powell was indeed on the MGM lot during the *Summer Stock* shoot, but not as a director. He was co-starring in the movie *Right Cross* (1950) with June Allyson and Ricardo Montalban. As for Bracken's looming Broadway deadline, that's harder to ascertain because the comedian didn't next perform on the Great White Way until 1955, when he replaced Tom Ewell in the stage version, and later the national touring company, of *The Seven Year Itch*.

In an interview Gloria DeHaven gave to *Buzz* magazine in 2003, she remembered her time with Garland as an immersive experience both on the set and off: "It was nothing but fun at work and then I'd go back to her house; have dinner with her or do something after. It was almost 24 hours a day. It was a great joy.

"My relationship with her was very different," DeHaven continued. "First of all, I admired her so much. For some reason, she trusted me. She didn't trust a lot of people—particularly women—she just didn't. Judy never felt she was pretty. She was always demeaning herself. We were sisters, we had a great relationship and I treasure every moment of it."[70]

LIGHTS, CAMERA, *IN*ACTION!

BY THE END OF 1949, IT WAS NOT JUST GARLAND'S ABSENCES THAT PUSHED the production back. Pasternak and his production team decided that the Warren-Gordon score of five songs were insufficient and new material was needed. It is partially because of this late decision that filming on the movie was pushed well into 1950. Kelly, for his part, was itching to start his next project, *An American in Paris*, a watershed movie that would cement his growing reputation as a true musical film innovator. But first he had to complete *Summer Stock*. "So that picture took seven to nine months to complete" [a slight exaggeration], he said. "She [Garland] wouldn't come in for a week at a time or maybe show up for an hour and we're all there with our makeup on everyday.

"She did excellent work in several numbers in that picture and in several scenes actually, but she couldn't take off weight," he continued. "I must say, at the time, and I still believe it, I may be naïve, the studio was very anxiously trying to care for Judy. All I know is that the same love and affection that existed long before between Judy and me still existed and I tried to use that to help her. She did some very difficult numbers in that picture if you look at them."[71]

Garland's performing genius, a brilliance that had been money in the bank for MGM for a decade and a half, seemed to circumvent her weight gain whenever the cameras rolled. "Judy had something extra-curricular that none of the other performers had, and she had a bent for everything," Kelly said. "Like she could learn a dance step quickly . . . anything, she could learn it well; she had a photographic mind . . . and it would almost drive you to distraction. She had a fantastic musical ear, which everybody knew about. I'd say to her, 'I'll come back in a week and I may know this song.' She'd know it in one minute, and that we'd just laugh about, you know."[72]

But as the weeks passed, the push-pull of Garland's absences versus the days when she felt centered and confident enough to perform fluctuated wildly. "Now in *Summer Stock*, I didn't see her at her best," Kelly admitted. "She just couldn't show up you know . . . but she'd come in at five o'clock some nights and let me know she was at the studio and have to come over and talk to me. And I'd just hold her in my arms and she'd cry because she hadn't been on the set that day. She wanted to work. She would have liked to have been there. Something was making her frightened. I was supposed to be doing that picture so she wouldn't be [frightened]."[73]

Dore Schary was not as patient as Kelly when it came to Garland and didn't believe in coddling the studio's high-priced talent, especially as the industry was facing a seismic shift that forced all Hollywood studios to implement austerity measures due in large part to the growing competition from television. Just as Walters had done regarding his concerns about the *Summer Stock* script, Kelly also opted to go directly to Schary (bypassing reporting to either Walters or Pasternak) when a sensitive issue arose that Kelly said jeopardized his ability to remain working on the film.

"Dore, I don't think I can continue," Kelly said when he met with Schary. "You can't stand next to her [Garland], the odor is overpowering." Schary asked Kelly to elaborate. "I don't know what it is, but when I have to play a love scene with her I almost die." Schary called Garland to his office and seated her next to him on his office couch. "And suddenly I knew it was some awful thing within her, it wasn't bad breath. It smelled like formaldehyde. I literally had to back away as I talked to her and she said, Gene was a little difficult and she's having trouble sleeping. I said, 'All right, honey, try to get yourself a rest and get in tomorrow.'"

Schary called a doctor to inquire exactly what type of drug could possibly smell like formaldehyde and was told it was probably a drug called paraldehyde, a powerful sedative used for people who have consumed too much alcohol or amphetamines. Both Schary and Mayer again advised their troubled star to check into the Menninger's Clinic for additional treatment. Garland declined the offer, telling Schary she "could get over it."[74] But, according to one of Garland's biographers, the production continued to be hampered by Garland's mood swings with the star acquiring medications through whatever clandestine means possible. "When she had begged Lee Gershwin [the wife of lyricist Ira Gershwin] for just one Seconal to help her get off to sleep, Gershwin was so distressed by her friend's anguish that she obliged, thinking that just one could do no harm. The plan was that Gershwin would leave the pill in her own mailbox from which it would be collected by Garland or someone else on her behalf. It was only later that Gershwin realized that Garland had made the same arrangement with other friends."[75]

When Garland would appear to have a meltdown on the set, Dr. Rose was always nearby to offer assistance. "Judy would go before the camera, animated, vital, then suddenly a cold sweat would come over her, she'd hurry offstage, to weep and cry," wrote Gerold Frank. "Dr. Rose would hold her hand, listen to her, give her 15 minutes of supportive therapy, and she would snap back. Benny Thau said Rose told him he was being forced to compete with people who gave Judy pills at five in the morning. His task was almost impossible."[76]

Phil Silvers not only provided comic relief in *Summer Stock*, he was also on stand-by as additional emotional support for Garland. Silvers wrote in his autobiography:

> Judy was unpredictable. For *Summer Stock* she would come in one day and miss two or three days when I wasn't on camera. I'd come in anyhow trying to keep her spirits up. We both enjoyed the visits on the set of her daughter, Liza, who came with her father. Judy was going through uncontrollable inner torments which studio people analyzed as spoiled self-indulgence.
>
> On top of all the terrible pressure of growing from childhood to womanhood, she felt unattractive. She felt she'd rather be a sexpot in the chorus than the exciting star she really was. As she became a woman physically, she remained a child emotionally.[77]

According to Silvers, his "big brother" to Garland role crossed the line briefly after yet another lament about being unattractive and unloved. "You know I'm a man, too. And I kissed her warmly. 'Alright!' she said, and gave me a throbbing kiss as if to say, 'What do you want?' That brief moment was the end of our romantic aberration."[78]

Carpenter, despite his dissatisfaction working with Kelly, who he said was downright "mean" to him, befriended Garland and did his part to help her make it through the filming. "It was marvelous," he said about when he learned he'd been cast in *Summer Stock*. "I was thrilled Garland was going to be in it. I didn't have the knowledge that it would be her last movie [at MGM]. It was wonderful to be with her. They gave me some nice credits considering I didn't have much to do in the movie."

Carpenter said that Garland made the experience tolerable. "She made up for everything," he said. "She was so terrific with me right from the beginning. And I watched her at the tail-end shoot 'Get Happy.' I got to know the guys in that number pretty well. That was wonderful for her." To ease her anxiety during the shoot, Carpenter said that he gave a party for several of the dancers whose work was completed on the film and wrote a special song for Garland titled "Let Go of Your Heart." "And Judy, when she learned of the party said to me, 'You didn't ask me to the party?' I said. 'Yes, of course,' and she ended up coming. There was a piano player and she sat down at the piano and played the whole song through and she added something in the middle, which was incredible. The party was in one of the rehearsal rooms on the lot. It was fun. Of course, she didn't show up on set for a couple of days after."[79]

Michael Chapin, born in 1936, is one of three siblings, all who gained some fame as child actors. He is also the last living actor who appeared in *Summer Stock*. His sister Lauren is best remembered for playing the youngest daughter (nicknamed Kitten) on the 1950s television series, *Father Knows Best*. *Summer Stock* was Chapin's last uncredited part before he landed the lead role in a series of Republic westerns starting with *Buckaroo Sheriff of Texas* in 1951. In *Summer Stock*, Chapin, along with fellow child actor Teddy Infuhr, are the two boys who stumble upon the wreckage of Jane's tractor and then scramble into the barn during the Wingait Falls Historical Society Dance (the "Portland Fancy") to ask her if they could play with the tractor parts.

For Chapin, age fourteen at the time, the memory of his brief screen time in *Summer Stock* is a blur, with one exception; lurking in the shadows of Stage 27, he remembers the dimly lit figure of Gene Kelly rehearsing a dance number during downtime on the set. "I was waiting around for my brief scene and just wandering around this massive sound stage," he said, "when I came across a nook and cranny in the back where I discovered somebody was dancing. I thought 'this is strange,' so I walked up to get a better look and saw that it was Gene Kelly. The best that I could surmise is that he was rehearsing his solo number [the squeaky board/newspaper dance] in front of a mirror. I was certainly impressed, which was no small feat because as a teenager I'd never heard of Gene Kelly and I was more interested in my bicycle, roller skates, and classmates. I was quite captivated by what I was witnessing in the shadows—Kelly was facing the mirror and looking at his body and foot placements. He appeared very focused."[80]

Bracken's recollections of Kelly during the filming of *Summer Stock* follow suit with Chapin's and were of a relentless worker always in pursuit of perfection. "You could very seldom find Gene in a position where you'd have a dinner party where you'd get up and play charades," Bracken said. "He loved that, but you'd see him maybe once in two or three years at some party doing that. The rest of the time he was working on routines. He was the guy who helped choreograph most of the stuff they were doing and was always working on his body and his physical strength. He was a perfectionist and a compulsive worker. So, you have nothing but high respect for a man like Gene Kelly. You bring up the name Gene Kelly, you have to salute. He's the admiral of the group."[81]

Producer Pasternak was charged with bringing the film in on time and on budget. According to a Garland biographer, even he—usually a softie, eternally upbeat, and an ardent supporter of Garland—began to have misgivings about her ability to complete the film, at one point suggesting to Mayer that the studio might want to consider cutting its losses and closing down production. Mayer would hear nothing of it. "Sit down," he [Mayer] said. "This little girl has been so wonderful. She's made us a lot of money, and she's in trouble. We've got to help her. If you stop production now, it will finish her."[82] In his autobiography, Pasternak wrote, "Never once did I hear a cross word, a tart comment, a bitter crack, on the part of any member of the crew or the cast. They all understood. Gene Kelly rates a special word. Gene said: 'I'll do anything for this girl, Joe. If I have to come here and sit and wait for a year, I'd do it for her. That's the way I feel about her.'"[83]

Despite his differences with the "front office," songwriter Harry Warren (like Pasternak and Kelly) believed that Mayer went to great lengths to placate his troubled star. "When she reported sick, he used to send her flowers," Warren said. "I think, too, they worked her too much, one picture after the other. They were making money with her, so they wanted to keep her working—like they did with the songwriters."[84] Warren said that if Garland had been under contract to Warner Bros., she'd have been dropped at the first sign of trouble. "You never would have heard of her again," Warren said. "First time she didn't show up at a rehearsal or a date for something, Jack Warner would have taken her right off salary! He did it with Bette Davis, anybody who argued with him—out! But Mayer was never like that. And she cost them a fortune over there. On *Summer Stock* nobody knew where she was. You think she could have done that at Warner's? Only with Louis Mayer."[85]

With frequent starts and stops in production, some members of the cast (mostly dancers) had to move on to other work obligations, which resulted in a spate of farewell parties. "Every time one of the kids left," Kelly remembered, "we'd have a farewell party. Judy was always invited, and she always came. And not only did she come, but the same woman who the day before was incapable of uttering a sound, would sing her heart out. We had about nine or 10 parties during *Summer Stock*; each time Judy was the star turn. She'd perform for hours and the kids just loved and adored her. Everybody did. As long as the camera wasn't turning, she was fine."[86]

Another member of Garland's inner circle at the time was her personal make-up artist Dorothy "Dottie" Ponedel (July 2, 1898–April 30, 1979), who worked almost exclusively for Judy throughout the 1940s and became her intimate friend. In her memoir, Ponedel wrote about a lighter moment on the set that concluded with a visit from two famous surprise guests:

> I remember when we were working on *Summer Stock*, the picture that turned out to be Judy's last one at MGM, Gene Kelly, Judy and I left the back lot walking slowly toward Judy's dressing room. You'd think the world was on our shoulders we had worked so hard that day. Judy was hoping that Tully [Myrtle Tully, Garland's secretary at the time] would have sandwiches and cold drinks for us to pump a little life into us, but there was no Tully. Gene threw himself into an easy chair, Judy on a blue satin spread across her bed. I threw myself across the foot of the bed as my day was pretty tough keeping the perspiration off of Judy—she had worked so hard that day.
>
> *Summer Stock* was a hard picture which seemed to take the life out of all of us. The room was so quiet you could hear the petal of a rose drop. All of a sudden, Judy asked me if I believed in God. It took me by surprise. I stopped for a moment and said, "Yes, Judy, I

believe in God, but I don't know what God is. God may be a great power that hovers over all of us, who keeps the oceans in their place so they can't swallow all the land; who put the millions of colors in the flowers, who gives us the trees, who gives the food out of the ground. God gives us a million things that we take for granted. I don't know, but I believe."

Just then, the door opened and in walked Tully with the sandwiches and cold drinks. After wolfing those down, we felt we were alive again. Judy asked Gene to practice one more hour on a particularly hard step and after an hour Judy had it down. Gene had a big grin and Judy said, "God or no God, he sure worked the pants off me today."

Just then, we were called to the set and Judy started clowning with Kelly. Gene handed her a bottle of Coca-Cola and a chocolate bar. He said, "This will give you the energy you'll need for the rest of the afternoon." While they were munching on a chocolate bar, in walked Frank Sinatra and from then on, the director couldn't handle any of them. The clowning that went on was unbelievable. Those three monkeys had everybody hysterical. A few minutes later, in walked Peter Lawford and the fun began all over again.[87]

IT'S A WRAP!

ACCORDING TO WALTERS, THE BETS AROUND THE STUDIO LOT WERE THAT *Summer Stock* would never be finished. "I would look at the dailies and say, 'How dare this look like we're having any fun!' How dare it when we were just sweating blood! I can't stand watching *Summer Stock*. I was on nothing but coffee and cigarettes during the filming. I ended up getting an ulcer on the film."[88]

Nevertheless, after fifty shooting days, filming on *Summer Stock* wrapped on April 5, 1950. The production schedule (when principal photography starts and when it ends, which is not always sequential) of nearly six months seems long, but not all the delays lie entirely at the feet of the film's star, Judy Garland. In fact, other MGM musicals made during this period and not featuring Garland experienced similar shooting timeframes. For example: *Take Me Out to the Ballgame* (1949), forty-nine days on a four-month production schedule; *On the Town*, forty-seven days on slightly more than a three-month production schedule; and *Annie Get Your Gun*, forty-six days (on an intermittent production schedule that experienced many delays).[89]

Finger-pointing during production delays was a common occurrence during the studio system era. In her autobiography, *Million Dollar Mermaid*, swimming star Esther Williams noted how "spies" were often embedded in production crews with standing orders to report back to the executives on the third floor of the Thalberg Building any blame that could be assigned for even the slightest delays. That was no doubt the case on *Summer Stock*, where studio lackeys were ready to rat Garland out for the slightest infraction.

In addition to Garland's absences, another reason for *Summer Stock*'s relatively long production window was that the filmmakers realized the five songs written by Harry Warren and Mack Gordon weren't sufficient enough to carry the film to the finish line. According to John Fricke, in December 1949, producer Pasternak, director Walters, and others involved in the production decided that instead of reprising the five songs in the show-within-a-movie finale, three more songs ("You Wonderful You," "All for You," and "Heavenly Music") needed to be written. With lyricist Mack Gordon no longer on the project, the task fell to Warren, Saul Chaplin, and Jack Brooks to come up with the new tunes in addition to the twenty-year-old Harold Arlen–Ted Koehler song "Get Happy," which was also added to the mix.

This scramble for additional songs added to production delays as the tunes needed to be written (with the exception of "Get Happy"), orchestrated, recorded, and filmed. However, they were imperative to *Summer Stock*'s eventual success, "Get Happy" providing Garland with her iconic showstopper and "You Wonderful You" the instrumental to Kelly's classic squeaky board/newspaper solo in the barn. In addition, "Get Happy" and Kelly's solo were the last numbers to be shot, added on after filming on *Summer Stock* had ostensibly finished. In terms of production, they were afterthoughts, but crucial ones.

Summer Stock received its nationwide release on August 31, 1950. As the film was garnering mostly positive reviews and strong box-office receipts, Garland traveled to New York City in September for a bit of shopping.

While there, on September 11, she snuck into the Capitol Theater in midtown Manhattan where *Summer Stock* was playing to packed audiences during an extended run. Her presence did not go unnoticed, and she was met with a near-riotous outpouring of adulation that was duly chronicled the next day by syndicated entertainment columnist Earl Wilson.

As she exited the theater to thunderous applause, a mob of cheering fans followed her car as it snaked back to her hotel. "At 1 o'clock the other morning," Wilson wrote, "a crowd on Broadway cheered movie star Judy Garland, shouting, 'We love you,' 'We're all for you,' 'Keep making pictures,' and 'Keep your chin up!' 'God love you all!' Judy was calling to the crowd, as she blew kisses to her fans from the back seat of the car. Wilson said he was tipped off about the commotion while holding court at Lindy's restaurant nearby and then ran over to Broadway and 51st Street to witness the unfolding situation firsthand. About her late-night sojourn to see *Summer Stock*, Garland told Wilson, "I didn't know anybody knew I was there. But when the picture was over, the whole balcony seemed to rise and start to applaud. Then the main floor became a sea of people cheering and then they came out into the street and over to the car. It wasn't like a mob, but like a lot of friends. I've been weeping every minute since—with joy. It's so encouraging."[90]

At that moment, buoyed by the heartfelt affirmation she felt from her fans, Judy could scarcely have imagined that less than three weeks later she'd be released from her MGM contract and leave the studio after fifteen years and more than two dozen films, never to return.

CHAPTER V

THE MUSICAL NUMBERS

A Brilliant Creation!

"IF YOU FEEL LIKE SINGING, SING"

Music by Harry Warren; Lyrics by Mack Gordon
Recorded by Judy Garland and the MGM Orchestra,
Johnny Green conducting, on October 13, 1949
Lyrics approved by Joseph Breen and the Motion Picture
Association of America on March 28, 1949

AFTER MORE THAN A YEAR'S ABSENCE FROM THE SCREEN, THERE WAS pent-up audience demand to see Judy Garland in another movie, and the earliest frames in *Summer Stock* were intended to give the audience what they craved—a Garland musical number. As soon as the opening credits dissolve, and before Garland comes into view, you can hear her start to sing the Harry Warren–Mack Gordon tune "If You Feel Like Singing, Sing." Director Charles Walters, using a crane shot over his giant soundstage farmyard set, passes over some foliage, and "invades" the privacy of the farm's owner Jane (Garland); the camera coming through Jane's second-floor bedroom window as she finishes her morning shower.

The peek-a-boo (albeit discreet) scene continues as Garland wraps herself in a towel and, behind a folding screen, makes a quick change into her farm work clothes—bib overalls, white socks and loafers, singing the entire time and at one point hitching up, from her foot to her free hand, her nightgown that was lying on the floor.

In *The Gay Divorcee*, sixteen years earlier and at a different studio (RKO), Fred Astaire did his own "getting dressed" number to "A Needle in a Haystack." In his routine, Fred (ably assisted by his valet) swaps his bathrobe for a suitcoat, tie, homburg, and umbrella, all the while singing and tap dancing around his London flat and vaulting over the furniture. Although Astaire's practiced excellence can't really be compared to Garland's stage movement in "If You Feel Like Singing, Sing" (Garland's hitch of the nightie is a far cry from Astaire's entrechat flutter kicks), the naturalness of how she gets dressed, smoothes the bedsheets, and puts away her clothes while simultaneously singing is, in its own way, just as synchronous and seamless.

Garland sings:

There's something about giving out with a song,
Makes you belong,
Helps you to find a peace of mindful day.

The lyrics reflect not just Jane's literal awakening from slumber, but a sunny determination to make a fresh new start to the day on her farm. It's optimistically upbeat and doesn't portend the disappointing news to come in the next scene, in which her longtime hired hands quit and leave her high and dry to tend to the farm with only Esme (Marjorie Main) for support.

Michael Feinstein, singer, pianist, and one of the foremost interpreters of the Great American Songbook, described songwriter Warren as a "chameleon composer":

> He had an innate ability to write-to-order. His general association at MGM was not as happy as his previous associations at Fox and Warner Bros., where he was happiest even though he was working much harder than he did at Metro. He used to do this party routine about what it was like working at Warner Bros. versus working at Fox versus working at Metro. He would do this routine at the piano where in Metro, you can take months to write a single phrase of a song, and they would have servants massaging your feet while you're working on a phrase—the excess of MGM. It was a very different atmosphere. It didn't necessarily serve Harry very well because he liked to do things quicker and get things going.[1]

The opening number in *Summer Stock*, "If You Feel Like Singing, Sing," said Feinstein, was an example of Warren writing a song specifically for the voice of Judy Garland, and crafting a piece that would musically fit well in her range and persona: "Harry was always mindful of writing for the character, even though he often was writing a pop song in a Tin Pan Alley thing. But after he had written *Summer Holiday* at MGM, which was the closest thing he ever came to operetta and having been raised on opera, 'If You Feel Like Singing, Sing' is more of an operatic sort of number in its musical construction. It also gives the kind of joyousness needed for that moment in the film."

Feinstein added that Warren would often get annoyed with his collaborator Mack Gordon, a frustrated melodist in his own right. "When Harry worked with Mack, generally, Mack was a guy who always liked to write melodies as well. He would sometimes fight with Mack because when Mack would come up with an idea for a song, he would sing it to Harry. Harry would say, 'Mack, I don't need your goddamn melodies! Just read me the lyric.' Harry worked equally well, writing music first or setting words to music, and I don't know which came first. But I would wager that in the case of that number, the music probably came first."[2]

A verse of the song that didn't make the final cut of the movie:

Good Morning, Mr. Tweet-Tweet—how are you?
You whistle in the shower
With your coffee and your toast
All day long and with everything you do
Philosophically, I like your point of view

"If You Feel Like Singing, Sing" didn't enjoy much of an afterlife following its appearance in *Summer Stock*. According to an ASCAP database, Garland is the only artist to have recorded the song. However, the song's title was cannibalized in the UK and Australia, where it did double-duty as the title of the film (*If You Feel Like Singing*) because the term "summer stock" had no equivalent meaning in those two countries.

"The bottom line for Warren is that he felt MGM was inexpert at 'exploiting' his music like what happened for him during his Warner Bros. and Fox tenures," Feinstein said. "That's not to say that the score for *Summer Stock* would have otherwise become a hit because those were songs written for situations that made it more difficult to exploit them. I mean, 'If You Feel Like Singing, Sing' is a nice song, but it's the love songs that were the money songs."[3]*

"(HOWDY NEIGHBOR) HAPPY HARVEST"

Music by Harry Warren; Lyrics by Mack Gordon
Recorded by Judy Garland, chorus and orchestra directed by Johnny Green, October 13, 1949
Recorded by Gene Kelly, vocal quintet, Johnny Green conducting (finale), February 2, 1950

SUMMER STOCK, AFTER BEGINNING ON AN UPBEAT NOTE WITH JANE'S (Judy Garland) optimistic aria in the shower, turns to panic in the next scene as her longtime farmhands tender their resignations, leaving Jane and her trusted housekeeper, Esme (Marjorie Main), all alone to tend livestock and harvest crops. But Jane has a brainstorm and wastes no time motoring into Wingait Falls, where she finagles her fiancé Orville Wingait (Eddie Bracken) into asking his father (Ray Collins), the town's leading citizen, for a tractor that could solve her manpower shortage.**

Orville must convince his father into green-lighting this "early wedding gift," but it's an easy sell; Jasper Wingait cagily consents, hoping that the move will bring Jane and Orville closer to marching down the matrimonial aisle. (Later, the tractor becomes a form of indenture that binds her to the Wingaits, and, when things get sticky, it's something they can hold over Jane's head to press their case for a wedding.) But in this early scene, happily bouncing behind the steering wheel of her new tractor on the way back to Falbury Farm, Jane launches into "(Howdy Neighbor) Happy Harvest."***

* In a royalties statement sent to Mack Gordon from Four Jays Music Co., Inc. (the rights-holder of the Warren/Gordon score for *Summer Stock*), "If You Feel Like Singing, Sing" remunerated Gordon a total of $6.57 in royalties for the six-month period of January 1–June 30, 1958.

** Jane's tractor that figures so prominently in the plot of *Summer Stock* is a 1949 Ford N8 model. The MGM Art Department covered that marking with the fictitious "Earthbuster" logo on the calendar page picture where Jane first sees it, and on the tractor itself in scenes where it appears.

*** The *Summer Stock* pressbook provided to the media included a photo of Garland behind the wheel of the tractor with director Walters. The caption read: "Every Ford dealer will be glad to use it (the photo)—both to sell tractors and for general star value and prestige."

A two-time Emmy-winning production designer for the daytime TV soap opera *Days of Our Lives*, Tom Early has spent hours sleuthing the location where Jane takes her tractor ride (ostensibly the Connecticut countryside but really the Iverson Movie Ranch in Chatsworth, part of the San Fernando Valley just north of Los Angeles proper).

"Happy Harvest" was shot in late winter/early spring of 1950, when the flora around Chatsworth was in full bloom; the likely location was directly below the ranch itself on either modern-day Bee Canyon Road or Farralone Avenue. According to Early, even today there are dirt roads and open parcels of land dotted with ranch houses in the area. The site is also where Garland and John Hodiak filmed "My Intuition," a number cut from *The Harvey Girls* that was shot directly up the hill behind the "Happy Harvest" location.[4]

As the song begins, Jane on the tractor is being towed by an unseen camera truck and is lip-synching to the playback machine which, during filming, would've been blasting at a high-decibel level since it was an outdoor shoot. Motoring along, Jane sings the salutation ("Howdy Neighbor") to a couple of guys in a hay wagon. They return the greeting in a kind of call-and-response that's repeated throughout the number as Jane makes her way down the road passing men on a milk truck and stopping at a vegetable stand to cool down an overheating engine where she also becomes an impromptu choirmaster to singing townsfolk admiring the tractor like it was a prize-winning heifer. Jane sings the last lyric (". . . you get paid by father time") and holds the last note so long that when she finally ends it, she does a comic take of consternation, in close-up, as if she's totally winded.

"(Howdy Neighbor) Happy Harvest" belies the effervescence we see projected on screen; shooting the number was often a touch-and-go situation. "You always had to keep her spirits high," said Charles Walters of Garland. "Once you had her in the mood for work, you had to keep her there. Not that it was always easy. What was that number on a tractor? Oh, 'Howdy Neighbor!' The days we spent on that. I can see her on the damn thing now, mumbling: 'What am I doing here? Please send for Vincente to bring me home.'"[5]

According to Walters's biographer Brent Phillips, the cast and crew endured the tough days, with Walters hoping for the best each day. "I can't say enough about Charles Walters and his patience," noted producer Pasternak. "When set to film her 'Happy Harvest' tractor ride through the San Fernando Valley, Garland announced she wasn't feeling well enough to face the camera. 'Hey Judy,' Chuck encouraged her, 'come listen to your playback for a minute.' Assistant director Al Jennings recalled, 'Well, she did. The music started, [and Judy] said, "Gee, that's great."' . . . She got on the tractor—and we did it! She had been on her way home, very ill, but she stood there and did the number. The funny part was that something went wrong with the playback, and I was furious. And Judy was calming *me* down! She said, 'They'll get it. Don't worry.'"[6]

In *Get Happy*, his book about Garland, Gerald Clarke tells a variation on that story. *Summer Stock*'s assistant director, Jennings, to calm Garland's misgivings, asked her to "climb into the tractor and rehearse for a minute?" She did as he requested, and just as he had anticipated, she soon forgot how sick she had been, not only remaining to finish the shot but even comforting him when a technical glitch forced her to do it again. "'Don't worry,' she earnestly assured him. 'We'll get it.'"[7]

In a kind of musical coda to end *Summer Stock*, "(Howdy Neighbor) Happy Harvest" is the final song that's sung (just a smidgen of it in reprise) by Joe (Gene Kelly) and Jane dressed in green flannels and straw hats as they stride on stage and embrace right before the end credits roll.

Phil Silvers, in his autobiography, contends that Garland banished him from the film's finale (although he does walk on stage with Joe and Jane before backing out of frame and taking his place among the rest of the assembled chorus). "Gene put me in the finale of *Summer Stock* for a reprise of a song-and-dance number, with him and Judy," Silvers wrote. "As I came on the set, costumed and made-up, everyone avoided my eye. When I walked over to talk to Judy, she broke into tears. Gene called me aside. 'She's more upset than you will be when I tell you. Judy doesn't think you should be up front with us.'"[8]

Silvers's memory of events is apocryphal, because MGM musicals characteristically had the two leads (boy and girl) embracing happily at the end—three would've been a crowd. Author and Garland historian John Fricke points out: "If he [Silvers] had been meant to appear 'up front' with Garland and Kelly and participate in the song, he would have been included on the pre-recording, which he is not. So, his recollection of being unceremoniously dumped on set doesn't make sense. Beyond that, it would have been Walters who would or should have circumvented such a situation, not Garland making the call and using Kelly as her intermediary."[9] Scott Brogan, who runs a popular Garland internet site (The Judy Room), concurs with Fricke's assessment: "It totally makes sense that Silvers wouldn't be up front. Judy and Gene were the big costars, of course, so, just like Judy and Mickey, it should be the two of them for the fade-out."[10]

Mack Gordon originally titled the song "Howdy Doody, Happy Harvest" and it was submitted as such to Joseph Breen and the Production Code Administration (PCA) for approval on June 1, 1949. Gordon (probably unconsciously) slugged the song with the name of the wildly popular freckle-faced marionette puppet that burst on the American scene in December 1947 in a children's television program that was also named *Howdy Doody*. Advised of the possible conflict of interest with the puppet, Gordon changed "Doody" to "Neighbor."

The song sent to the PCA (with "Howdy Doody" phrased as "Howdy Doo Dee" but still a problem phonetically) also included a verse that was never recorded or used in the film:

Come on along and take a ride
And look at life from the cheery side
Oh, things are gonna jell for the farmer in the dell
And how—and how
Keep the road a-clear—it's "go to market" year
And how—and ho
They'll be a prosperous swish to the tail of every cow
We'll sow—and plow—and hoe—and how—how, how

Chorus: Howdy Doo Dee—Happy Harvest

The Gordon lyrics submitted to the PCA, also contained the following lines:

And in crowded country chapels
every farmer will be prayin'
And as sure as God made little green apples
You'll hear them sayin'
Let's be thankful, for a happy harvest time

In a letter dated, June 3, 1949, to Louis B. Mayer at MGM, Joseph Breen at the PCA wrote: "We must ask that you revise the line, 'And as sure as God made little apples,' for the reason that this use of the word God does not seem quite reverent."[11] Gordon complied with Breen's decree and removed the "objectionable" wording.

Noodling with the lyrics to the song, Gordon typed out a page of notes—a rough draft—that he later refined with Warren's melody to come up with the final lyric sheet. A look at those preparatory notes—the couplets and rhymes—provides an insight into the development of the final song:

All our cares are gonna end
There's a great big, purty rainbow
'round the bend, friend
Corn and wheat and rye
Will be wavin' high, Reuben

Come on along
'Twon't be long
'Twon't be long
Until there won't be nothing wrong

Hay in every hayloft
Corn and wheat in every bin

Pay day—Hay day

Quaint countryside chapels
You'll hear farmers prayin'
And as sure as God made little green apples
You will hear them sayin'
Howdy doo dee to a HAPPY HARVEST Time.

Things are going to jell
For the farmer in the dell

Bells of plenty are going to chime

Rainbow in the sprinklers

Aplenty
Just like you'll change a twenty

That's the farmer's hallelujah

Wheat and corn and rye will be wavin'—Hi Rueben.
We'll be sayin' to the sun, Mr., where've you been?

Grin full—bin full

Gonna be—whopper
—cropper

Sun and the rain—Shake hands
Partners are in on the plans

Plowing, hoeing, and raking it in
Plantin' seeds aplenty

Freezers will be stocked
Cackle—Burlap sack'll

Mother Nature and Father Time
Pockets in our jeans

Girls wear prettiest ginghams
Sunday one percent wool

Taters, Turnips—Radishes

Gosh all Hemlock—Holy Smokes
Throw in a couple of artichokes

Hale and hearty
Complete the party
We'll throw in a couple of artichokes

To top it all
Barrels of moonbeams
And bushels of stars

Toil—Soil

Market at Rainbow's End

Ridin' through the furrows
On your horses, mules and burrows

'Twon't be long—'Twon't be long
'Til there won't be nothin' wrong
—Troubles end
Rainbow around the bend, friend

Cousin Myrtle
Fertile soil to till
Change a twenty dollar bill

If you're a bettin' man, then bet us

We're ridin' to a hay-day
Every day is gonna be pay day

This year's crop will be a whopper

And how—And how—
They'll be good luck
Written on every plow

No mortgages or losses
You'll be pullin' with your bosses
Mother Nature and Father Time

Farmer Jones
No more mortgages or loans

Howdy doo dee

—Grinfull
—Binfull

Hayloft—growing
Overflowing
Sowing

Crop gonna be—a whopper
Comes a cropper
Topper

Planting seeds of plenty

We'll see Mother Earth
Giving birth to
Money's worth

Mother Nature and Father Time are
Farmers just like we are

Pockets in your jeans will be full

Girls in the prettiest gingham
Boys—Sunday suits—100% wool

Will be barrels of moonbeams
And bushels of stars up above

Farmer boy and farmer girl will say
Howdy doo dee to a HAPPY HARVEST of love

Pecks
Maybe a crate of tomatoes
Maybe a peck of nectarines

Tractors—important factors
Toil in the soil

See our troubles end
Rainbow around the friend
Weather man will be our friend

Write your cousin Myrtle
We've got fertile soil to till

If you're a bettin' man just bet us

Good luck written on every plow

Things are gonna jell
For the farmer in the dell
And how—and how

Farmer in the dell did
Does

A prosperous swish to the tail of every cow

For a change
We can change a $20 bill

The tractor is quite an important factor

You'll be hearing no more
Banker's groans
Loans
Farmin' will be charmin'
Farmer Jones

Come on along
Join the crowd
Mighty slick
Mighty proud

Cake
We can break a $20 bill[12]

On October 6, 1963, more than a decade after *Summer Stock* was released, on the ninth episode of *The Judy Garland Show* on CBS, Garland reprised

"(Howdy Neighbor) Happy Harvest." The number begins on a minimalist set with a windmill, a weathervane, a fence, and the outline of a shed. Dancers costumed like Raggedy Anns and Andys—or possibly a hybrid of scarecrow—toss each other acrobatically about before Judy twirls into frame to sing the song.

Dressed in white slacks and wearing a checkered shirt, Garland appears at one point to muff the lyrics, but pro that she is, saves it by mugging with the dancers. Comic Jerry Van Dyke then enters with a file folder and hectors her about cost overruns for the number. The set vanishes (carted off by the dancers) and a perplexed Barbra Streisand appears (Judy's special guest that week) dressed in the same slacks and patterned blouse as Garland. They sing the last line of the song together and then sit on a couple of stools as Judy commiserates, saying: "Well, there's one thing they can't cut out of the budget and that's our voices."

"DIG-DIG-DIG DIG FOR YOUR DINNER"

Music by Harry Warren; Lyrics by Mack Gordon
Recorded by Gene Kelly, Phil Silvers, and chorus, and the MGM Orchestra, Johnny Green conducting, on November 4, 1949;
Additional recording done on April 29, 1950, and June 8, 1950
Lyrics approved by Joseph Breen and the Motion Picture Association of America on April 13, 1949
Special materials for the song credited to Saul Chaplin and Gene Kelly were approved by Breen and the MPAA on December 8, 1949

WITHIN THE STORY LINE OF *SUMMER STOCK*, ON THEIR FIRST NIGHT AT THE farm, the cast and crew of *Fall in Love* (the show-within-the-movie) sit down to a farm-to-table supper prepared by Esme (Marjorie Main). It's a dour affair, with a noticeable pall in the air as the despondent troupe has just been informed by Jane (Judy Garland) that they cannot stage their show in the barn and will have to vacate the premises the next morning.

After a quick confab with her sister Abigail (Gloria DeHaven) in which she learns how much the show means to her, Jane changes heart and reluctantly consents to let Joe and his troupe stay and put on their show with one stipulation: each morning, before rehearsals, they must pull their weight and pitch in with the chores. "Farms don't just run by themselves," she declares. Those duties include feeding chickens, slopping pigs, stacking hay, milking cows, and—worse—a 6:00 a.m. wake-up call, cataclysmic for gypsies more accustomed to late nights and noon rehearsal calls. But Joe, with his sidekick Herb (Phil Silvers), convinces them that ". . . making with a hoe" is a small price to pay for theatrical immortality, and they launch into "Dig-Dig-Dig Dig for Your Dinner" to convince them.

The number parodies southern revival meetings and starts with Herb, in a "Come to Jesus" moment, slapping the dinner table in an exaggerated burlesque—like Billy Sunday thumping on a lectern—that soon leads to role-playing between him and Joe:

> ***Herb to Joe:*** *(in a southern drawl) Save me, SAVE ME!*
> ***Joe:*** *Well, I don't want to sound like I'm preachin' a sermon.*
> ***Herb:*** *Oh, preach to me, PREACH!*

Much of the patter that precedes the actual song and resumes after the first verse as Joe tries to restrain Herb's hammy fervor is not the work of lyricist Mack Gordon. In fact, credit for that dialogue (termed "Special Materials") is attributed to Saul Chaplin and Gene Kelly. It's perhaps Kelly's only known contribution to the lyrics of a song. The Warren-Gordon tune is interpolated with the Chaplin-Kelly spoken word add-ons and is underscored at times by the chorus clapping a backbeat to the music and yelling emphatic, "Digs" as if the word was the heavy, percussive stomp of a foot-pedal on a bass drum.

Warren was not pleased with Chaplin and Kelly's contribution. "When we did 'Dig for Your Dinner,' Mr. Kelly decided that he would like to have Saul Chaplin, or somebody, write some extra material for him and Phil Silvers, who was in it," Warren said. "I was burned by that time. I wouldn't even go on the lot to look at it."[13]

The recording had a few modifications, but the final cut kept most of the Chaplin-Kelly wordage:

Chillun' are you listening to the man?
This is the man who saved me
This is the man who showed me the way

This is the man who took me by the hand
Up to the glory road
I was wicked, I was bad
This is the man who gave me the beat
He made me righteous—this man here

Ya gotta—pull the weeds
Ya gotta—rope the steer
Ya gotta—bag the tiger
Gotta—hunt the deer
Ya gotta—see your dentist twice a year
And dig, dig, dig
Ain't it the truth

Warren had this to say about writing a patter (fast to very fast tempo) song such as "Dig-Dig-Dig Dig for Your Dinner":

> When I write, I think of the way the lyric writer is going to put in his lines. Of course, you can always put a lyric to a melody. If you have to put a melody to a lyric, you're stymied right away, because you have to write, if it's four-and-four and five-and-five or six-and-six lyrics, something like that, how are you going to do it? Sometimes it's tough.
>
> It's different if you're going to write a comedy version of something or a patter. That's easy. You can set that to music right away, or you can chord it. If you write a patter, I always think the music shouldn't interfere with the patter. All you have to do is just write chords against it, so you can hear the lyric.[14]

As author Brian Seibert noted, Kelly showcases his best tapping in *Summer Stock*: "One number ('Dig') is a pep talk in the form of a mock Holy Roller service. Kelly testifies with his feet, and for once his rhythms have drive."[15] However, the "Down South Camp Meeting" feel of the song didn't sit well with some. After *Summer Stock* was released, MGM had to address mail accusing the studio of blasphemy for its supposed mocking of evangelical gatherings.[16]

Walters did not have the color palette of Vincente Minnelli, but he did have a strong suit when it came to directing musicals, one that Minnelli or few others could boast of. As a dancer/choreographer himself, Walters innately knew how to frame a number—especially a dance—for maximum impact and fluidity. In "Dig-Dig-Dig Dig for Your Dinner," Walters's camera tracks Kelly and Silvers around the long dining table as they sing the song. When Kelly continues alone, gyrating around the table a second time, the camera shadows his every spin, providing an ideal point of view whenever Kelly makes a choreographic flourish. At one point, Kelly, sitting on Silvers's lap, is bucked off and lurches in a full body extension to a wall on an emphatic beat in the music and to a quick and faultless camera cut. But instead of being jarring, the moment is seamless. Before the number has even begun in earnest, the audience has been primed by the buildup for Kelly's explosive tap dance that follows. Walters achieved that intricate effect routinely in dozens of numbers in different films over many years.

"That number was 100 percent created for the camera," said Mandy Moore, choreographer of *La La Land* (2016). "It feels very three-dimensional without it being 360 degrees. It's like you're an audience member observing the number but then you feel like you're one of the troupe sitting around the table. It creates a kind of intimacy with a film audience that is difficult to pull off."[17]

It's at this point in "Dig," when Joe circles the table the second time, that he briefly links arms with dancers Jeannie Coyne (who would become Kelly's second wife) wearing a tucked-in white shirt and cuffed blue jeans and Sarah (Nita Bieber) in a light brown polka-dotted dress and wearing eyeglasses with owlish frames. It's also impossible to miss Carleton Carpenter standing at 6′ 3″ and playing jack-of-all-trades Artie, who forms the apex of the human pyramid whenever the chorus* is grouped for framing purposes during "Dig."

"Kelly was just mean to me," Carpenter recollected of his time shooting *Summer Stock*. "He'd say: 'Is that where you're going to be?' I'd respond that this is where Walters [the director] put me. He'd say, 'This is where I think you should be, over here.' It was very strange. I didn't understand what was going on with him. He was just mean to me all the way through, which was fine. I really didn't have that much to do in that picture." Carpenter further speculated that Kelly's coldness could have emanated from their height differential—he visibly dwarfed Kelly.[18]

* Numbered among the chorus boys in "Dig-Dig-Dig Dig for Your Dinner" is Arthur Loew Jr., grandson of Marcus Loew, one of the founders of MGM.

Truth to tell, if—during Kelly's ceaseless quest for perfection, which was deeply ingrained and informed everything he did—alienation of affection occurred and feelings were hurt by his brusque single-mindedness, it was a small price to pay for what resulted, an enduring legacy of brilliant choreography and classic movies. Personal acclaim as a movie star mattered more to the pollsters at *Modern Screen* magazine than it ever did to Kelly, and that extended to his likability on set. For Kelly, always in the vanguard was his urge to advance the film musical to a new creative capstone; nothing was more important. As Bracken said, Kelly was admiral of the group, and sometimes he pulled rank.

No one, not even Astaire, could circumvent the limits imposed by a confined space better than Kelly could in a tap number (think of his "Tra-la-la" tap dance in the doorjamb of his flat in *An American in Paris*). But perhaps nowhere else does Kelly fully explode in a cramped space quite the way he does adjacent to and on top of the dinner table in "Dig-Dig-Dig Dig for Your Dinner."

The fact that Kelly was compact, with a low center of gravity (as Carpenter can attest), presented a marvelous dichotomy when he danced; it brought a kind of tension that sprung from his controlled and highly disciplined movements that were, at the same time, hyperkinetic and could appear almost frenzied when he was dancing in close confines. "You have to be aware of your surroundings when you're working in such a confined space," Mandy Moore said. "I think it is interesting in 'Dig' that you never feel like Gene is prohibited because of his space—like he's making his movements smaller. He is still grand even within a small movement or a small space. That's fascinating because I think if you have a smaller space to work in, the natural instinct would be to make the dance smaller. But because he was such a pro and is so aware of his space, he could open it up and fill it."[19]

At the urging of Herb, Joe climbs on top of the dinner table and to a squelching blast of brass (a recurring motif in Skip Martin's arrangements), he lays the iron down, alternating from one foot to the other with small lightning-fast pivot steps that don't take him beyond the width of the very narrow table and that are punctuated with heel drops on the beat and to chants of "Dig!"

"His footwork feels a little bit more dug into the ground so you get a lot more heel-toe work," said Corey John Snide, a tapper who trained at Juilliard. "In 'Dig' he does what's called a running cramp roll (flap-heel-toe). And then he throws in a move called a Cincinnati circle (brush-heel-shuffle-heel-step). And yet he remains so buoyant."[20]

Eventually Joe travels downstage and leaps off the table into the foreground where he pulls trenches (slides that exchange one leg for another) that build into another tight, rhythmic pattern of, in the words of author and tap expert Brenda Bufalino, "complicated small footwork" to a double-time tempo. The chorus continues harmonizing the song as an overlay to Joe's rapid-fire footwork that sounds like a pneumatic drill gone berserk.[21]

Joe's big finish employs a series of acrobatic barrel turns (a mainstay in Kelly's repertoire of killer flash steps), variations of which appear in most of his musicals, perhaps most famously as the "aeroplane" spins he does, arms outstretched like a propeller, to culminate "I Got Rhythm" in *An American in Paris*. But here, Kelly executes the barrel turns as jumps from left leg to right leg and back again, a gymnastic move that doubtless took great strength as well as perfect balance to pull off.

"When Gene does the barrel jumps, he uses repetition for a 'wow' factor because he did the move to the right, to the left, to the right, and to the left," Moore said. "The fact that he did them from both sides is herculean. I also love the syncopated chorus handclaps to keep time. Gene is a master of building a dance to really show off at the end, and, as an audience member, I wanted that big finish."[22]

After the barrel jumps, "Dig-Dig-Dig Dig for Your Dinner" climaxes as Joe, back on the table, pirouettes down its length ending in a final flourish on his knees framed on all sides by his troupe as they shout one last "Dig!" in unison. It's a rousing finish to a number to which even Elmer Gantry in all his messianic zeal might have borne witness with a praise break that—just like this dance—raises the rafters.

"MEM'RY ISLAND"

Music by Harry Warren; Lyrics by Mack Gordon
Recorded by Gloria DeHaven and Hans Conried (dubbed by Pete Roberts), chorus and the MGM Orchestra, Johnny Green conducting, on November 17, 1949
Lyrics approved by Joseph Breen and the Motion Picture Association of America on June 9, 1949

NEAR THE BEGINNING OF THE SONG "MEM'RY ISLAND," SHOT ON THE makeshift rehearsal stage in the barn, the dulcet baritone of Harrison Keath (Hans Conried), dubbed by Pete Roberts, elicits a double-take from a flustered cow in the stable that's befitting of a cockeyed glance by Jimmy Finlayson in one of his many Laurel and Hardy film appearances. The bovine is expressing its corny reaction to a number intended to mockingly jibe the pompous leading man Harrison I. Keath and his high-maintenance leading lady, Abigail Falbury (Gloria DeHaven), rehearsing their duet among the barnyard chaos of cackling chickens and dancers who miss their cues.

Conried, sartorially, is pitch-perfect as the New York "name," wearing a tweed coat and ascot that contrasts with DeHaven's garb decked out as she is for the rehearsal in a pair of short-shorts that would have put Catherine Bach's "Daisy Dukes" in TV's *The Dukes of Hazzard* to shame and that miraculously passed muster with the Breen censors.

"Mem'ry Island" is aptly described as "a hammy spoof of summer stock heroes" and a "spoof of old-fashioned theater ballads."[23] The song is the reason for the rehearsal scene in which virtually everything that can go wrong does, much to the chagrin of the show's director Joe Ross (Gene Kelly).

Songwriter Harry Warren had an affinity for classical music, enjoying throughout his long life the works of Puccini and Verdi. As an opera aficionado, "Mem'ry Island" can also be construed as Warren's homage and affectionate send-up of this more classical art form. Although the song probably never was intended to enjoy a life beyond *Summer Stock* (and it didn't), its campiness works perfectly within the context of the film.

Summer Stock commenced production a few months after Kelly had just come off of co-directing (with Stanley Donen) his first feature film, *On the Town*; so playing the frustrated director Joe Ross going through the motions of staging a troublesome number with his two temperamental leads and a chorus of singers and dancers is a bit of art imitating his real-life aspirations as a filmmaker. In the scene, Joe thrusts his head in frustration and grimaces during the rehearsal—undoubtedly what Kelly did more than once when actors or crew members in movies he directed missed their marks. The humorous bits of business (when the camera pulls back to show the lanky Conried gently clunk his head on a hanging lantern as he and Abigail are wheeled offstage on a tractor trailer) is attributable to the man behind the camera, Chuck Walters, who brought his own experiences as a director, dancer, and choreographer to the scene.

Pete Roberts, who performed the vocals for Conried, also handled dubbing chores for one of the Blackburn Twins on "Thou Swell" in the MGM Rodgers and Hart biopic *Words and Music* (1948), and he was a vocalist in *Brigadoon* (1954).

A verse in the song that never appeared in the film reads:

What happened to this love of ours?
We care—but carelessly
Although the spark we gave it—isn't really gone
The afterglow is fading fast
Before this love is lost in a storm
And tossed on a restless sea
We can save it—By depending on
The warm nostalgia of the past
So let us board—Our ship of dreams
And head it toward—The shores of used-to-be

"THE PORTLAND FANCY"

"The Portland Fancy," a traditional New England dance instrumental
Recorded by Johnny Green conducting the MGM Orchestra on
November 5, 1949

FALBURY FARM, THE FOCAL POINT IN *SUMMER STOCK*, IS THE SITE OF A longstanding tradition: the annual Wingait Falls Historical Society Dance, where townsfolk get all gussied up to trip the light fantastic in Jane's (Judy Garland) expansive barn, which is decorated for the occasion in festive bunting. But this year's gathering will be different because the farm is occupied by Joe Ross (Gene Kelly) and his troupe of interlopers. As the prim and proper locals robotically clop across the floor to "The Portland Fancy," a traditional New England square dance tune,* the actors watch the "squares dance" from the loft above the barnyard floor.

But when they spot Joe promenading with Jane, they consider it a license to "join in on the fun" and swoop down on the makeshift dance floor. One chorus boy shoos away a geezer from behind the drum kit and takes over, accelerating the beat. And that's all a young trumpeter (who's been flirting with a cute blonde chorus girl in the loft) needs in order to cut loose with a lick that announces to all present that the Historical Society Dance is about to go from sedate to swing. As the music shifts, members of the troupe breakout into a Lindy Hop while the locals—shuffled to the sidelines—watch in horror, aghast at how a staid reel dating from the 1840s could possibly transform into a rhythmic, hepcat jam session (courtesy of orchestrator Skip Martin's pulsing big band–inspired chart).

At first, Joe is reluctant to participate in the jazzed-up atmosphere, but caught up in the groove, he begins to improvise tap steps during his circular stroll with Jane around the dance floor. Jane doesn't immediately take the bait but finally succumbs and duplicates a tap combination that Joe rattles out. The floor clears and the battle is joined! With the exception of a barrel roll that Jane can't duplicate, that is played for comic effect and that leads to the number opening up into a duet, she mirrors Joe step for

*Instead of the "Portland Fancy," the *Summer Stock* script dated October 24, 1949, called for a genteel round dance on the order of "Put Your Little Foot (Right Out/There)," which was an old-time fiddler's waltz.

step (no mincing allemande left and right for these two). The spontaneity that unfolds from the first challenge steps to the final flourish is delightful, and by number's end Joe is rightfully gobsmacked by his partner's terpsichorean prowess.

Kelly (with incidental assistance from choreographer Nick Castle) really put Garland to the test with steps far more difficult and physical than anything they did together in *For Me and My Gal* (they didn't dance together in *The Pirate*). "Wonderful, wonderful Judy, she was the greatest," Kelly told us during a visit we had with him in 1978. For a moment, he seemed lost in a kind of reverie as he remembered. "She wasn't a trained dancer, but she was such a hard worker. We did a number in *Summer Stock* in a barn called 'The Portland Fancy.' She was terrific, picked up the steps so quickly. And it wasn't an easy dance to do. Really, I never worked with a trained dancer who was so quick to learn steps as Judy was. You would run through a combination twice—and some were difficult—and she would have it down pat."[24]

To his biographer Clive Hirshhorn, Kelly added that Garland performed admirably in the routine despite the perceived challenge of her weight gain. "We did a number in the barn together called 'The Portland Fancy,' and though she was pretty overweight at the time—obese might be the more appropriate word—she danced magnificently, far better than in *For Me and My Gal*, and it wasn't an easy routine. I gave her some very difficult turns to do. But she was fine, just fine. She was in a good mood that day, and it was hard to believe she had anything else on her mind but her work. The only thing she couldn't lick in that number was her size."[25]

SOMETIMES A GREAT NOTION

Choreographer Nick Castle was an "idea man." When working with dancers and directors the caliber of Gene Kelly and Charles Walters close collaboration was key, and Castle's suggestions were incorporated into at least four musical routines in *Summer Stock*—"Dig-Dig-Dig Dig for Your Dinner," "The Portland Fancy," Kelly's solo routine on a newspaper and squeaky floorboard, and the "Heavenly Music" hillbilly number. It's impossible to know what steps or gestures are or aren't directly attributable to Castle.

Kelly biographer Clive Hirshhorn called *Summer Stock* a "hodge-podge," citing how the dance numbers were parceled between Kelly, Walters, and Castle, who Saul Chaplin described as a "meat and vegetables choreographer."[26]

"I have no idea what the exact working relationship was during the numbers," said Castle's son, Nick Jr. "I'm sure my dad—because Gene would do the bulk of his own stuff—came up with little gags in the context of the numbers. Not joke gags—little bits of business. He definitely would have been heavily involved in the 'Heavenly Music' number."[27]

As with any convergence of talent, differences and on-set flare-ups are almost inevitable and *Summer Stock* was no exception. Kelly's feistiness on the set one day almost resulted in he and Castle exchanging blows, according to Walters's biographer Brent Phillips: "As [the assistant director Al] Jennings observed, Kelly and Castle never quite jibed. Gene was proud of Gene . . . and Castle was a little hot-headed, too. They got into a little kind of thing . . . I thought they were about to come to fisticuffs. I stepped between them and said, 'You two little boys!' I really let them have it."[28]

Born Nicholas John Casaccio in Brooklyn, New York, March 21, 1910, the son of a cabinetmaker, Castle began performing at an early age, teaching himself how to dance by watching various vaudeville acts, eventually forming his own partnership with Frank Starr and traveling the vaudeville circuit. In 1935 he came to Hollywood and worked as a dance director primarily at Twentieth Century-Fox.

Castle's longest and most fruitful collaboration was with the dancing Nicholas Brothers in the early 1940s. The brothers (along with the Berry Brothers) were the greatest flash act to ever trod the boards at Harlem's Cotton Club during the 1930s where they tapped, twirled, back-flipped, and leg-split to the swingin' bands of Cab Calloway, Chick Webb, and Duke Ellington. Later on, while under contract to Twentieth Century-Fox, their specialty numbers in such movies as *Down Argentine Way* (1940), *Tin Pan Alley* (1940), *The Great American Broadcast* (1941), *Sun Valley Serenade* (1941), *Orchestra Wives* (1942), and *Stormy Weather* (1943) drew wild applause in movie houses from coast to coast.

"The only time we worked with someone who gave us something was Nick Castle," said Fayard Nicholas. Upon their first meeting, Castle remarked to the brothers, "I'm happy to meet you guys. Now there's somebody who can do my ideas." The infusion of Castle's ideas (including moves drawn from ballet, modern dance, and ballroom dance) into the brothers' rhythmically complex repertoire transformed their routines into spectacular musical performances.[29]

In one such number in 1943's *Stormy Weather*, the brothers end their routine by leap-frogging over each other into splits down a flight of stairs. "We did that in one take," said Fayard Nicholas. "We never did rehearse coming down those stairs jumping over each other's heads. Our choreographer at that time, his name was Nick Castle, and Nick said, 'Don't rehearse it, just do it.' He just thought we could do it in one take and that's the way it happened."[30]

Summer Stock was not the only time Castle worked with Garland. "My dad got along with Judy really well because she wound up hiring him for her TV show in the early 1960s," said Nick Jr. "He was working on *The Andy Williams Show* at the time and she had him come over to start her series. I got to meet her then. I was about fifteen. She was a character. My dad pointed out her car. I looked in it and there was a holster—a gun holster—with a liquor bottle in it!"[31]

Castle spent the latter part of his career choreographing for television and various nightclub performers while operating his own dance studio. He died of a heart attack on August 18, 1968, at age fifty-eight while driving to work on the Jerry Lewis television show. In 1989, as a homage to his father, Nick Jr. wrote and directed the film *Tap!*

The tap dance challenge has roots going back to the beginning of the twentieth century and is loosely defined as "any competition, contest, breakdown or showdown in which dancers compete before an audience of spectators or judges . . . motivated by dare, focused by strict attention to one's opponent, and developed through the stealing and trading of steps, the tap challenge is the dynamic and rhythmically expressive 'engine' that drives tap dancing—our oldest of American vernacular dance forms."[32]

Choreographer Mandy Moore agrees that "The Portland Fancy" is a variation on the age-old challenge dance, akin to a dance version of the Irving Berlin "Anything You Can Do" braggadocio tune from *Annie Get Your Gun*. However, instead of trying to one-up each other in a singing duel, Joe and Jane engage in a battle of what Fats Waller might term "the pedal extremities."

"Judy keeps doing the cakewalk and Gene tests a new step," Moore said. "He breaks away from the cakewalk partnership and she responds with a look that telegraphs: 'Anything you can do, I can do better.' 'No, you can't,' he taps out. 'Yes, I can,' she responds. What's more, the dance flows naturally out of the narrative where Jane starts turning from a serious farm woman and begins to express her less inhibited inner artistic side. In this number, she's making the transition from the soil to the stage."[33]

According to tapper Corey John Snide, numbers like "The Portland Fancy" induce an almost out-of-body experience that still resonates with contemporary audiences. "What I love so much about watching Gene dance and all of those brilliant artists from that time period is that what you get is an almost a 'trippy' experience where you forget that you're watching or listening to their footwork and watching their bodies. It's this crazy cross-over visual experience."[34]

There's a story about legendary tap dancer Bill "Bojangles" Robinson performing before a group of journalists and dance experts whose attention was riveted on the intricate rhythms he was pounding out with his famed feet. He is said to have remarked, "They should've been watching my face, because that's where I was sellin'." Dancer Honi Coles is even more succinct: "Bo's face was about 40 percent of his appeal."[35]

Kelly and Garland are the personification of what Robinson and Coles were driving at. Stanley Donen, Kelly's frequent collaborator and co-director on *On the Town*, *Singin' in the Rain*, and *It's Always Fair Weather*, reckons: "Gene was the only song and dance man to come out of that period who had balls," he said. "There were other good dancers around, like Don Loper, Jack Cole, Gower Champion, Charles Walters, and Dan Dailey—even Van Johnson. But they somehow weren't as dynamic as Gene. It was the athlete in him that gave him his uniqueness."[36]

Some, like the great MGM contract dancer Tommy Rall, were arguably more technically proficient than Kelly. But none of them had the indefinable star quality—call it *chutzpah*—Kelly had. His reactions while he danced (and Garland's too, for that matter) are indelible in every one of his performances. And in "The Portland Fancy," Kelly and Garland are "sellin' it" in spades with every gyration and expression of delight. As they orbit the dance floor and the steps become more challenging, all the while keeping pace with the up-tempo brassy swing of the music, Walters's camera glides with them, becoming an almost weightless third presence, unobtrusive and fluid, that never fails to capture every nuance they exchange with each other. Noted Snide:

> No one does barrel turns like Gene. In the number, they start this back-and forth conversation between their feet. He tries a step, and she mimics it. He's already interrupting her, not really giving her a chance. I mean, they're doing this back and forth, where Judy has her arms folded, slightly exasperated. It's like, who's going to make the first move and then Gene dives out and takes control. He introduces this syncopated rhythm with the heel step, heel step that feels a bit more like an interruption and is more assertive. It's like they went over each other's phrasing or finished each other's phrasing. The beauty of this dance is how they begin in opposition to each other in keeping with the story, but by the end of the number they fall into synchronicity.[37]

Mandy Moore said it's obvious to viewers who watch intently that Garland is not a trained dancer "but she looks like how a real woman would move and I like that. I also think it's brilliant that she can stand next to somebody like Gene who is ultra-trained, ultra-professional, and still hold her own because those steps were tough.

"Gene was a taskmaster and he should be," Moore continued. "I'm sure he really coached Judy. You could tell there was a real connection. I really appreciate not only how the number is executed, but also its DNA, how it was created. Yes, Gene was amazing. Judy was amazing. They are stars. But if they were doing movement in a number that had not been crafted so well, I don't think it would be as memorable."[38]

At the end of "The Portland Fancy," as Jane is receiving kudos from Joe and his troupe (the locals have fled and the barn is largely empty), an angry Jasper Wingait (Ray Collins) rebukes her for allowing the thespians to crash the dance: "A fine finish to the meeting of the Historical Society," he fumes. Wingait doesn't know how spot-on that assessment is—talk about understatement!

"YOU WONDERFUL YOU"

Music by Harry Warren; Lyrics by Jack Brooks and Saul Chaplin
Recorded by Judy Garland and Gene Kelly and the MGM Orchestra
conducted by Johnny Green, February 3, 1950
Lyrics approved by Joseph Breen and the MPAA on December 9, 1950

THE SCENE IS THE BARN. JANE (JUDY GARLAND) FURTIVELY, HESITANTLY climbs stairs to the stage, steps into the halo of a spotlight, and imagines for a moment what it would be like to be a performer in front of an audience. Her daydream is interrupted when Joe (Gene Kelly) enters from offstage and says, "Wait until opening night when the people come in, even the air gets exciting . . . it's like electricity." Jane doesn't quite understand, so Joe opens a tube of greasepaint and gives her a whiff but cautions that although you can wipe it off your face you may never get it out of your blood. He then gives Jane a showbiz tutorial that includes a song-and-dance demonstration to "You Wonderful You." At one point she joins him singing and dancing. The number culminates when Joe sings the lyric, "My arms around you, that's wonderful too," lifting Jane off a wooden crate into a loving embrace that ends in a consensual kiss abruptly cut off by an overwhelmed Jane, who exits quickly.

For Kelly, "You Wonderful You" follows a trajectory that was used in two other films to win the affections of his leading lady. In *Anchors Aweigh*, in a dream sequence, Kelly performs a Spanish dance to "La Cumparsita" in a courtyard to romance Kathryn Grayson, a beautiful contessa, as she looks on from her balcony above. In *Singin' in the Rain*, a vacant soundstage, "5,000 kilowatts of stardust," and the song "You Were Meant for Me" are all that Kelly requires to steal the heart of Debbie Reynolds. The *Anchors Aweigh* courtship scene—essentially a Kelly solo number with Grayson looking on—is fairytale romance writ large; his song and dance with Reynolds, although less contrived, is appropriately played tongue-in-cheek, a loving pastiche of the cornball innocence that defined the era as silent films transitioned to "talkies."

But neither is as less self-consciously theatrical (and therefore honest) nor emotionally intimate as what transpires in the barn between Joe and Jane with "You Wonderful You." The scene doesn't feel "acted" or even rehearsed. It's as if all the weekend parties at 725 North Rodeo Drive (Kelly's Beverly Hills home), to say nothing of Kelly and Garland's two previous pairings, coalesced into the unforced tenderness—even playfulness—Jane and Joe have with each other here.

No less a film critic than Pauline Kael noted the palpable chemistry that existed between the two performers: "Garland and Kelly bring conviction to their love scenes and make them naively fresh. She joined her odd and undervalued cakewalker's prance to his large-spirited hoofing; and he joined his odd, light, high voice to her sweet deep one. Their duets together especially, 'You Wonderful You,' have a plaintive richness unlike anything in the Astaire-Rogers pictures. They could really sing together. There was a vulnerability both Gene and Judy brought out in each other and which neither had with anyone else."[39]

Author and tap dance expert Brenda Bufalino said the soft shoe dance that follows Kelly's vocal is "the most romantic dance that one can tap out and the bare stage and use of spotlights serves as the 'ultimate private environment.' Kelly executes what's called an essence step as he softly glides over the floor in triplets [another tap combination] like a lover's hands might smooth the hair of his lady. Holding hands in the traditional grapevine, this playful, gliding move joins the lovers together and develops into a foxtrot embrace."

The entire "You Wonderful You" song, dance, concluding kiss and embrace, and the dialogue that precedes the number was captured in three extended shots, with the dance filmed in one continuous take. "Normally," said Charles Walters, "when I do a really long take, it's because what's happening seems really interesting to me, and I don't see the point in cutting it. It's not because I'm looking for a certain visual effect."[40]

"You Wonderful You" came as an add-on late during production when it was determined that three new tunes were needed to complement the original Warren-Gordon score. "What Harry [Warren] told me was that Mack went dry on that film," said Michael Feinstein. "I don't know if it was the pressure of the studio or what circumstances led to that. I don't know what was going on in Mack's life at the time. He could not come up with an idea; he couldn't come up with the lyrics. So, they canned him. I don't know if they officially fired him, but they shunted him aside and that's when Jack [Brooks] and Saul [Chaplin] came in."[41]

"She [Garland] and I discussed what songs she should do," Chaplin told Garland biographer Gerold Frank. "Mack Gordon had left. When Harry was there, they wanted an old-fashioned song, and he wrote the tune and I and a guy, Jack Brooks, wrote the lyrics to 'You Wonderful You.'"[42]

THE BRITISH ARE COMING!

When Jack Brooks was brought in to contribute new lyrics to "You Wonderful You" in *Summer Stock*, he had never actually met the composer of the melody, Harry Warren. According to Warren biographer Tony Thomas, "At Metro, he [Mack Gordon] suffered a blow to his pride when his lyrics to 'You Wonderful You' were dumped and a new set were supplied by Brooks and Saul Chaplin. Warren was off the picture by this time and had no say in the matter."[43]

The British-born (February 14, 1912) Brooks had enjoyed a modest career as a lyricist writing special material for Bing Crosby, Fred Allen, and Phil Harris, with one major song hit under his belt before he worked on *Summer Stock*: the 1946 tune "Ole Buttermilk Sky," written with Hoagy Carmichael for the film *Canyon Passage*.

It was in 1953—three years after Brooks's work on *Summer Stock* with Warren in absentia—that the new songwriting team of Warren and Brooks would officially form thanks to an unlikely matchmaker—Jerry Lewis. At the time the comic, along with his partner Dean Martin, were enjoying a successful run in a series of comedies that featured Lewis's spastic brand of buffoonery and Martin's languorous ballads.

After Warren left MGM in 1952, he began a long tenure at Paramount working on a picture-by-picture arrangement. It was Lewis (a longtime admirer of the composer's work) that kept Warren at the keyboard throughout much of the 1950s and into the early 1960s.

"Lewis asked Warren to come and see him and talk about writing songs for *The Caddy* (1953)," Thomas wrote. "The question of a lyricist came up, and Lewis suggested Jack Brooks, a man with a considerable background as a pianist-accompanist and a writer of nightclub songs and skits for Las Vegas performers. At the mention of Brooks's name, Warren shrugged and admitted that he knew nothing of the man or his methods (understandable, as he and Warren had still never met in person). Lewis suggested that they try collaborating and that if it didn't work out, he would arrange for another lyricist."[44]

The association proved fruitful, giving *The Caddy* the Oscar-nominated "That's Amore," a kind of parody of a Neapolitan organ-grinder's song that became a signature tune for Martin and his first gold record, with two million sales. Brooks, with and without Warren, continued to pick up lyric-writing movie assignments, including three more films with Jerry Lewis, ending in 1964 with the rock 'n' roll lampoon "I Lost My Heart in a Drive-In Movie" from *The Patsy*. He died in Los Angeles November 8, 1971, at the age of fifty-nine.

In an interview he gave to the American Film Institute, Warren recounted recording the song: "I had the misfortune to have Miss Garland when she wasn't feeling so good," he said, "and she sang a song in there called 'You Wonderful You.' The day she came in to record it, she couldn't sing so they sent the whole orchestra home. Then they waited a month, and they kept a couple of tapes that she made, singing like a basso (a low vocal range)."[45]

"You Wonderful You" is one of two songs reprised in *Summer Stock*, the other being "(Howdy Neighbor) Happy Harvest." The reprise (clocking in at a mere 1:17) is performed in the show-within-a-movie finale in front of the stage curtain with Joe and Jane in quaint costumes, Joe wearing a red-and-white-striped blazer with beanie to match and Garland with a large bow in her hair.

This meta-song-and-dance brings to mind the comic "Snooky Ookums" routine that Garland and Fred Astaire performed in *Easter Parade*. Both show-within-a-movie numbers are brief (Astaire and Kelly embracing Garland from behind as they stroll). However, Joe and Jane are restrained in their counterpoint singing—a look of innocence on their faces, with none of the facial mugging that was part of "Snooky Ookums." On the Judy Room website (www.thejudyroom.com), you can hear take thirteen of the pre-recording of this reprise, with some unintelligible conversation just prior to the song and what sounds like a jubilant Garland laughing and in high spirits.

Taking their cue from Kelly and Garland, Dick Van Dyke and Mary Tyler Moore performed a soft shoe rendition of "You Wonderful You" in a 1961 episode of TV's *The Dick Van Dyke Show*. In 1981, Kelly revisited the song for obvious comic effect with Miss Piggy in a TV episode of *The Muppets*.

"FRIENDLY STAR"

Music by Harry Warren; Lyrics by Mack Gordon
Recorded by Judy Garland and the MGM Orchestra,
Johnny Green conducting on October 27, 1949
Lyrics approved by Joseph Breen and the Motion Picture
Association of America on May 26, 1949

JUDY GARLAND'S "FRIENDLY STAR" BALLAD (IT'S ALMOST A TORCH SONG) reflects the dilemma confronting her character Jane as her fiancé Orville (Eddie Bracken) and his domineering father (Ray Collins) ramp up Orville and Jane's engagement by giving her a bracelet (the elder Wingait actually puts it on Jane's wrist!). Problem is, just prior to this ham-fisted declaration of intent by the Wingaits, Jane and Joe (Gene Kelly) share a tender scene in the barn when he sings and performs a soft shoe dance to "You Wonderful You," then embraces and kisses her. Although long in coming, in the plot it's an awkward moment and Jane abruptly exits, leaving a flustered Joe trying to sort out what just happened as well as his own feelings.

"Friendly Star" begins in the farmhouse after the Wingaits leave, with Jane turning off the lights (similar to what she did with co-star Tom Drake in the "Over the Banister" number from *Meet Me in St. Louis*). As if in a reverie, Jane sings the introduction and first verse of the song in the darkened foyer, her fingers absently running along the mesh of the screen door. She continues singing onto the porch, her face upturned and bathed in moonlight that, in a lovely effect, also illumines passing clouds.

Crucial to the success of any musical is that the songs and dances, in essence, "say" what mere dialogue would fall short trying to explain or affirm. Nothing provides better emotional counterweight to a scene than a beautifully crafted song well placed and well sung. In "Friendly Star," Harry Warren's gentle melody and Mack Gordon's lyrics, filled with yearning as Jane looks to the stars for answers, heighten the stakes of what just occurred between her and Joe in the barn:

Lead me to my lover,
Just point him out, and whisper,
There you are, there you are

Then my love, you will be
Standing here, close to me
In your eyes, I will see my friendly star

As the song draws to a close, Charles Walters's camera tracks away from Jane so that the audience (but not her) discovers Joe sitting in a wicker chair, lost in thought, as he, too, realizes he's in love. The camera then centers into a medium close-up of Jane as she concludes the song, whereupon she notices that Joe has been listening all along.

"Friendly Star" is a good example of how Walters methodically staged ballads in his movies. As author and film historian Gerald Mast observed: "For Walters, space is centripetal, not moving outward from the performer into space but moving inward from the edges of the frame toward the performer. When Walters's camera moves, it keeps the performer as the fixed foot of a compass, traveling around him or her, attracted to the performance as if magnetized or hypnotized."[46]

"The one song from the film that should have had the most life is 'Friendly Star,'" said Michael Feinstein. "But Harry was very angry at the music publishing arm of MGM because he felt that they absolutely did not know how to exploit songs and he said that they were not good music publishers. He was so upset that he complained to the executives at MGM, saying that he was going to leave the studio. They said, 'Well, how would it be if we give you your own publishing company?' He said, 'Well, that would be very nice.' So, they established Harry Warren Music Company which co-published some of the songs.

"At one point," Feinstein continued, "Harry was called to New York to have a meeting with the people at Loew's Inc. (the parent company of MGM). In a big board room they thundered at him, 'What do we say to our shareholders when we tell them that your music company lost a million dollars?' Harry thundered back, 'The same thing you tell them when one of your goddamn lousy movies has lost five million dollars.'"[47]

"Friendly Star," as Feinstein suggests, was initially considered to be the film's "money song," a ballad filled with longing that Warren, Gordon, and others felt sure would become a Garland standard, but it was not to be. Any plans to reprise the number were jettisoned when Mack Gordon came off the film and a new song, "You Wonderful You," was composed by Warren, Saul Chaplin, and Jack Brooks. Indeed, "You Wonderful You" was used three times in *Summer Stock*—as accompaniment in the brief soft shoe Kelly and Garland do together in the barn right before "Friendly Star," as the jazzy instrumental for Kelly's "Squeaky Board/Newspaper" solo and in a slower, waltz-tempo reprise duet for Kelly and Garland in the show-within-a-movie finale.

Director Walters remembered shooting the number and particularly Judy's reaction to *his* reaction: "There's a number in that film, 'Friendly Star,' which I think is one of the best things she ever did. I remember, at one point, I was on a boom just above her head, and we were moving in for a giant close-up. Judy looked up with those great liquid eyes of hers and it was the most fantastic shot in the world. 'Cut!' I yelled. 'Will someone please hand me a towel. I've just cum!' Now that might be thought indelicate, but Judy loved that kind of foolishness. It really turned her on. 'C'mon, what's next?' she'd ask."[48]

Joan Ellison, a singer of classic American popular music who has also made it her mission to restore and preserve the original arrangements of Garland songs, finds "Friendly Star" and how it was filmed to be mesmerizing. "I do think that it's underrated," she said. "I mean it's not one that would have been even in my top twenty songs for Judy, but it's so beautiful in the movie. Then, when it cuts to Gene's face listening at the end, it's quite moving."[49]

Garland's daughter, Lorna Luft, said that her mother always had a fondness for "Friendly Star." "It's a pretty song, a *very* pretty song and she thought it was a beautiful song. She knew it wasn't going to be a classic—it was filler, but *beautiful* filler. It was also shot beautifully and that's because of Chuck."[50]

According to the American Society of Composers, Authors and Publishers, to date only a handful of artists besides Garland—Feinstein and Margaret Whiting among them—have recorded "Friendly Star."*

*The melody for "Friendly Star" was originally written in 1944 for a song entitled "Fools Rush In" that was to be part of the score of *Yolanda and the Thief* starring Fred Astaire and Judy Garland, who eventually ceded the co-starring role in that film to Lucille Bremer. Although Warren wrote the melody for Garland, six years would elapse before she sang it in *Summer Stock* with a new set of lyrics by Mack Gordon.

THE SQUEAKY BOARD/NEWSPAPER DANCE

Music by Harry Warren
Recorded March 31, 1950, by the MGM
Orchestra, Johnny Green conducting
Additional add-on recordings (the whistling)
made on April 27 and 29, 1950

WHEN INTERVIEWERS INVARIABLY ASKED GENE KELLY TO NAME HIS FAVORite dancing partner, he was the diplomatic soul of tact and avoided divulging any names. As a feint, to throw questioners off-track, he often cited his diminutive cartoon partner in *Anchors Aweigh*—"Jerry the Mouse." But Kelly *was* forthright about naming his favorite solo routine—not the "Alter Ego" number in *Cover Girl*, his bravura roller-skating spree in *It's Always Fair Weather*, or even his justly famous titular song and dance from *Singin' in the Rain*. For Kelly, it was tapping on a squeaky floorboard and an errant page of discarded newspaper on a deserted stage in *Summer Stock* that he cited repeatedly through the years as his favorite. "It was certainly the hardest one to rehearse," he said.[51]

The number begins after Kelly's character Joe admonishes Abigail (Gloria DeHaven) in front of the cast and crew for having a "star complex" during a rehearsal in the barn. Jane (Judy Garland) witnesses the ruckus and, as the protective older sister, takes exception to Joe's "tough love" professionalism toward Abigail. Joe promises Jane that going forward he will treat Abigail with "kid gloves." As the troupe calls it quits for the night, Joe tells Artie (Carleton Carpenter) to "Let everything go, I'll clean up." On a dimly lit stage with just a wooden table and chair, two ladders, a wooden three-level riser/staircase, and a rehearsal piano off to the side, Joe, in a contemplative mood, reflecting on the discord with his leading lady and his growing feelings toward Jane, starts whistling "You Wonderful You."*

*Maurice "Muzzy" Marcellino dubbed Kelly's whistling that begins and ends the squeaky board/newspaper dance. An American musician and orchestra leader with Gloria DeHaven as his featured singer in 1938, Marcellino himself was perhaps best known for his melodious style of whistling, a talent later heard to iconic effect in Ennio Morricone's score of Clint Eastwood's 1968 classic "spaghetti western" *The Good, the Bad and the Ugly*.

The dance is happenstance, evolving by accident when, lost in thought, Joe slowly walks across the stage and steps onto a loose floorboard that gives off a creaking sound. The perspective is a crane shot from high above the stage. The next shot cuts up close to Joe who, after noticing the creak, steps onto the board a couple more times to confirm his discovery.

Joe starts experimenting with the sound, tapping all around the creaky board and then stepping on it for declarative emphasis when finishing a combination of steps. "It's a meditative dance of discovery and all dancers would be fascinated by the sound the loose floorboard makes,"[52] said author and tap dance expert Brenda Bufalino. When Joe, with an amused grin, steps away from the creaky floorboard, he backs accidentally into a sheet of newspaper lying on the stage floor and it rustles a bit. It's a second unexpected revelation of an aberrant sound and from them both the routine unfolds and slowly builds, climaxing into an athletic and explosive number.

In order to make each of his routines exciting and innovative, Kelly (like Fred Astaire) would often introduce props or "gimmicks" to create an unforgettable moment. Examples abound: Astaire partnering with a hat rack in *Royal Wedding*, Kelly with a broom in *Thousands Cheer* (1943). But the squeaky board/newspaper dance broke new ground that neither dancer had fully explored before in their solo routines because, in addition to the exciting visual aspect of the dance, the number integrated (actually showcased) the disparate *sounds* of a squeak (the floorboard) and rustling (the newspaper). It was as choreographer Mandy Moore said, a purely cinematic moment, one that could never have been duplicated as effectively in a live stage performance.

"I loved that they were long shots—head to toe—that really allows the libretto of the dance to develop within the frame," said Moore. "You could see his lines. The colors look great within the space. I love when he goes up onto the stairs and then you see his shadow to the side, the backlit shadow. It was just like his alter ego, a little bigger than him. It was a beautiful shot, but I also love the lighting of that. I love that the camera did not comment on anything. It was not its own character; it just uniquely captured what was happening. Walters and Kelly let the story evolve within the frame."[53]

To put himself into the mood—cinematically—for this number, Kelly said that he channeled Buster Keaton, and a hint of the great stone-faced comedian from the silent film era can be seen when Joe circles the newspaper his body tensed and arms locked to his sides. "Keaton had a great influence on me," Kelly said. "A lot of his moves I intuitively copied in doing some numbers. I know I was thinking of him when I did a dance with a squeaky board and a newspaper. I didn't look like him, but I often wish I did. He was a complete genius and there was a lot of dance inherent in his movements."[54]

"I feel like this whole number was born in this idea of finding play within a space, finding play within how a space responds to you, and how you respond to what is in your space," said Moore. "It really told the story of Joe being alone, and maybe what you might do alone when you do not think anyone is watching versus what you might do when, say, an audience is watching.

"The most brilliant part of the entire routine for me is the discovery of the squeak, because that is everything. Kelly was such a master at what I would call 'falling into the dance.' He found the squeak, then he discovered more about the squeak, and then he played with the squeak. Then he started introducing rhythms and patterns, sonically to us as an audience; then (always the punchline) the squeak. The tap is all built off of patterns and rhythms."[55]

Kelly augments the natural squeak and rustle the floorboard and the newspaper make with his own footwork, at one point in the dance extending just his foot onto the newspaper with a step called a nerve tap (a rigid tensing of the foot at the ankle) which sounds like the flutter a piece of construction paper makes when it's caught in an electric fan; Kelly's two-toned loafer beating as fast as a hummingbird's wings.

Breaking down the routine further, tap dance expert Bufalino said that Kelly begins to syncopate the rhythm by playing with the squeak and then sliding the newspaper around the stage with a simple shuffle-ball-change. "This dance is very reminiscent of a classic sand dance where the newspaper and the squeaky board become the motivator of the dance," she said. "His tap steps are not complicated, they are swinging and stylish. His jazz moves are syncopated and dynamic."[56]

Tap dancer Corey John Snide also saw elements of a traditional sand dance in the routine. "I think the solo is so brilliant because it really trains your ears to hear the waltz clog, but Kelly does it using the creaky floorboard filter over it. When he gets to the scrappier tones of the newspaper, they feel a little 'sandier' sounding to me. Then, as he's tapping on it, his soft shoe work underneath is really so manipulative. We've lost that full body aspect of tapping that I think was so brilliant about the Golden Age musicals. If I were to write it down on paper and hand it to a beginner, they'd be like, 'I can do that.' But it's the way that Gene does it with his whole body that gives those steps a character."[57]

Snide said Kelly's last visit up the steps to the top of the wooden riser is where the number reaches its most thrilling stage and where it also creates a brilliant cinematic moment. "He's standing on top of the pedestal [riser], doing his 'Maxie Fords' and 'Bombershays' and he's able to take those two steps and stretch that rhythmic idea over several phrases of music. Then he'll also come back to some of those steps. It's just brilliant. A brilliant, almost lost skill is that ability to stretch a rhythmic idea over a very long phrase."[58]

He leaps down the stairs and onto the newspaper, the orchestra peals, and the tempo shifts into overdrive as Joe halves then quarters the newspaper with his feet into neat squares. Suddenly, he spots an item of interest in another sheet of newspaper littering the floor. The crescendo fades and he picks it up and exits the stage reading it, but not before walking over the squeaky board one last time while again whistling, "You Wonderful You," the scene ending as quietly as it began. "That's another Gene 'Oh-my-God!' moment," said Judy Garland's daughter Lorna Luft in describing the squeaky board/newspaper dance. "He knows his body and what works for him because he was so athletic. And if you take the number out of the context of the entire film, it stands fantastically alone."[59]

Kelly told actor Roddy McDowall in a television interview that the initial idea for the number came from choreographer Nick Castle:

> One day when Judy was not feeling well, we [Castle and Kelly] went to his home, we broke early and we had a couple of drinks. We were sitting there tired from rehearsal, a couple of hoofers. And Nick said, "Listen to this sound." He put a newspaper on the ground and said, "Isn't that a great sound, if only it can be used." I said, "Nick, that's the number, we'll use that."[60]
>
> The next morning, we bought a lot of newspapers and started working on it and we found out that it wasn't a number by itself. So, we said we need another sound. We went around town the two of us together and people would stare at us because we would kick gutters, and we'd scrape along sewer tops, we'd go down steps dragging our

> heels. We tried every kind of sound, and nothing worked. And then about a week later I was on the set where we were going to play a scene and it was in a theater and the theater was in a barn and the stage was bare wood and I said, "That's it—a squeaky board!"
>
> We had to experiment with paper, and the squeaky sound. It wouldn't tear properly. We tried to score it with a razor blade which is the usual movie trick, but I would jump on it and my legs went out and I almost ended up with a hernia. We finally found an old, old newspaper and one year that was perfect and we sent the poor prop man around town looking for something like a 1935 edition of the *Los Angeles Times* and again they thought we were crazy, but at any rate the number got on.[61]

Creating the number became a family affair, with Kelly's daughter Kerry being enlisted to help.

> One of the very distinct memories I have about *Summer Stock* has to do with the squeaky board number. Dad had to figure out how to get the newspaper to tear for that number so he and I actually spent a lot of time together experimenting with folding newspapers different ways, scoring newspapers, wetting them, drying them, ironing them, trying various ways to generate a newspaper that would dependably tear the way he needed it to do. I think I just thought it was fun. He was probably just involving me in the project because it was fun. But it's a very distinct memory for me about *Summer Stock*. I think it's one of his classic numbers that go with the "Alter Ego" number in *Cover Girl* and other amazing tour-de-forces like the roller-skating number in *It's Always Fair Weather* that are specifically him—the Gene Kelly brand.[62]

Nick Castle Jr., just four years old at the time, recalled a story that his mother told him: "Gene would come over to our house, my mom would cook. My dad and Gene were friends during the course of making the movie. We were living near Fox at the time. My mom was talking about my dad rehearsing the number in the barn, the squeaky board. She remembers my dad tearing paper for hours trying to figure it out."[63]

When it came time to decide what music would accompany the routine, Kelly turned to *Summer Stock*'s lead songwriter Harry Warren's "You

Wonderful You," a tune Garland and Kelly sang and danced to (twice) in the film. In an interview, Warren, said he tried the best he could to deliver the type of tune Kelly requested: "Oh, he does a soft shoe to 'You Wonderful You.' We had trouble with that. He kept . . . I don't know what he wanted. He wanted some kind of tune. I finally said, 'Do you want a schottische (a slow polka) type of tune, or something like that?' And he said, 'Yeah,' and that's how that tune got written."[64]

The routine left an indelible impression on a young dancer named Tommy Tune, who was directed by Kelly in the 1969 film *Hello, Dolly!* Tune recalled:

> When we made the movie, I had to ask him about how the newspaper number worked because I tried it and I couldn't make it work. Kelly told me, "Well, first of all, I could not let the property master at MGM do it; he tried to perforate it and it would not work. What you have to do is take the newspaper, fold it one way, run it between your index finger and your thumb, run your finger down all the way, not stopping, and then you flip it over and do the reverse, you flip the paper, do the other side of it, run your finger down, and you have to do that many times until it is so fragile but still holds together, and then it works." That number was just outrageously inventive, and it made such an impression on me that, of course, when I met him, I had to talk to him about it.[65]

After the actual filming of the number was completed, the real, painstaking work began—dubbing in the taps and adding in the squeaky board sounds. Just like singing in movies, taps were recorded and dubbed by the dancers in post-production and it was considered one of the most onerous tasks in show business. "You are hearing a post-dub of the taps," Kelly said. "The reason for that is when you have the playback on set, you take a record, because you can't have a 40-piece orchestra there playing with you—they'd get in the way."[66]

By 1950, the time of *Summer Stock*'s release, the tap dance musical had reached its zenith. "Tap dance was in vogue, and the reason that we did a lot of tap dancing—we put a little bit of it into most numbers—was to show that it was an American form of dance," said Kelly. "We'd pretty much always have it somewhere in a picture unless it was something like

The Pirate, where it didn't belong at all. But to dub the taps you looked at yourself up on the screen and added the taps afterward. It was a pain in the neck and we all hated it."[67]

Much has been written about the number of months it took to complete *Summer Stock*, beginning in November 1949 and not finishing until April 1950. Garland wrapped her work on the film, shooting "Get Happy" in mid-March, and it was not until the following month when Kelly completed filming his solo routine that the film finally wrapped. Carleton Carpenter remembered that Kelly's solo was the last sequence filmed as he (Carpenter) had wrapped his own work on *Summer Stock*, but was called back to exchange a few lines with Kelly as the preface to the squeaky board/newspaper dance.

It's impossible to state definitively the exact dates the squeaky board number was shot and if Charles Walters was actually behind the camera directing it. "Chuck may not have been present for the filming of Gene's solo as he trusted Gene completely," said Walters's biographer Brent Phillips. "Chuck may have needed a rest, but perhaps more so from having to create 'Get Happy' so swiftly and get it before the cameras."[68] If, in fact, Walters was not behind the camera, and Kelly was essentially directing his own routine, it was just another extension of Kelly's desire at that period in his career to grow into a complete filmmaker—director, choreographer, and performer.

"I think that Gene was a master at storytelling through movement, not only as an actor but as an athlete and a dancer," said choreographer Moore. "He is one of the greatest as far as understanding when to push things and make things 'wow' moments coupled with moments of intimacy. I think this number, in particular, is a perfect representation of how good he is at that."[69]

Sarah Crompton, writing in the British *Telegraph* in 2012, summed up the appeal of Kelly's squeaky board/newspaper dance. "He creates a dance of infinite invention and perfect poise. His jaw jutting just a little, his hands relaxed, he conjures magic out of thin air. It is sublime."[70] A banner headline, for sure!

"ALL FOR YOU"

Music and Lyrics by Saul Chaplin
Recorded by Judy Garland and Gene Kelly, vocal quintet and MGM Orchestra, Johnny Green conducting, on February 2, 1950
Lyrics approved by Joseph Breen and the Motion Picture Association of America on January 23, 1950

"ALL FOR YOU" IS THE RAZZMATAZZ NUMBER THAT KICKS OFF JOE ROSS'S (Gene Kelly) show, *Fall In Love* (the show-within-the-movie in *Summer Stock*). It comes right after Judy and Gene's most tender scene in the movie. Minutes away from the opening curtain and gripped by stage fright, Jane (Judy Garland) confesses to Joe that she's drawing a blank and can't remember her lines. Joe, showbiz veteran that he is, puts her at ease, and tells Jane she's everything he ever hoped for in a leading lady and confesses his love for her, to which Jane replies: "Now I won't remember a word."

The scene dissolves into a shot of a transformed barn with the camera tracking up the center aisle to the stage. A follow spotlight hits various chorus girls and boys singing the first verses of the song. Then the spot illuminates the top of a staircase at the precise moment Kelly leaps into it from the darkness, taking over the singing of "All for You." Judy soon joins him on the staircase and they trade verses.

Kelly (for the only time in the movie and one of the few times in his career) is decked out in top hat, white tie, and tails and carries a cane. He looks a bit bulky in evening clothes, underscoring his own belief that as the "Marlon Brando of dancers," he always presented better in loafers and chinos. Judy is dressed in a black gown with an intricate, lacy fringe and she wears a tiara. The costume has a rather slimming effect on her as she and Kelly descend the stairs, whereupon she takes over the vocal as Kelly tap dances around her. They circle around singing, make their way up an incline to the top of the staircase and then descend down again framed in an overhead shot with the chorus boys and girls joining them on the periphery to deliver the last measures of "All for You."

The song itself is performed as an upbeat, anthemic rouser with feel-good lyrics about the simple pleasures that money can't buy:

It's a lovely world that's all around you
Count your treasures you are well-to-do
There's so much to see that's absolutely free
And it's all for you

Lyrically, "All for You" echoes "The Best Things in Life are Free," a 1927 hit written by Ray Henderson, Buddy DeSylva, and Lew Brown with its celebration that "The moon belongs to everyone" and the unalloyed delight of hearing "The robins that sing." Saul Chaplin's couplet even parallels that imagery:

If you should fall in love the moon is yours
A bird's tune is yours take your choice

However, that's where the similarity ends. Renditions of the Henderson-DeSylva-Brown song are usually covered in a slow tempo filled with wistful yearning; "All for You," orchestrated to a brassy rhythm section, comes on like gangbusters—a high-octane optimist's creed.

Beginning with "All for You," each musical number that subsequently appears in Ross's show (the reprise of "You Wonderful You," "Heavenly Music," and "Get Happy") is treated as a standalone set piece, like songs and dances threaded together in a revue, without the need for any number needing to cohere with what came before or after it.

"'All for You' [in which Saul Chaplin wrote both the music and the lyrics] is a perfectly fine song that is—even in 1950—reminiscent of other songs of that ilk," Michael Feinstein said. "But the general feel of the thing is, I think, it's a serviceable song. It's pleasant, but it has no fireworks in it or a particularly brilliant or clever turn of phrase. That's not to denigrate the song in the sense that it works very well in the film, and it's absolutely fine. It's not something I would call inspired."[71] Inspired or not, "All for You" led to some frazzled nerves for Chaplin when it was given an inadvertent "sneak preview" before being introduced to Garland, Kelly, and director Charles Walters. Chaplin recalled:

At the time I wrote "All for You" André Previn was occupying the other room in my bungalow (at the studio). When I finished the song, I played it for him. He liked it, and we spent the morning playing it four-hands. That night I went to a crowded, smoky, Hollywood-type cocktail party. I was about to leave when I thought I heard someone whistling the opening phrase of "All for You." I looked around to see who it was, but there was such a mob that it was impossible to tell. I decided I had only imagined it. I was saying goodnight to my host when I heard it again. After at least an hour of hearing it sporadically, I finally caught the culprit. It was Arthur Jacobs,* a casual acquaintance. I grabbed him firmly by the arm and shouted at him, "What are you whistling?"

"I don't know, I whistle it all the time."

"Just now you were whistling a certain song. Can you do it again?"

"Oh, you mean—" and he indeed whistled the entire first phrase of "All for You."

"Where did you hear it?" I asked irritably.

"I don't know. It must be a pop tune I heard on the radio."

"Are you sure?" I asked.

"Well, I sure as hell didn't write it."

"Yeah—well, I sure as hell thought I did," I moaned.

I spent a sleepless night trying to devise ways of changing the melody and retaining the lyric. Nothing sounded right. I got to my office very early the next morning and spent two hours experimenting with changes until I eventually faced the inevitable truth: I had to write a new song. At some point during my struggle, I heard André arrive and go into his office.

I was in the midst of writing my new song when he came into my office. "What are you doing?" he asked. I told him of the events of the preceding evening. He burst out laughing.

I was furious. "What the hell is so funny?"

Between bursts of laughter, he explained: "You've been framed, but I never dreamed it would work out this well. Arthur Jacobs is a good friend of mine. I knew you were going to the same cocktail party. I spent most of yesterday afternoon at his office teaching him 'All for You.' He couldn't learn the lyrics, so we decided that he would whistle it. He's such a lousy whistler that I didn't think you'd recognize the tune. But you did, and I think it's hilarious." He dissolved into gales of laughter.

I was so relieved I didn't even get angry. In the cool light of day, I think if I had killed them both, it would have been justifiable homicide.[72]

*Arthur P. Jacobs began his career in show business as a courier at MGM. Later, he became a publicist with Judy Garland as a client and in 1964 produced the film *What a Way to Go!* featuring Gene Kelly in a co-starring role opposite Shirley MacLaine.

GETTING THE RIGHT FEEL

Although he was often unheralded, Saul Chaplin played an integral part in the evolution to sophistication of the MGM musical from the moment that he was hired at the Culver City studio in 1949 after a long tenure at Columbia Pictures.

Born Saul Kaplan in Brooklyn, New York, February 19, 1912, he majored in accounting at New York University, all the while looking to pursue his true passion, music. Chaplin's first success as a songwriter came when he changed his name to Chaplin and teamed with another New Yorker, lyricist Sammy Cahn. The team's first published song was "Rhythm Is Our Business" in 1934. Chaplin and Cahn struck paydirt in 1937 when they adapted a Yiddish theater song into English, "Bei Mir Bist Du Schoen," which became a big hit for the Andrews Sisters.[73]

Chaplin's most popular songs written with Cahn were "Until the Real Thing Comes Along" (1936) and "Please Be Kind" (1938). In 1940, he and Cahn became in-house songwriters at Columbia Pictures, working on multiple films at a time (mostly low-budget musicals), many featuring tap dancer Ann Miller. Their partnership ended in 1942 as Chaplin began to hone skills in what would become his main specialty—scoring and arranging.

Chaplin first worked with Gene Kelly and Phil Silvers when he served as assistant musical director on Columbia's *Cover Girl* in 1944. His first three projects at MGM were with Kelly: *On the Town, Summer Stock* (where he received musical director credit with Johnny Green and for which he contributed three songs—"You Wonderful You," "All for You," and "Heavenly Music"), and *An American in Paris,* which netted him the first of three Oscars for best musical score. Chaplin's other Oscars were for *Seven Brides for Seven Brothers* (1954) and *West Side Story* (1961).

When Chaplin arrived at the "gold standard" studio for musicals, MGM, he immediately noticed the stark differences between Metro and his previous employer, Columbia. "In the beginning, I couldn't believe the leisure," he said. "I just couldn't believe it. I mean I was doing only one picture at a time, *On the Town*. That's insane! Then later, I got used to it. I think during the 1950s when I was there, they had the greatest collection of musical talent that ever existed in the world."[74]

As the public appetite for dance musicals waned, Chaplin continued to contribute to the genre as a producer or associate producer, starting in 1957 with *Les Girls* starring Gene Kelly and extending to *Merry Andrew* (1958), *Can-Can* (1960), *The Sound of Music* (1965), *Star!* (1968), *Man of La Mancha* (1972), and *That's Entertainment, Part 2* (1976).

"Starting way back with, I guess, *High Society* [directed by Chuck Walters], the people in my films were never just singing," he said. "They're always part of a scene. I don't care about great vocal power; I care that they have the right dramatic feel for the character—more important. Every time I've done a musical, I have long discussions with the director as to the intent of the song. What are we trying to prove? And if we start at this point, where should we be at the end of the song—where have we progressed? If we haven't progressed, the song doesn't belong in the picture. Because, unless it's something special, such an unintegrated song will fall out, be cut, when we find out the picture's too long. That's generally what happens."[75]

Chaplin died on November 15, 1997.

"HEAVENLY MUSIC"

Music and Lyrics by Saul Chaplin

Recorded by Gene Kelly, Phil Silvers, six women, and dogs, Johnny Green conducting the MGM Orchestra, on March 6, 1950

Lyrics approved by Joseph Breen and the Motion Picture Association of America on December 7, 1949; additional lyrics approved on March 6, 1950

"HEAVENLY MUSIC" AS PERFORMED IN *SUMMER STOCK* IS ANYTHING BUT—it's a contradiction in terms. It's a comic novelty song and dance featuring Joe (Gene Kelly) and Herb (Phil Silvers) as country bumpkins, with shapeless felt hillbilly hats, wigs, blacked-out teeth, humungous rubber bare feet, and threadbare shirts and overalls that, with a strategic pull of the suspenders, expose them in their boxer shorts. Set against a painted stage flat of a ramshackle cabin, it's as if they just stepped out of Al Capp's *Li'l Abner* Sunday comic strip. About the only ingredient missing to make this a spot-on proxy for "Dogpatch, USA" is Mammy Yokum puffing on her corncob pipe.

The song arrives as part of the show-within-a-movie ending to *Summer Stock* and was one of the new tunes written by Saul Chaplin for the final section of the movie. It was conceived as a duet and intended for Garland and Kelly in the same vein as two other comedy set pieces she performed, "Be a Clown" (with Kelly) from *The Pirate* and "A Couple of Swells" (with Astaire) in *Easter Parade*, both released in 1948, the year before filming started on *Summer Stock*.

The number begins in contrast when six elegant young women, dressed to the nines in evening gowns, enter the stage through the parted curtain, wax lyrical about their privileged lives, enunciate a bit of French, and exit oblivious of the two aromatic hayseeds that have joined them and are baffled by the ladies' perfect poise and classy mien. Joe and Herb then proceed to guffaw, mug, and cavort with a pack of mangy, barking dogs while extolling the a cappella marvels ("Heavenly Music") to be heard on the farmstead, specifically, assorted cock-a-doodle-doos, quacks, gobbles, baas, and moos. Talk about "a little barnyard entertainment" . . . Harrison Keath (Hans Conried) might've been clairvoyant after all!

According to Kelly biographer Clive Hirschhorn, it is possible Kelly himself might have conceived the idea of including the pack of howling canines in "Heavenly Music" by recalling his childhood in Pittsburgh when younger brother Fred hatched an idea to stage a dog show in their backyard, charging the neighbors three cents each to watch. Fred stood the dog on a rickety wooden box, "put a piece of exotic Eastern music on the phonograph, probably 'The Sheik of Araby,' introduced 'Little Fatima—the Egyptian Hound' and watched delightedly as the dog shimmied hysterically," Hirschhorn wrote. At the end of the show, the animal was rewarded with choice bits of dog food, and in the ensuing scramble, chaos reigned.[76] And that's just how "Heavenly Music" ends, with the yelping dogs bounding on Joe and Herb as they walk giggling offstage.

As stated, this barnyard symphony was originally intended to feature Garland, but there's conflicting information on why she never recorded or filmed "Heavenly Music," or how Phil Silvers came to replace her. According to Charles Walters's biographer Brent Phillips, Garland's work on the movie was considered complete by early February 1950 (others put the date as mid-February), and when Garland opted out of playing a hillbilly, Phil Silvers filled in.[77]

Looking at the approval dates for the song provides additional clues. The lyrics were sent to Joseph Breen at the Motion Picture Association of America in two parts; the main song was sent over on December 7, 1949, and approved the next day. Chaplin wrote additional lyrics (the preamble to the song performed by the women in gowns), which were sent to Breen on March 3, 1950, and approved on March 6.

Garland was in the middle of shooting the movie when the original lyrics to the song were approved in December, but had wrapped her work on *Summer Stock* when Chaplin's additional lyrics were delivered three months later. Memorandums show that the song was recorded by Kelly and Silvers on the same day they were approved, March 6. If that's the case, to appear in the number, Garland would have had to return to the studio to record and shoot it. That never happened.

Another account has producer Joe Pasternak losing patience with his often-tardy star and making the decision to shoot "Heavenly Music" without her. To add to the mystery, in the final release print that audiences view today, Garland is seen backstage wearing the hillbilly costume she would have worn in the number. According to Hirschhorn, the scene showing Judy in her costume had previously been shot as it was necessary to the plot, and although she never performed the number, the impression given in the film is that she did.[78]

Yet another conflicting version, this one given by Michelle Vogel in her biography of Marjorie Main, hypothesizes that from the outset, the number was intended as a trio with Garland, Kelly, and Silvers all performing the song. "However, when Judy Garland failed to show up for work that day it was to be shot," Vogel writes, "they went ahead and did it without her."[79]

Chaplin, who composed the tune, supported this claim: "During the body of the picture there's a shot backstage of Judy, Gene and Phil Silvers in tramp outfits; and behind them are the chorus kids—backstage. When you see the picture there are only two people in that number, only Phil and Gene. They waited so long, and Judy didn't come back, they shot it without her. But in the picture, you still see her backstage as though she'd been in the number. What happened, she wasn't coming back so they shot the number without her."[80]

Understandably, memories recalled decades after the fact can be fuzzy, and Chaplin's insistence that the number was slated as a trio featuring Garland, Kelly, and Silvers seems unlikely because she never recorded the vocals and was off the shoot in March when the song was recorded and filmed with Kelly and Silvers.

Garland herself opting out of the number (for whatever reason) on or before December 7, 1949, seems the most plausible explanation for her absence and why "Heavenly Music" was never envisioned to be performed as a trio; that and the fact that following suit with her earlier show-stopping duets with Kelly and Astaire in *The Pirate* and *Easter Parade*, it's safe to assume that Chaplin, Walters, and others thought a like-and-kind rematch with Kelly (not as part of a trio with Silvers) would perhaps be capturing lightning in a bottle a third time. But with Garland gone and the song written and approved, Silvers was her logical replacement, the number being a low-brow comedic turn with plenty of hokum (or "Yokum" as the case may be) that would've been an easy stretch for him to perform.

In Michael Feinstein's view, "Heavenly Music" works well as a comedic number. "Saul was a guy who was so interesting because if you met him, he was very facile and sort of unemotional," Feinstein said. "He didn't betray deep emotions. Saul was a guy who was very quick and glib and very New York in his manner. That concealed his tenderness and his heart in a certain way. It's always like that, though, with songwriters where you meet them and they look like lawyers or accountants, and then they end up writing these incredible songs."[81]

The introductory lyrics written by Chaplin (and trilled by the six regally dressed debutantes) were modified when it came time to record the song. These lines were omitted from the release print:

From the outset we hastily explain
That our lives are like bubbling champagne
Of all things unpleasant it's free
We live it—we love it—mais quo

"GET HAPPY"

Music by Harold Arlen; Lyrics by Ted Koehler

Recorded by Judy Garland, with a male sextet and the MGM Orchestra, Johnny Green conducting, on March 15, 1950

Perhaps in part because of the religious slant of the song, Joseph Breen and the PCA readily approved the "Get Happy" lyrics for the film's US release. Not so in the United Kingdom: in a confidential memo to MGM dated November 17, 1950, the MPAA requested a change in the lyrics (petitioned most likely by the British Board of Film Censors reacting to what some in the UK might've construed as lyrical sacrilege). Marked "deletion," the memo read: "Reel 12 The words and song 'Come On and Get Happy,' especially 'Get Ready for the Judgment Day,' 'The Lord Is Waiting to Take Your Hand,' 'Going to the Promised Land,' 'Wash Your Sins Away,' are unsuitable."[97]

NEAR THE END OF *SUMMER STOCK*, THE CURTAIN OPENS TO A SQUEAL OF brass revealing eight male dancers in black tuxedos against a pink backdrop with cottony clouds that could have sprung directly out of a Thomas Hart Benton painting. As the vamp continues and the dancers tumble to the stage floor, the person they've been shielding, standing with her arms nonchalantly crossed, is no longer a woman consumed with thoughts of farm mortgages and tractors. Like a butterfly freed from its chrysalis, Jane (Judy Garland) has transformed from farm girl into sophisticated chanteuse, dripping with glamour and supple as a teenager. Costumed (following form with the men) in a shortened tuxedo, but topped by a swanky fedora, black pumps and hose that flaunt endless legs complete Jane's wondrous makeover. It's truly a *va-va-voom* moment! What follows for approximately the next two minutes and forty-five seconds is one of the most iconic showstoppers ever committed to celluloid—Judy Garland's MGM swan song "Get Happy."

The jury will be forever deadlocked as to what musical moment Garland fans consider her greatest. But virtually all would agree that "Get Happy," a song in the show-within-a-movie that effectively concludes *Summer Stock*, makes everyone's short list. "It's definitely in my top five," said Michael Feinstein. "I don't know what my top five are, but it's one of her numbers that immediately comes to mind, so it's right up there."[82] But it's one that almost didn't happen. Garland's work on the film was considered complete in February 1950 when Charles Walters, at the end of the editing process, realized that a show-stopping number by the film's star was not only missing, but essential to solidify Jane's transition from farm owner to powerhouse entertainer. Producer Pasternak agreed.

"We finished cutting the picture [not including Gene Kelly's solo dance, which was filmed after 'Get Happy'] and realized that we needed another number," said Walters. "Judy had gone to Carmel [other sources say Santa Barbara] with a hypnotist to rest and recoup and she said, 'I want "Get Happy" and I want to wear the costume that was cut out of *Easter Parade*. And I want you to do it.' So that's a nice challenge! What the hell am I going to do with 'Get Happy'? What does it say, what does it mean? So, I used the pink backdrop with the white clouds that had been used earlier in the picture because it signified nowhere or anyplace."[83]

In a way, the song's lyrics speak to where Judy (not Jane) was at that point in her life:

Forget your troubles, c'mon get happy,
you better chase all your cares away.
Shout hallelujah, c'mon get happy,
get ready for the Judgment Day

It's almost as if, when Garland selected the song to perform, she instinctively knew that her days at MGM were numbered but that, just possibly, happier days lay ahead.

Accounts differ on how "Get Happy" was chosen as Garland's big payoff song. According to Garland biographer Gerold Frank, who cited Walters as his source, Judy had been at a party with (composer) Harold Arlen when he played a song he had written years before called "Get Happy." "'Just wonderful! Chuck, you get "Get Happy" for me, we build the dance around that, and I'll do it,'" Garland told him. "'I'll give you a week—otherwise forget it.'"[84]

Saul Chaplin said that when Garland was told that the studio wanted her to do another number for the film, she was delighted. Rather than have a new song written, she suggested a Ted Koehler–Harold Arlen tune that she had always wanted to sing, "Get Happy." Chaplin remembered:

> I made a three-chorus arrangement for her that ranged over four ascending keys. We never did rehearse "Get Happy." When I finished the arrangement, we called her, only to find out that she was ill. She wanted to hear the arrangement anyhow. Chuck Walters and I went to her house to do it for her. She was lying on a sofa. She loved the arrangement. She kind of mouthed it when I went through it again but didn't sing because she wasn't feeling well enough. I did it a third time and we left. That happened on a Friday. The recording session was set for the following Thursday. We suggested that we postpone it, but she wouldn't hear of it. She arrived at the recording session looking pale and tired. With nothing but a lyric sheet in front of her [she couldn't read music], she made a perfect take the third time she sang it. That is a most incredible feat that one has no right to expect from mere mortals. But then, Judy was never "mere" anything.[85]

Garland's return to the Culver City studio a few weeks later to shoot the sequence turned heads and drew catcalls from the crew. Whatever she did during her brief time away worked; she had shed "a couple of stone" and Walters described her as "thin as a string."[86] It's this abrupt "before-and-after" transformation in Garland's figure that for years helped perpetuate the myth that "Get Happy" was an outtake from an earlier film, while others, in trying to explain the jarring weight loss, erroneously claimed that the number was shot "several months" after *Summer Stock* wrapped, not just a few weeks later.

Walters stated rather matter-of-factly: "I got some boys together, staged it in three days, got Judy back, she rehearsed it in a day, we shot it in two, and she was back in Santa Barbara by the week's end."[87] According to John Angelo, one of the dancers in the number: "Chuck came into rehearsal knowing what he wanted. He showed us our part—and *he* did Judy's part. Chuck was what I call an 'ape-er.' He could 'ape' anyone. So when Judy would come in, she'd say, 'Chuck, would you mind running through it with the boys,' and he'd do it—and you thought he *was* Judy Garland! He did everything."

Walters's insouciance notwithstanding (see earlier remarks in his biography where he tells an insecure Judy to "channel" Lena Horne during "Get Happy"), the reality of shooting the number played out differently; with the camera rolling, Garland faltered on her first take. Brent Phillips wrote:

"Walters told her she seemed too tentative, and the discouraged Garland retreated to her dressing room. Her fearful director followed. 'I hated to say it that way,' he ventured, 'but . . . it was your first crack at it.' Judy remained silent, prompting Walters to return to the set, kicking himself—'me and my big mouth!' Garland soon re-emerged, headed straight for her critic. Hands on her hips, she quipped, 'You know Chuck, if you had any class, you would use that travel clock the crew gave you.' It was a classic Garland non-sequitur. 'Alright, fellas!,' she announced, 'let's do this.'"[88]

If ever a musical number was staged, orchestrated, costumed, and performed that fully embodied the sentiment of its title, it's this one. "Get Happy" is an infectious exhortation to do precisely that! Adjusting her hat at a cockeyed angle, Jane strikes poses that make Madonna's "voguing" decades later seem wan by comparison. She's a veritable juggernaut of controlled confidence, strutting and posturing around Walters's finger-snappin' chorus boys, who perform eccentric choreography (rubberleg high-kicks and knee-drops) as if their limbs had suddenly liquefied. At one point in the number, crouching on stage, they percussively beat the floor with their fists in time to the tom-tom drumbeat—hipsters rhythmically repenting to a spiritual-shoutin' diva bewitching them in song.

Fred Astaire once said that many of his musical numbers were built for applause reactions from movie audiences (witness the silent bows he takes with his hat-rack dance "partner" at the end of the "Sunday Jumps" number in the ship's gymnasium in *Royal Wedding*). As "Get Happy" finishes, a radiant Jane, in closeup, modestly tips her hat to a clapping audience we don't see. But that canned soundtrack effect (admittedly a rather modest ovation) was amplified a hundredfold by the applause of exuberant, real-life moviegoers, which contemporary accounts report was thunderous. For Jane, "Get Happy" clearly addresses the question that may have still lingered in a few minds: How Ya Gonna Keep 'Em Down on the Farm (after they've caught the showbiz bug)? The emphatic answer: You can't!

In stark contrast to the ebullience of the number, for composer Harry Warren, the interpolation of "Get Happy" into his score was a slap in the face that provoked bitter feelings he harbored for the rest of his life. Ironically, the song would never have existed if Warren had not introduced Arlen and Koehler to each other more than twenty years earlier. Warren and Arlen first met in New York City in 1927 outside the Park Central Hotel when they were both budding songwriters. Arlen played Warren the vamp that would become "Get Happy" and Warren responded saying he knew "just the guy to write this up." The "guy" was lyricist Ted Koehler.[89]

"One day along comes a guy I've met named Harry Warren, and he introduces me to a guy named Ted Koehler, who writes lyrics," said Arlen. "Koehler sits down and writes a set of words to my little vamp, and he calls it 'Get Happy.' I didn't seek it out or ask for it—it just happened. The song was auditioned for a lady named Ruth Selwyn who was preparing to produce *The Nine-Fifteen Revue* (1930). She promptly took it for her first-act finale, where it would be sung by a popular vocalist of the day, Ruth Etting."[90]

"Get Happy" became a hit for Etting, whose photo appeared on the cover of the sheet music, but it wasn't until Garland's rendition in *Summer Stock*, two decades later, that the tune secured its place in the popular song pantheon. It was also no accident that Garland elected Arlen's "Get Happy" to sing in *Summer Stock*; he was her good luck charm. In 1939, Arlen with Yip Harburg wrote Garland's signature ballad, the Oscar-winning "Over the Rainbow" for *The Wizard of Oz*. In 1954, Judy turned again to Arlen who, with Ira Gershwin, composed "The Man That Got Away" for her comeback film, *A Star Is Born*.

In his 1975 autobiography, Vincente Minnelli claimed conceptual credit for Garland's famous "Get Happy" costume. "I suggested she try a bit of costuming I'd seen Tamera Geva [a Russian-born actress, ballet dancer, and choreographer] wear on the stage," he said. "Judy fell in love with the idea. She sang 'Get Happy' wearing a man's black fedora tipped rakishly over one eye, a man's tuxedo jacket altered to fit her form and leotards beneath which revealed her great-looking legs. The number was a smash, and Judy was ecstatic."[91]

In actual fact, the "Get Happy" costume was hanging in the MGM wardrobe rack from a Garland number called "Mr. Monotony," shot (by Charles Walters) and cut from *Easter Parade* two years earlier. Minnelli, who was married to Garland at the time, was originally assigned to direct *Easter Parade*, but citing personal reasons, he was taken off the film after five days and replaced by Walters.

Minnelli's origin story of how Garland's "Get Happy" costume came to be received a totally different accounting in a biography of MGM's principal costume designer known as Irene. (Her full name was Irene Lentz Gibbons.) According to Irene's colleague and confidante at MGM, Virginia Fisher, Walters and producer Arthur Freed told Irene to design a costume for one of Garland's *Easter Parade* solos, "as the movie-going public was ready to see Judy's legs!" Added Freed: "After all, that's why the [Betty] Grable movies are so popular at Fox."[92] Fisher said it was actually Marlene Dietrich (not Tamara Geva) who just happened to have called Irene the day before, and who served as the inspiration for Garland's "Mr. Monotony" costume. "As we discussed a New York showgirl look for Judy, Irene, with Dietrich's call fresh on her mind, suggested that we create an 'homage to Marlene' by giving Judy a tuxedo jacket, black tights and a fedora for the number."[93]

"We know that the costume was ready because it had already been shot for 'Mr. Monotony' and then cut out of *Easter Parade*, so they had the elements in place," said Garland's daughter Lorna Luft. "It's the one number that really solidified and legitimized *Summer Stock*. You go to any of my mom's other films and there's always that gold star moment. And even if you think, 'This is a silly story,' there is that moment and you come away thinking, 'Okay, this movie was worth it for you to watch and to learn from and to realize just how incredible her talent was.'"[94]

According to Michael Feinstein, "Get Happy" presents a kind of perfect storm of elements that make it great:

> Judy, at the moment, was fresh and in wonderful shape and raring to go. Saul [Chaplin] was still relatively new at MGM and it was his first opportunity to create something for her, and his arrangement was magnificent. It's a brilliant creation. I also believe it's the first orchestration that Skip Martin did at MGM after previously working for the Les Brown Band.
>
> It's MGM at its finest, even though it was a factory. André Previn once told me that the music department at MGM was no more or no less important than the "Department of Fake Lawns." It was just a component. But when they came together, man, they were the greatest! Many of these creators, especially in the music department, were creating for their own sake, because they knew that the higher-ups wouldn't appreciate it nor would the people seeing the movies necessarily have the capacity to appreciate the intricacies of what they created. Viscerally and emotionally, they felt it. That's one of the reasons that "Get Happy" and the other numbers are so great.[95]

Garland's brilliance aside, according to Feinstein, it's Skip Martin who's the "unsung hero" of the number: "Clearly, Judy was thrilled by what Skip Martin did with 'Get Happy.'" I don't think they had worked together previously, so that demonstrates the impact that that arrangement had on Judy. And she also used that same arrangement in her live performances right after she left MGM. I have a set of MGM charts that are marked out from the live performances, which is why it's one of the few MGM charts for which the original arrangement exists, because Judy saved it."[96]

Garland would go on to perform "Get Happy" in many concert performances and the song has been recorded by dozens of artists throughout the years, including Stevie Wonder, Frank Sinatra, Jerry Lewis, Art Tatum, Mel Tormé, Benny Goodman, Rosemary Clooney, and Michael Jackson. It was also memorably sung as a duet with Barbra Streisand (paired with "Happy Days Are Here Again") on the October 6, 1963, airing of *The Judy Garland Show* on CBS. Judy's *Summer Stock* rendition of "Get Happy" finished #61 in the American Film Institute's "100 Years . . . 100 Songs" survey of top tunes from American films. Arlen's name appears five times on the list, including as the composer of two other Garland standards: "Over the Rainbow" (#1) and "The Man That Got Away" (#11).*

THE CUTTING ROOM FLOOR—TWO SONGS THAT DIDN'T MAKE IT

THE DEEP FACILITY OF SONGWRITERS LIKE HARRY WARREN AND MACK Gordon to write to any mood or situation is a hallmark of their collaboration and a testament to their versatility. If the script called for a heartwarming wartime ballad, the duo responded with "You'll Never Know" for Alice Faye in *Hello, Frisco, Hello* (and won a Best Song Oscar in the bargain in 1943). Perhaps it was a swing tune needed for *Sun Valley Serenade* featuring the Glenn Miller Band; the team weighed in with "Chattanooga Choo Choo" (a defining gold record hit for Miller).

But like the very best songwriters from that era, and Warren and Gordon certainly numbered among them, not every tune they wrote made the grade. Case in point: "The Blue Jean Polka," which the team wrote for inclusion

*For the record, Harry Warren with partner Al Dubin (not Mack Gordon) makes the AFI survey once with "42nd Street" at #97.

in the barn dance sequence. (It was replaced minus any sung verses by the traditional—albeit jazzed-up—folk tune, "The Portland Fancy.")

The song was sent to Joseph Breen at the MPAA on June 20, 1949, for approval, but there is no evidence that it was ever recorded or filmed. However, Gordon's verse and chorus have survived.[98]

Verse
Come on and do a square dance
To the blue jean polka
Like people everywhere dance
To the blue jean polka
So hurry up and have your supper
Or you'll miss the warmer-upper
To the blue jean polka

Chorus
Take a look at all the old blue jeans
And gingham pinafores
A-crowdin' through the door
The caller just said "Won't you honor me?"
So what are we waitin' for
Swing your partner with ease
Steal a hug if you please
That's providin' that she's your own
If you're coy and sly with one nearby
By and by you'll be going home alone
And don't you dare to look into her eyes
For if you do you're gonna miss the call
So keep your mind on what you're doin'
Till you're promenadin' all
It's a barrel of fun
When a five-foot-one
Swings a partner six foot tall
So sip your cider—sip your coke
Tomorrow night your feet will soak
But tonight ya gotta do the blue jean polka

Another song Warren and Gordon composed for *Summer Stock* titled "Fall in Love" had a slightly better fate than "The Blue Jean Polka." The tune, written as a duet for Phil Silvers and Gloria DeHaven, gave its name to the show that Joe Ross (Gene Kelly) mounts in the barn, but, like "The Blue Jean Polka," never appeared on film. However, after approval by Breen and the MPAA on May 9, 1949, it was recorded by Silvers and DeHaven with Johnny Green conducting the orchestra on November 15, 1949.

The pre-recording of the song survives and is on a version of the *Summer Stock* soundtrack CD, but, again, there is no record that the number was actually filmed; the liner notes for the soundtrack CD saying it was axed during rehearsals. The melody for "Fall in Love" was originally planned to accompany Kelly's squeaky board/newspaper solo dance but was replaced by "You Wonderful You" which was anticipated to be the breakout hit from the score before "Get Happy" was interpolated into the film.[99]

Verse
Are you peaceful and relaxed
No ill feelings or resentments
Do your nerves remain untaxed
Are you the picture of contentment
Well, life can be dull that way
So if you want the picture changed
Believe you me, it can easily be arranged

Chorus
Fall in Love
It's lovely when you start out
Ah! 'Tis spring
But wait till you feel the frost
You'll be sorry
Fall in Love
And you'll eat your heart out
When "Oh, My Darling" turns into "go get lost"
Go on and be sincere
Tonight you're softly sighing
Tomorrow night you're crying in your beer
Oh, you fool, you

Fall in Love
Better not try not to
For you'll find out that it's just got to be
And as long as misery loves company
Be an idiot and give your all
Bang your pretty head against the wall
But you know you're gonna fall
In spite of it all
So won't you please fall for me

2nd Chorus
Fall in Love
Just promise to be loyal
And the joy of living will then begin
That's what you think
Fall in Love
Comes that battle royal
You pace the floor and wonder what town you're in
Just make yourself at home
Around her little finger
And you'll go through the wringer, wait and see
Ouch, it's painful
Fall in Love
And here comes the topper
No longer is your life your property
In between those make-up kisses you will be
Pulling out another new gray hair
Till you haven't any hair to spare
But you know you're gonna fall
In spite of it all
So won't you please fall for me

Alternate (after "No longer is your life your property" in 2nd chorus)
Anytime that you've been hooked your goose is cooked
You'll be pulling out a new gray hair
Till you haven't any hair to spare
But you know you're gonna fall

In spite of it all
So won't you please fall for me

Looking at the storyline for *Summer Stock*, it's hard to see where "Fall in Love" would have fit into the plot, especially as a duet between Silvers and DeHaven. According to George Feltenstein, WarnerMedia library historian, the "Friendly Star" lyrics were originally meant to be coupled with the "Fall in Love" melody. "The words and music fit perfectly," Feltenstein said, "but my assumption is that Mr. Warren came up with something better, hence the final result of that song."[100]

Although "Fall in Love" never had an afterlife, an earlier, similarly titled tune, "Let's Fall in Love" written in 1933 by the "Get Happy" composers Harold Arlen and Ted Koehler, is a standard in the American song repertoire and has been recorded by dozens of artists. Such was the fickleness that befell some songs destined for obscurity and the bottom of a composer's trunk while others generated kudos and monstrous royalties for their creators—all part and parcel of being a tunesmith during songwriting's Golden Age.

CHAPTER VI

MARKETING, REVIEWS, REVENUE, AND REVIVALS

The Voice of Garland and the Feet of Kelly Are at High Tide in *Summer Stock*

LONG BEFORE THE INTERNET, DIGITAL MEDIA, AND EVEN BEFORE TELEVISION became a promotional tool, much of film marketing was the responsibility of a studio's publicity department, a vital cog in the factory system. Under the watchful stewardship of longtime studio publicity chief Howard Strickling, perhaps no other studio hawked its movies better than MGM. In addition to the coming attractions preview trailer screened in theaters prior to release, Strickling and his army of publicists, photographers, and graphic artists provided theater owners and journalists with a publicity tool kit that included a pressbook of sample reviews, feature stories, radio scripts, behind-the-scenes tidbits, posters, images, print ads, and an "exploitation" section of ideas to generate buzz for both the film and the soundtrack album. Some of these exploitative ideas—or "stunts"—have common cause today and are known as guerilla marketing techniques.

Pressbooks were foundational tools used by film distributors to work with theater owners in order to maximize the reach and profit of their films. Since theater owners received a percentage of the box-office receipts and were directly vested in the success of the films, it was in their best interest to use content and ideas in the pressbook to increase movie attendance. It was also partially the responsibility of the theater owners to share the pre-written copy in the pressbooks with local print and radio outlets. Since record sales were another important revenue source for Metro, marketing ideas to promote the soundtrack were also included.

For *Summer Stock*, MGM's publicity effort focused heavily on the fact that it was Judy's first feature film since *In the Good Old Summertime*, released thirteen months before *Summer Stock*, and her reteaming with Gene Kelly, who was growing in popularity with each starring turn. And like the hokum referenced in the movie, much of the content generated in the pressbook leveraged the earthy likability of its two stars and supporting players and the homespun plotline of the picture.

The following examples of promotional ideas to encourage exhibitors are pulled from the pressbook. Though some of the ideas may land as, well, outlandish, they seem as well intentioned as they are screwball!

—

CONTEST—"JUDY GARLAND'S MUSICAL MEMORY ALBUM"
Run a disc jockey contest in conjunction with the MGM record album. Offer prizes for biggest lists of picture titles in which Judy had a singing role. Or—ask contestants to name one song in each picture—awarding prizes for biggest combined lists of songs and movie titles.

ELECT A QUEEN OF THE HARVEST!
Run a contest in the name of Judy Garland to elect a local "Queen of the Harvest" in observance of a successful harvest in, or adjacent to, your community. The official song for it could be "Happy Harvest"—sung by Judy in the picture and MGM album.

HAYRIDE ON STREETS
Load a horse-drawn wagon with hay—and guys and gals costumed as farmers and farmerettes. Banner it and amplify hit songs from the MGM album. Send it around your city's streets.

FARMER AND FARMERETTE COSTUME PARTY
1. Announce that patrons wearing these costumes to a specified performance will be eligible for prizes for the best.
2. Tie the contest up with a disc jockey with finalists to appear on theater stage and to be judged by audience applause for the best costume.
3. Promote merchandise prizes with stories.

LOCAL JUDY STROLLS INSIDE A SHOWER CURTAIN OR, HOW ABOUT A REAL SHOWER WITH WATER IN YOUR LOBBY?

Some theaters are going to put a "shower girl" on their streets. Construct it of canvas, hung from circular ring which supports shower rod and head (no water, of course). Girl wears a swimsuit.

Another idea consists of rigging up a real water shower in theater lobby, with cutout figure of a girl (made locally) under it. MGM record album contains "If You Feel Like Singing, Sing." Play it with the display.

WHAT YOU CAN DO WITH THE NAMES OF JUDY AND GENE

These two first names, together, have an attractive and pleasantly repetitive sound. Reading them, people are tempted to speak them. Cash in with this personal element.

FIRST BABY BORN—AND NAMED JUDY AND GENE

Promote a page of local store ads. It announces that first baby born after midnight of picture's opening date and named either Judy or Gene will be entitled to all the advertised gifts.

JUDY AND GENE DATE CARDS

These cards must be printed locally. Make the men's one color and the women's another. Copy: "If the 'GENE' (you) holding this card, finds a 'JUDY' with a card containing a similar number, both of you will be admitted free to see Judy Garland and Gene Kelly in MGM's Technicolor musical 'SUMMER STOCK,' etc. Your copy on the woman's card is the same, except you substitute the word Judy for Gene. All cards must be numbered."

KALL OUT ALL THE KELLYS!

There must be a million Kellys, more or less, in the country. City theaters, with large populations, might want to do something about it.

1. Contact Ancient Order of Hibernians, Friendly Sons of St. Patrick, or other Irish society. Arrange for theater "Irish Night" in honor of Gene Kelly.
2. Local Kelly families (if not too many) to be theater guests at a picture performance.

3. Place a scroll of appreciation in your lobby hailing Gene Kelly's contribution to the screen, asking local Kellys, and the rest of the Irish, to sign in. Mail it to him, care of MGM Studios, Culver City, California.

PAIR OF "RUBES" IN YOUR LOBBY—OR AS A STREET BALLY
Gene Kelly and Phil Silvers perform a hilarious singing and dancing number to the engaging tune of "Heavenly Music."

1. Dress men in "rube" or yokel clothes, with amusing copy on oversized bare feet (make out of flesh-tinted cardboard, papier-maché or obtain from local costume shop) and play the "Heavenly Music" record (Gene and Phil sing it) from the MGM album.
2. Send out two similarly-dressed men for street clowning purposes. One can carry a small portable machine for playing above record, and other album numbers.

MY FUNNIEST EXPERIENCE ON A FARM!
Funny things happen to the city actor-folk on the farm in *Summer Stock*. Likewise, to summer vacationists who go rural for two weeks. Offer prizes for most amusing experiences in a newspaper, radio or theater contest.

WATCH OUT FOR FALL FAIRS AND CARNIVALS
Lots of communities hold country fairs at the end of summer. Picture's rural background makes it possible for theaters to tie-in with a contest of ballyhoo. If there's a carnival in, or coming to town, a similar opportunity exists.

IS THERE A SUMMER STOCK SHOW PLAYING NEAR YOU?
There's always a chance that a real theatrical summer stock company might still be in operation in your community. If so, invite its players to be your special guests at opening picture performance. Pass out comment cards to them so that your engagement will benefit from the endorsements.

The pressbook even had canned copy for radio disc jockeys. Here's a sample script (note the special mention of "brand new dancing star—alluring Nita Bieber"):

> Announcer: Judy Garland's latest picture, *Summer Stock,* is a musical who's *whoosical!* . . . Yes, MGM presents a terrific team—Judy and Gene—that's Judy Garland and Gene Kelly with glamorous Gloria DeHaven, hilarious Eddie Bracken, riotous Phil Silvers, lovable Marjorie Main, and a brand new dancing star—alluring Nita Bieber in *Summer Stock*! What a cast! What a picture! It's packed with Technicolor magic . . . eight new hummable, strummable tunes . . . dazzling dances . . . and a warm and wonderful romance! Judy Garland sings her way into Gene Kelly's heart . . . as Gene dances his way into Judy's life. *Summer Stock* is a zingy, swingy, singy thing with a story as fresh as a new-baked pie! But why go into lots of details? . . . surely, you'll want to hear Judy Garland sing . . . see Gene Kelly dance and have fun with all the delightful cast in MGM's newest merriest Technicolor musical—*Summer Stock*!

Some ingenious theater owners went "off script" and created their own promotional gimmicks. *Boxoffice* covered one stunt and slugged it with the headline: "Two Dancers Ballyhoo *Summer Stock* at Shops": "Paula Gould, publicity director for the Capitol Theater in New York, arranged an unusual tie-up with the distributors of MGM records to ballyhoo *Summer Stock*, reported the magazine. Two models dressed to resemble the stars of the film production, made the rounds of the music shops in the Times Square area. In front of each store, the duo did a song and dance on the sidewalk, to the tune of one of the song numbers from the picture. Signs on the back of the dancers brought the picture playdates to the attention of curious groups which gathered to watch the performance."[1]

WHAT THE CRITICS SAID

SUMMER STOCK WAS RELEASED ON AUGUST 31, 1950, TO MOSTLY FAVORABLE reviews, with critics virtually unanimous in their celebration of a third Garland-Kelly pairing; some, however, took note of Garland's plumpish figure and her slender transformation in the "Get Happy" number. The added heft to Garland's small frame (she was 4' 11") paid a certain dividend in that it gave her vocals in the film an even more powerful vibrato. It should also be noted that in addition to the universal given of it being impossible to appease all critics, Garland was severely underweight in her two previous films (*Easter Parade* and *In the Good Old Summertime*), and so the fluctuation of her adding a few stone for *Summer Stock* would have come across as jarring or at least noticeable.

Prior to the film's general release, on August 5 the movie was screened before the invited Hollywood press, or "tough critics" as they were described in a *Boston Globe* article. Most of the reviewers decided that the story and tunes were just so-so. But Judy, they agreed, saved the movie—her first in nearly two years. "She was her old bouncy, happy self. She looked so happy in the picture that the audience, if it hadn't read all about it in the papers, never would have guessed the tough time she had working in *Summer Stock*."[2]

Ironically, considering the film had been lambasted from the start for its hackneyed plot, the only award for which *Summer Stock* was ever nominated was in the category of Best Written Musical at the 3rd Writers Guild of America Awards (WGA) in 1950. Sy Gomberg and George Wells shared the honors but their screenplay for *Summer Stock* lost out to *Annie Get Your Gun*, which, in a further twist, had originally been earmarked for Judy Garland to star in the role of sharpshooter Annie Oakley. Indeed, Wells came up short twice. His other WGA-nominated musical script, for *Three Little Words* starring Fred Astaire, also lost that year.

Unsurprisingly, most stars (from any era) have healthy egos, and some go out of their way to feign indifference to their notices, publicly announcing that they never read reviews or even care what the critics write about them. That was apparently *not* the case with Gene Kelly, who received a note from his MCA agent Harry Friedman on September 7, 1950, along with copies of several *Summer Stock* reviews ("The notices are really terrific," wrote Friedman), including several from Kelly's hometown newspapers in Pittsburgh.[3]

In 1950, the show business trade publication *Boxoffice* regularly ran an aggregate of reviews based on seven different publications—*Boxoffice*, *Harrison's Reports*, *Variety*, *Film Daily*, the *Hollywood Reporter*, *Parents' Magazine*, and the *New York Daily News*. The compilation of reviews used a grading system of "very good," "good," "fair," "poor," and "very poor" and then assigned a numerical score for each film based on those grades. Since "very good," the highest rating, was given two points, the most points any movie could accumulate (based on the seven publications) was fourteen. *Summer Stock* scored thirteen out of fourteen possible points, higher than other box-office hits at that time such as *The Black Rose* (11), *Three Little Words* (12), *On the Town* (11)* and *Fancy Pants* (10).[4]

*It's interesting to note that *Summer Stock* scored higher with movie reviewers in the *Boxoffice* aggregation than Kelly's groundbreaking musical *On the Town*, the dancer's personal favorite of all his films.

The New York Times

As a tardy salute to summer and to the troupes of ambitious young folks who hie themselves off to rural theaters and "thesp" for the bland vacationists, Metro has brought along a passel of its more amiable and talented kids to give out with merriment and music in a Technicolored lark called *Summer Stock*. Headed by Judy Garland in high good spirits and health and Gene Kelly in a state of perfection that finds his legs as lithe as rustling corn, this gang is currently to be witnessed on the Capitol's screen, which is not exactly a cow-barn but serves to project the air of the same. Best spots in the show, however, are a solo dance which Mr. Kelly does to "You Wonderful You," and the finale, "Get Happy," in which all eventually join. Mr. Kelly's dance, accomplished with a newspaper and a squeaky board as props, is a memorable exhibition of his beautifully disciplined style. And "Get Happy" finds Ms. Garland looking and performing her best.[5]

Pittsburgh Post-Gazette

The voice of Miss Judy Garland and the feet of Mr. Gene Kelly are at high tide in *Summer Stock*. It's a good thing they are too, for the lightweight musical at the Penn needs their best. . . . When Miss Garland bursts into song, however, or Mr. Kelly puts on his tap shoes, the ayes have it. *Summer Stock* can do no wrong while these two are concentrating on their specialties. Miss Garland does things to a song that nobody else can do half as well and something mighty good comes out whenever she opens her mouth. . . . Mr. Kelly at ease is always a pleasure, and his light-hearted hoofing has a tap-happy incandescence. Although the grits of Miss Garland and Mr. Kelly are entitled to something much better than *Summer Stock*, let's not quarrel too strenuously with anything that has them aboard at all. Be grateful for big favors and overlook small containers.[6]

Los Angeles Evening Herald & Express

That Judy Garland lights up like a Christmas tree in *Summer Stock*, a Technicolor musical she and Gene Kelly largely share on Loew's State and Egyptian Theaters. It's pure delight to watch her edge into the singing and dancing routine and start the personality fireworks going. Right along with her is Mr. Kelly, who imbues his role of a Broadway song and dance man, producing a straw hat revue with the joy of showtime. Miss Garland's best solo number is "Happy Harvest," sung driving a tractor. Kelly's best is "Dig-Dig-Dig," done with Silvers and the troupe. Their best duet is "You Wonderful You," which winds up with Kelly doing a novel dance solo.[7]

Milwaukee Journal

Once every four or five years a great movie musical show comes along. Between times Hollywood presses out dozens of technically excellent Technicolor jobs like *Summer Stock*. Each has music, each has merit, and they're almost as hard to tell apart as a bunch of little new-born cans of beer. The current item is funnier than most of the lot, with Marjorie Main, Eddie Bracken and Phil Silvers hatching top-grade bucolic clowning. Also on the credit side are the dancing of Gene Kelly, the singing of Judy Garland and a lively pace. Contrariwise, this listener thought the music was not very good. *Summer Stock* will give you a pleasant hundred odd minutes in the theater. You may not remember much about it later. At the conclusion of its first early afternoon showing, many of the youthful audience burst into wild applause. Whether this was because of what they had just seen or because it was over and they could now see the co-feature, Roy Rogers in *Trigger, Jr.*, could not be determined.[8]

Miami News

As movie patrons don't particularly worry too much about shortcomings in musicals anyway, this one—*Summer Stock*—should hit the jackpot because of other advantages. The advantages are primarily the lively talents of Judy Garland and Gene Kelly. Ms. Garland, rounder fore and aft than usual, plays with her infectious enthusiasm and scores a hit. Her rendering of "Get Happy" is almost worth waiting for throughout the overlong story. Kelly is fine, too, and his clowning with Phil Silvers is the highlight of the film. They're dressed as hayseeds with missing teeth, oversized bare feet, and loose pants. They perform in vocal harmony and hoofing while a pack of dogs, growing in number with each chorus, joins in the fun.[9]

Chicago Daily Tribune

Judy Garland proves that she can still sing with a lilt and dance with exuberance, that she can be winsome or wistful if need be, even though she has gained considerable weight. Her excess poundage unfortunately is accentuated by generally unbecoming costumes—overalls and slacks are not kind to any but the slimmest of figures.[10]

Asheville Citizen-Times

Judy Garland, who, with a great fanfare of publicity, has recovered her own bouncy health, is featured in a new MGM musical soundtrack album, *Summer Stock*. She sings four of the eight songs in the group from the movie made just before her front-page suicide attempt. Her best side, recalling her superior performance in *The Wizard of Oz*, is "Friendly Star"—a slow-paced ballad that points up a message of hope.[11]

Ekstra Bladet (Copenhagen Denmark)

Judy Garland is certainly a bit chubby in her new film *Summer Stock*, so chubby that you are impressed when she throws herself into the big dance scenes, but despite the chubbiness she is a very nice girl, and a sweet girl you can like her . . . Gene Kelly is—when he's not dancing—more human than he used to be, but the film is first and foremost Judy Garland's—let's see her again, thick or thin, it really does not matter.[12]

• • •

Not only did her legions of fans enthusiastically welcome Judy's return to the screen after her one-year absence, nationally syndicated columnist Dorothy Kilgallen was so overjoyed that she devoted a column in the form of a personal fan letter to the star of *Summer Stock*:

> Dear Judy:
>
> You have had a bad time in your private life recently, but take a look at your latest picture and cheer up. You could not sit through that picture without realizing the girl up there on the screen—warm,

vivid, vital, tremendously appealing—has a combination of qualities no other actress in Hollywood can match.

But there is more than that. The big extra, which has always been there, is her great personality. It is there whether she is thin or plump, laughing or sad, whether she is in a good picture or a so-so picture. It shines in her eyes and it makes people believe in her and it makes people care. It is a rare, rare thing to own, Judy. Cherish it. Take care of yourself.

Sincerely,
A Fan[13]

A CONTEMPORARY TAKE

MORE THAN SEVENTY YEARS AFTER ITS RELEASE, *SUMMER STOCK* IS BEING discovered by a new generation of fans and is considered an important enough work in the cinematic canon of Garland and Kelly to merit critical reconsideration. It's a reckoning that only the clarity that comes with the passage of decades can truly provide.

"In some ways, *Summer Stock* feels like an ignobly small-scale end to Garland's run at MGM. The plot is—to quote the film itself—pure hokum," opines Caroline Siede in a blog she wrote for Avclub.com. However, she goes on to say: "In its final cut, the film is an effervescent, delightfully corny salute to the theater in which Garland keeps up with Kelly step for step, ending her MGM run with her iconic performance of 'Get Happy'—a brassy, sexy highlight of her entire career.

"In its own goofy, homespun way, *Summer Stock* is a celebration of musical theater's ability to provide a beam of sunshine on a cloudy day, and a tribute to the artists who work so hard to make it look effortless."[14]

CRUNCHING THE NUMBERS

SUMMER STOCK HIT SCREENS AS A LATE SUMMER RELEASE AND WAS TIMED to capitalize on the pending Labor Day weekend crowds. In an internal MGM document, titled "Schedule of pictures with estimated final costs and budgets" as of March 30, 1950, *Summer Stock* was listed with a budget of $1,981,218 and an estimated final cost of $2,231,899, a cost overrun but not a significant one by Hollywood standards. Since the film officially wrapped production on April 5, 1950, these numbers reflected an estimate. It has also been reported that *Summer Stock* came in at a final cost of $2,024,848, an overrun of just $43,630 from the original budget.

If initial box-office grosses are any indication, *Summer Stock* seemed like another profitable film for MGM. According to *Variety*, "Labor Day week upsurge is carrying film theater biz in key cities to highest peaks since early this year. Reports from *Variety* correspondents in 22 key cities show the top eight pictures grossing over $1,852,000 or a pickup of nearly $900,000 over recent weeks."[15]

According to the article, the top four films were *The Black Rose, Fancy Pants, Sunset Boulevard*, and *Summer Stock*. Two weeks later, in the September 20 edition of *Variety, Summer Stock* was still holding its number four spot at the nation's box office.

MGM ran a full-page ad, under the title "Stock Soars," in *Variety* on September 13, 1950. The ad included a graphic of a lion strumming a guitar singing, "J-U-D-Y, they're simply w-i-l-d about you J-U-D-Y." The ad boasted that the film generated the second highest (receipts) in the first five days in 2½ years at the Capitol Theater in New York. Other copy points included:

- Tops *Annie Get Your Gun* in fourteen comparable spots
- In five cities it tops *Father of the Bride* July 4th business
- In five cities it beats Thanksgiving records of *Adam's Rib*
- Six-day gross in Worcester is $184 less than *Battleground*[16]

Ledgerdemain

The promising citations from *Variety* notwithstanding, it's impossible to ascertain the exact profitability of *Summer Stock*. The "Eddie Mannix Ledger" housed at the Margaret Herrick Library in Los Angeles lists every film produced by MGM between 1924 and 1962 (more than 1,000 films in all), and for each one cites domestic and foreign earnings, production costs, and itemized profits and losses. According to the financials in the ledger, *Summer Stock* initially took in $2,498,000 in the United States and Canada and an additional $859,000 overseas for a total gross of $3,357,000 or a loss of $80,000.[17]

Mannix (February 25, 1891–August 30, 1963), a longtime executive at MGM, was known as the "fixer" and was expert at quelling potentially disastrous situations that could harm the "bankability" of the studio and the popularity of its high-priced talent. As a loyal company man, it's possible that the financial numbers in Mannix's ledger were also "fixed," because accurate accounting during the studio system era was often sketchy.

The origins and purpose of the Mannix Ledger are murky at best. It was found amongst the many files and documents donated to the Academy by Howard Strickling. However, the ledger bears the name of Edgar J. "Eddie" Mannix, one of three administrative vice presidents at MGM. He was hired in 1925 by Nicholas Schenck, the president of Loew's Inc. (MGM's parent corporation), to act as a liaison between the corporation's financial headquarters in New York City and the production facility in Culver City, California.

Mannix was at first regarded in Culver City as a spy for the New York executives, but he soon became a confidant of MGM studio chief Louis B. Mayer. In addition to his sobriquet of "the fixer," Mannix was known as the "general manager" of the studio, and also as "Mayer's right-hand man." As such, Mannix reportedly gave Mayer a daily briefing on the studio's financial affairs. Thus, there is little doubt that Mannix had the status and access to compile such a ledger; but just why he compiled it, what sources and accounting procedures he used, and how the ledger ended up among Strickling's papers remains a mystery.[18]

According to archivists at the Margaret Herrick Library, Mannix was part of an elite group that would have been entrusted with a copy of the ledger for his personal use. However, they disagree with the assertion that Mannix compiled the ledger himself (or had it expressly compiled for himself). The Herrick Library believes that the ledger was a standard studio reference, available to numerous MGM executives and other company personnel on a "need-to-know" basis.

In a preface to the Mannix Ledger, the Herrick Library archivists state that they cannot definitively advise on how the data in the ledger should be interpreted. There is no "key" or other explanatory document available that explains what all the various numbers mean or how they should be read, individually or in combination with one another. While a number for

"Cost" or "Est. Final Cost" would seem self-evident, the precise meaning of the other numbers—the "revenue" or "billings" figures, and the "profit (loss)" value—is mysterious. There does not appear to be a single formula that can be consistently used to calculate the profit/loss number from the other numbers, nor is it clear how the "O.H." (Overhead) days are calculated (if they are) into the individual picture's cost. There is also no indication whether the revenue and profit/loss figures reflect gross receipts (that is, the amount taken in at the box office) or rentals (the studio's share of the gross).[19]

To further add to the quandary of whether *Summer Stock* ended up in the red or the black, MGM's parent company, Loew's Inc., fiscal year ended on August 31, the day *Summer Stock* was released, so its financial results would not have been reported until Loews' books closed a year later on August 31, 1951. Despite the encroachment of television and the dismantling of the studio-owned chain of theaters, Loew's still reported a healthy net income of $7,804,370 for the fiscal year ended August 31, 1951 (the reporting period that would have reflected *Summer Stock*'s revenue loss). That was almost unchanged from earnings of the previous fiscal year: $7,854,557.[20]

So, it's impossible to say conclusively that *Summer Stock* turned a profit or showed a loss during its initial theatrical release. What's more certain is that when revenue from television airings, ancillary markets (non-theatrical, ships at sea, armed forces), plus soundtrack sales from MGM Records and other more recent revenue in the form of DVD and streaming sales is added up, the film has likely become profitable.

Stock Optioned!

Almost all MGM musicals were original works conceived for the big screen, not the proscenium stage. However, that hasn't prevented some from attempting to adapt them into a live theatrical experience, while at the same time capitalizing on nostalgic audiences who fondly remember the Golden Age of Metro musicals. *Summer Stock* has proven to be no exception to that wistful longing for simple, goodhearted entertainment.

Over the last few decades, several MGM musicals were re-envisioned for the stage, with varying degrees of success once they eventually hit the Broadway boards. Examples include *Meet Me in St. Louis*, 252 performances; *Singin' in the Rain*, 367 performances; and *Seven Brides for Seven Brothers*, five performances. Arguably the most successful stage adaptation of an

MGM film was *An American in Paris,* which closed on Broadway in 2016 after 623 performances.[21]

It was while directing *A Chorus Line* for the Western Stage, a theater company at Hartnell College in Salinas, California, that Roxanne Messina Captor first pitched the idea of a *Summer Stock* stage musical to the group's artistic director, Tom Humphrey. Later, when Captor was working for Turner Entertainment, she met Sy Gomberg, original story creator and co-screenwriter of the film, and pitched her idea to him for a stage version of the movie. Gomberg was receptive and he and Captor worked for about eighteen months adapting the screen version to the stage, adding seven new songs from the Harold Arlen-Yip Harburg songbook, including "Paper Moon," "I Like the Likes of You," "That Old Black Magic," and, oddly, the Groucho Marx comic novelty number "Lydia, the Tattooed Lady," which was performed by the Esme character onstage.

Captor said the show became a passion project, almost a tribute to Gene Kelly, whom she had gotten to know after working with him on the musical films *Xanadu* (1980) and *One from the Heart* (1981), for which Kelly served as a technical advisor. She recalled at one point during her collaboration with Gomberg that a "ghost-writer" with a high profile (none other than Carl Reiner) suggested a few bits of business. "Sy and Carl were very close friends," said Captor. "One day during a work session at Sy's house, Carl came over and gave us some ideas for the script."[22]

The *Summer Stock* stage version that was Captor and Gomberg's brainchild enjoyed a limited engagement September 1–17, 2000, at the Western Stage. The reviews for the show were generally kind. "Simple, in a classic sort of way," wrote the critic for the *Monterey County Weekly*. "*Summer Stock* is not an outstanding show, but it is fun and entertaining. Give it three stars and an 'A' for effort."[23] Although the creators of the show had bigger aspirations for it than to reside in a regional theater, Captor and Gomberg's version of *Summer Stock* never enjoyed an afterlife after its initial run at Western Stage. "Sometimes you think a show is going to go to another level, but it doesn't," said Captor. "I have no idea why. It's the nature of what we do. You're not at the right place at the right time; you don't have the right person to champion it. Who knows?"[24]

Ten years later, in October 2010 another incarnation of *Summer Stock* for the stage emerged. The Skyline Theatre Company in New Jersey's Bergen County presented a concert adaptation of what was billed as "the new stage musical *Summer Stock*, inspired by the MGM movie musical." According to a story on Playbill.com that dates from that period, the show "has been in development as a stage property (with new songs mixed into the film score) in the past year under the direction of Sam Scalamoni, Skyline's managing artistic director. He co-wrote the new libretto and continues to shepherd the project as director. It was previously read in a Manhattan industry reading in August 2009."[25] Scalamoni told Playbill.com on September 16, 2009, "The response to the material has all been very positive from both commercial producers and regional theaters. We feel we are at the peak of our development process and we are ready for a full stage production."[26]

To date, a second stage version of *Summer Stock* under Scalamoni's stewardship has yet to materialize, but at last report, after more than a decade in limbo, Scalamoni says the show is being resurrected for a possible Broadway opening and touring show by way of a new licensing agreement with Warner Bros., which owns the rights to the movie. According to Scalamoni, new producers (Steve Peters and Michael Londra of VenuWorks Theatrical) have been engaged. The fact that their company, VenuWorks, is domiciled in Ames, Iowa, located in America's heartland and in a region filled with barns, is purely coincidental.[27]

Before this book went to press, the Goodspeed Opera House in East Haddam, Connecticut, announced that in the summer of 2023 (July 7–August 27) it would mount its own stage version of *Summer Stock* with music and lyrics from some of the same disparate set of composers that contributed to the Western Stage version of the musical in Salinas, California. But, according to Dan McMahon, director of marketing for Goodspeed, "We are creating a brand new adaptation, so it will not be the same as was done in California."[28]

And finally, an item announcing plans to adapt *Summer Stock* into a television series appeared in the *Hollywood Reporter* in November 1978. Edward A. Montanus, president of MGM-TV, was quoted saying that the studio was at work adapting the movie into a half-hour comedy series with a talent search then underway for the roles of a struggling young actress (the Garland character) and a well-known recording star who wants to break into the legitimate theater, a role that, according to the story, was "originally essayed by Gene Kelly, as a song and dance man." The squib in the *Reporter* was the first (and last) mention of *Summer Stock* ever becoming a TV property.[29]

OH, YOU BEAUTIFUL DOLL!

IN 2001, THE MADAME ALEXANDER DOLL COMPANY IN NEW YORK MANUfactured a sixteen-inch collectible doll of Judy Garland in her "Get Happy" costume from *Summer Stock*. The doll's outfit featured a black three-quarter-length tuxedo jacket, sheer black hose, black pumps, a white silk ascot, rhinestone pin, earrings, and the iconic black fedora Garland wore during the number. It also included a clear plastic posing stand and was sold exclusively at FAO Schwarz, America's oldest toy store, located in Manhattan. On the back of the box was an endorsement from Judy's daughter, Lorna Luft, extolling the doll's beauty and craftsmanship with the wish that "every time you look at it, you will just forget your troubles and get happy."

New Yorker Beatrice Alexander founded her doll business in 1923 and it became renowned for replicating famous personalities like the Dionne Quintuplets, Scarlett O'Hara, the characters from Louisa May Alcott's *Little Women*, and even first ladies of US presidents. Alexander, who started out designing and sewing cloth dolls herself, ran the company for sixty-five years before selling it in 1988.

FROM VIDEO TO DIGITAL AND BEYOND

BEFORE THE ADVENT OF VIDEOCASSETTE TAPES, *SUMMER STOCK* COULD largely only be seen as part of late-show programming on TV or if the viewer was fortunate enough to live in a city populous enough to accommodate a revival house or repertory cinema that specialized in screening vintage films. For instance, in the mid-1970s, the local CBS affiliate in our hometown of St. Paul, Minnesota, would broadcast *Summer Stock* annually as part of a week of musical films during the dog days of summer. Other films that week invariably included *Singin' in the Rain*, *In the Good Old Summertime*, *Royal Wedding*, and *It's Always Fair Weather*. And all were shredded by commercials, with some films marred by aspect ratios that didn't fit the images to the small TV screens. Nonetheless, musical week marked the only airing of *Summer Stock* on TV in the Twin Cities by any of the network affiliates in a given year.

But that situation was altered forever with the invention of videocassettes. For the first time, individual consumers who couldn't afford to pay hundreds of dollars to buy copies of movies in 16mm could purchase for an affordable price, their own VHS cassettes of their favorite films. The first US videocassette release of *Summer Stock* was in the fall of 1987, along with other MGM musicals including *Anchors Aweigh*. It was part of the "Musicals Great Musicals" collection brought out under the auspices of MGM/UA Home Video.

The story of the movie during this period of technological innovation involves some rather serpentine business negotiations between corporate entities and is worth encapsulating briefly here.

In 1986, Ted Turner and his Turner Broadcasting System purchased MGM from its then-owner Kirk Kerkorian for $1.5 billion. Four months later, Turner sold the MGM name, Culver City studio lot, and other assets back to Kerkorian but kept the library of vintage MGM movies (including *Summer Stock*), which subsequently formed the nucleus of his Turner Entertainment Company. MGM/UA Home Video (initially retained by Turner but then sold back to Kerkorian) obtained a fifteen-year home video rights agreement with Turner Broadcasting System to distribute videocassettes of the classic MGM library (which had remained the property of Turner Entertainment). Two years later, in 1988, Turner Broadcasting launched the TNT network; and in 1994, they created Turner Classic Movies (TCM) in order to utilize the company's catalog of films—a move that introduced new generations to the merits of these classic movies. In 1996, Turner Broadcasting System was bought by Time Warner and its distribution functions were largely absorbed into Warner Bros., which now controls the rights to *Summer Stock*.[30]

Amid the buffeting of these various corporate buyouts, *Summer Stock* kept pace and adapted to the new technological advances when Warner Home Video transferred it to the DVD format in 2006 in its original 1.37:1 standard aspect ratio.

As an added attraction, special features on the disc included *Summer Stock: Get Happy!*, a sixteen-minute featurette that chronicles, by way of Garland historian John Fricke, the film's tumultuous production history, salutes its superb cast, and analyzes its musical impact. Cast members Gloria DeHaven (who idolized Garland) and Carleton Carpenter (who jokes about having either "an elbow or an earlobe in every other shot") also share their fond *Summer Stock* memories. The seven-minute Tex Avery cartoon *The Cuckoo Clock* supplies plenty of slapstick while *Did'ja Know?*, a live-action "Pete Smith Specialty," humorously depicts the differences between new and expectant fathers and demonstrates why yawns are contagious. An audio outtake from the movie, "Fall in Love," featuring DeHaven and Silvers, and a theatrical trailer wrap up the rich trove of supplements. In 2019, the film got the full high-definition treatment from Warner Archives when it was transferred to Blu-ray with the same extras imported from the DVD.[31]

At the time of the publication of this book, *Summer Stock* is also available for purchase or rental on such streaming platforms as YouTube, where individual scenes and numbers from the movie can be watched free of charge. One way or another, whether via continued airings on TCM, DVD and Blu-ray purchases, viewings via streaming services, or through theatrical showings in the dwindling number of repertory cinemas in the United States, *Summer Stock* endures!

CHAPTER VII

STRAIGHT UP ALL THE WAY

SHORTLY BEFORE *SUMMER STOCK* WAS SCHEDULED FOR NATIONWIDE release, Garland returned to MGM to begin work on her next film, *Royal Wedding*, again co-starring Astaire. Garland reported for rehearsals and wardrobe fittings for eighteen days between May 23 and June 16, 1950, arriving late for half of those dates. With Louis B. Mayer's power fading at the studio and production costs mounting, MGM's new head of production, Dore Schary, was unsympathetic. On June 17, Garland, suffering from a migraine, missed her rehearsal call and later that day she was notified by the studio that she was again placed on suspension.

Garland's dismissal from *Royal Wedding* hit her like a prizefighter's knockout punch. That was on Friday, June 17, 1950. On June 20, she had been scheduled to start recording the score with cameras set to roll on June 26. Instead, on June 21, the nation was shocked to wake up and read this headline in the newspaper: "Judy Garland Slashes Throat after Film Row."[1] As reported in the *Los Angeles Times*, "Judy Garland slashed her throat with the broken edge of a water glass Monday night [June 20] in an emotional blowup over career troubles, her film studio disclosed yesterday." The article continued, quoting Garland's physician, Dr. Francis E. Ballard, who termed the suicide attempt "an impulsive act" and the cuts "very minor."[2] The wound, described as "superficial," did not require stitches and happened at Garland's Los Angeles home on Evansview Drive.

Howard Strickling and his publicity team immediately went into damage-control mode. MGM prepared a 600-word statement that took no responsibility for aiding or abetting the situation: "Miss Garland has been under nervous strain since Saturday when she was suspended for failing to report to work," the statement read. "We did everything we could to make her comfortable and keep her happy."[3] It is estimated that the studio spent more than $100,000 on doctors, hospitals, and various types of treatments to improve Judy's health. "Several times against our better judgment, at her insistence, we have started films with her, and her consequent illness has caused us embarrassment, delay, inconvenience and a loss of morale to coworkers," the statement said. Strickling also emphasized that Garland's suspension from *Royal Wedding* was "not a hasty move, prompted by pique or irritation," but was "arrived at with great regret."[4]

TOUGH LOVE

A SOURCE OF ENCOURAGEMENT FOR THE TROUBLED STAR SOON CAME from an unlikely source—Katherine Hepburn. At the urging of Mayer, Hepburn was tasked with trying to buck up Judy's spirits. Mayer felt that "anyone who could cope with Tracy's [Spencer, Hepburn's life partner] drinking, would understand Garland's problems."[5]

"Now listen, you're one of the three greatest talents in the world," Hepburn was reported to have told Garland at her bedside, "and your ass has hit the gutter. There's no place to go but up. Now, Goddamnit, do it!"[6] After several hours visiting with Garland, Hepburn ducked most of the media by exiting out the back door and hopping a fence. She evaded a few reporters still in pursuit by retreating down a side street and scaling a wall into the garden of her friend Greta Garbo, who was not home at the time.

In September 1950, Metro agreed (by mutual consent) to cancel Garland's contract, which had more than a year left to run, and forgive the several thousand dollars she still owed the studio for her trips to Boston the previous year. On September 29, less than a month after the release of *Summer Stock*, MGM officially released Garland from any further obligations, "with reluctance and regret," as Mayer generously phrased it, "and with a view to serving her own best interests."[7]

Over the next few years, Gene Kelly would cement his fame with brilliant dancing and choreography in *An American in Paris* and *Singin' in the Rain*, to which he would also add directing laurels. Charles Walters would continue to put his special directing stamp on a string of successful musicals and Joe Pasternak would produce more movies that endeavored to help audiences forget their troubles. After fifteen years of almost constant work at MGM, which included starring in twenty-eight feature films (including one loan-out to Twentieth Century-Fox for *Pigskin Parade*) and numerous shorts, Garland would embark down her own road without the protective cover of the studio that made her a star. In the intervening years—a span in which Judy's name would achieve near mononym status—there would be many triumphs (her concerts at the Palace, Carnegie Hall, and the London Palladium with her daughter Liza, to name just three), but the public would not see Garland back on the screen until her Academy Award–nominated performance in *A Star is Born* in 1954.

On the face of it, *Summer Stock* seemed destined to be a dated throwback to the kind of wholesome movies that had been Metro's bread and butter two decades earlier—a lifeline thrown to Garland at a difficult moment in her life and a transitory way-stop in the careers of Kelly and Walters. But along the way, helped by affecting performances from a gifted cast and the deft hand of Walters at the helm, the movie transcended those inauspicious beginnings and became something more. "I think during shooting, Gene and Chuck had time to meditate on the script," Brent Phillips said. "I think very calmly they decided to say something pithy about show business, the need for self-fulfillment, and of not being subservient to your father-in-law or fiancé or farm or family tradition. It's about following your own journey, wherever it leads. And that, ultimately, is what the audiences fell in love with. *Summer Stock* is literally about if you feel like singing, then just sing! It's about being the star attraction in your own world just as Judy was in her barnyard."[8]

And yet . . . "There are no auteurs in musical movies," Kelly said, in accepting his AFI Life Achievement Award in 1985. "The name of the game is collaboration."

And so . . . In *That's Entertainment!* Liza Minnelli, plaintively at first, eulogizes her mother: "Whatever rocks or bumps there were, she never let it show in her films," she says. Then in a tone more defiantly triumphant, she expounds on Garland's ethic of professionalism, declaring: "For mama, it was straight up all the way!"

For the cast and crew of *Summer Stock* that labored through all the problems and delays that ultimately led to the creation of a joyous musical, MGM production #1477 was a film that defied the odds. Working together, they personified the inherent strengths of the studio system at its apex, particularly MGM with its unmatched pedigree in conjuring musical escapism. Garland, Kelly, Walters, Pasternak, and the rest never let the challenges that loomed almost daily stand in the way of delivering the goods, creating out of that turmoil a film that continues to delight audiences decades later. They got the job done.

Straight up all the way.

CHAPTER VIII

TAKING STOCK

Who's Doing Anything Remotely Like It Now? I'll Tell You Who—Nobody!

SUMMER STOCK IS VINTAGE NOW, A SEPTUAGENARIAN. BUT THE PASSAGE of time, more than seven decades at the time this is being written, enables a perspective that would have been difficult (if not impossible) to achieve when the movie came out. Like the overwhelming amount of films released in any given year, *Summer Stock* was topical to the era in which it was made; in its particular case, the late 1940s and early 1950s. And, thematically at least, it strictly adheres to the litmus test of formulaic film musicals made in that postwar period: the guarantee of a boy-gets-girl happy ending.

Plot aside, we wondered what current-day performers might say when queried about the movie's musical numbers and on-screen chemistry between Judy Garland and Gene Kelly, and if those ingredients might hint at some kind of enduring legacy for *Summer Stock*. To that end, we asked a number of actors, singers, dancers, choreographers, and others to weigh in with their thoughts on Garland, Kelly, and the movie.

LORNA LUFT

Lorna Luft is the second daughter of Judy Garland (and Judy's husband-producer, Sid Luft), and like her half-sister Liza Minnelli has enjoyed a successful career as a stage, television, and screen performer and best-selling author. Luft's cabaret shows are a mixture of song interpretation from the Great American Songbook as well as anecdotes and insights about what is was like growing up in a legendary show business family.

My mom didn't share a lot with me about working on *Summer Stock* or "Get Happy" because she was a live-in-the-moment person. She wouldn't sit and reminisce or play her own movies or do any of that, but I know that she adored Gene and she discovered him, and they had worked together and they really liked one another a lot. They loved working with each other and I think that that's one of the reasons that Gene did *Summer Stock*—because she was involved and I know that when she was getting ready for it, she was tired. She should not have had a schedule like that but you can't say that to the powers that be at MGM. Unlike Bette Davis, who would throw down scripts and say, "I'm not doing this!" mother didn't. She tried and then they would threaten her and she would get scared. She thought the idea was hokey, like, "Oh, my God, it's another thing where I put a show on in a barn."

The biggest thing (and most people know this, of course) In the film is that her weight went up and down, and that's a pretty normal thing for people to do when they are stressed out and people don't listen to them. And they didn't listen because they didn't have the knowledge, they didn't have the facilities, didn't have any kind of help for the talent. The actors (especially my mother) truly were like mice on a treadmill. They just kept going and going and going and going. Nobody knew the effects of what that pressure would do to people. It made them massive stars, household names, movie icons, and it also destroyed them.

I have to say I like *Summer Stock* a lot. I don't love the movie. And that's just me, because I think that the numbers in the movie are phenomenal but, as a whole, the story was like I'd seen her do this before. I'd seen her on a farm. I thought the score was very good. I think "Get Happy" certainly ranks in mother's top five. You can't really say what's number one because everyone has a different opinion of what their favorite moment is in any of her films.

Mom had her own space because she was a child star. It wasn't like all of the other people—the Annie Millers and the Cyd Charisses—they were adults when they became famous so nobody grew up with them. They weren't "Dorothy Gale," do you know what I'm saying? That was where my mother was so unique because her career went from a child all the way through her adult life as a star. She was the whole deal. It was really my mom and Elizabeth Taylor and that was it.[1]

KERRY KELLY NOVICK

Kerry Kelly Novick is a child, adolescent, and adult psychoanalyst. She did her academic training with Anna Freud in London in the 1960s and her adult training at the Contemporary Freudian Society in New York. She lectures nationally and internationally and is the author of numerous papers and five books with her husband, Jack Novick. She is Gene Kelly's first child with wife Betsy Blair.

I think they all approached *Summer Stock* as funny and fun to do. You do it a tiny bit tongue-in-cheek. But people of that level of talent, even when they do something slightly tongue-in-cheek, do it to the best of their ability. I don't know if my father agreeing to be in the film was necessarily a "comfort factor" to prop up Judy, but as I understood it as a child, it was to help take care of Judy and that it was important because people help their friends out. Everybody that loved her was worried about her and wanted to do anything they could do to help. *Summer Stock* was an attempt to put her in the safety net of familiar people and try to get her through an entire film. My father was trying to be supportive, but also felt for her to get on with it. They all worked so hard. They knew if she would keep working, she'd go on. "The show must go on" is a phrase that has a lot of utility.

At the same time, my father didn't experience the kind of stress that Chuck Walters went through on *Summer Stock*. He was pretty demanding as a choreographer and co-star, but at the time he thought it was good for Judy to have high expectations. My father was always an intense person.

Dad owed an enormous debt to her for helping him learn how to be in a movie in *For Me and My Gal*, because he was a Broadway star where you do it big. He always said that Judy taught him how to make it the right size for the camera. She taught him how to act for the screen, how to make a smaller and more focused performance rather than reaching for the third balcony.

After the war, at our house at 725 North Rodeo Drive [in Beverly Hills], from 1945 on, Judy was there all the time, practically every weekend. Looking back, those parties were astonishing, but to the people involved, it was a group of friends like any group of friends getting together on the weekend. It just happened to be a group of people with extraordinary talents. They would play games, sports, play music and sing. It was fun for them and relaxing. Always there was somebody at the piano and always somebody singing, often it was Judy. People at the piano would be Saul Chaplin, Lennie Hayton, or André Previn. Judy was comfortable singing because she was among friends. She felt safe, she felt loved. It was the weekend.

Judy would sing anything and everything at those parties, all the popular tunes of the day—sometimes new songs or songs with some original lyrics. People like Jule Styne used to try out new songs, as would Adolph Green and Betty Comden. The parties would evolve organically from late afternoon, when there were the volleyball games in our backyard, the food, the drinks, and the singing. Everybody knew it would be that kind of sequence. Sunday nights we'd show films in 16mm in the living room.

After *Summer Stock*, we saw Judy in many places—New York, London, and at her various stage performances. Liza was only four years younger than me. I was almost like an older cousin to her. I was an only child, as was Liza. Liza and I would visit Judy in the dressing room before a show and she would ask if Liza had eaten her snack. Judy tried the best she could to be as motherly as she could even though she didn't have that kind of upbringing herself. When she was married to Vincente Minnelli, they lived around the block from us, so on Christmas morning we'd go over to the house and deliver presents in person. Whenever she was in a film, Judy would have one of the costumes made in miniature for Liza, very sweet. Liza was thrilled.

So much is made of Judy's difficult times and difficult life. I think in the Freed unit and with my father she really found a kind of family. It was very important for her as a grown-up to have colleagues like that—different from when she was a kid at MGM.[2]

BEN VEREEN

On screen, Ben Vereen has appeared in such musicals Sweet Charity *(1969) with Shirley MacLaine,* Funny Lady *(1975) with Barbra Streisand, and* All That Jazz *(1979). On Broadway, Vereen starred in* Wicked, Fosse, Hair, Jesus Christ Superstar, Chicago, Pippin, Grind, *and* Jelly's Last Jam. *His role in* Pippin *in 1973 garnered him both the Tony Award and the Drama Desk Award for Best Actor in a Musical.*

Gene Kelly was a natural. He represented male dancers in a beautiful way. He was so masculine and cool. He was this cool guy, like, "Wow! This guy, I know this guy. I run the street with this guy." When I met Gene, he made you feel that way. He had that way about him.

What I love about him is his tenacity. For example, in his movie *The Pirate*, with the Nicholas Brothers, people didn't want Gene to use them in the film [they cut Gene and the Nicholas Brothers' "Be a Clown" number out at a lot of theaters in the South] but Gene was adamant about doing the number with them. When I was on *The Mike Douglas Show* in Los Angeles with both Gene and Fred Astaire, I asked them—point-blank—I said, "The numbers that you did; did you guys go up to Harlem and study the dancers?" Gene was the first to say, "Yes, we did!"

I would love to have been a fly on the wall during rehearsals for *Summer Stock*. What chemistry he and Judy had! That chemistry was going on before they got on the set. He developed how he would work with her. He got her to move a certain way to be so in-synch.

Gene Kelly is one of those cats that you got to be honoring and paying homage to. Gene would be on the stage with nothing—like in the "squeaky board" number in *Summer Stock*—and create a whole environment with magical rhythm. Young people need to see that. So my vote would be to get the film out there and let the nation see it again, and get the young people to see it maybe for the first time.

You cannot discuss films and musicals without discussing Gene Kelly, from where he came. Once you know from where people like Gene and Judy came, then we know how to move forward, because if we do not look to our past and understand it, we will be stuck in the past. Gene gave us a pathway forward. He knew his work and did his homework, and if we have more people who do their homework and follow his example we will have much better art.[3]

MARIO CANTONE

Mario Cantone is a comedian, writer, actor, and singer with numerous credits on stage, screen, and television, including his years-long arc as Charlotte York's gay wedding planner, Anthony Marentino, on TV's Sex and the City. *Cantone's standup style is fast paced, with much of his humor stemming from impersonations of various characters ranging from family members to celebrities, including a spot-on take of his childhood idol, Judy Garland.*

My mother Lizzy thought that Judy was the greatest entertainer in the world. She saw her on tour in Boston when Judy performed there, and she saw her again in 1957. She said she was not as good the second time, but even at her worst, Judy was great. My mother had the Carnegie Hall album and it was a double album set, as you know. I memorized it all when I was two years old and would sing the whole thing standing on a coffee table in front of people. They would make me *do* her! My mother was not very happy about the fact that I was gay and I was like, "Okay, you made me sing Judy Garland at two years old, I got obsessed with her."

In performance she was honest and real and in pain and hilarious. Everyone says that Judy was one of the funniest people that they ever knew—bitingly funny. She does the thing Liza doesn't do. Liza is very veiled and she is not funny. For me, she is incredibly talented, but she is not funny; like she is afraid of her anger. And I do not think Judy was.

Judy has that typical "fat" voice, you know, fat, like Whitney Houston—that fat voice in her prime, fat and distinct. It's like when you listen to Mariah Carey, even when she was younger they fattened her voice when they recorded her. When you heard Mariah live, her voice was thinner. I do not care how much range she had. It was thin. Judy's voice was big and fat and real and powerful and was like no other voice. As far as *Summer Stock* goes, every time it's on TV, it draws me in and I watch it. I love "Happy Harvest." I love that song. I just like the movie. I think it is good—it looks good. And Judy is a great actress.

Harry Warren is a good songwriter, but he was no Harold Arlen. Harold Arlen was great and who knows how it would have been if Arlen wrote the whole score instead of just "Get Happy." I'd rank "Get Happy" number two after Arlen's "The Man That Got Away" for Judy. I mean, I love "Over the Rainbow"; it's lovely, but it does not have that theatrical excitement that those two other numbers have. She had a gorgeous voice in 1939 during *The Wizard of Oz*, but she was not singing like she does with "Get Happy" or "The Man That Got Away."[4]

TOMMY TUNE

Tommy Tune is one of the country's most prolific performer/director/choreographers. He has received ten Tony Awards, including the 2015 Tony for Life Achievement in the Theatre, and he's the only person in theatrical history to win Tonys in four different categories. Tune has also received the National Medal of Arts, eight Drama Desk Awards, two Obie Awards, three Astaire Awards, and multiple lifetime achievement awards, including the Stage Directors and Choreographer Foundation "Mr. Abbott" Award. In the 1969 film Hello, Dolly!, *directed by Gene Kelly, Tune played the role of Ambrose Kemper.*

Gene has been part of my life from, I think, the first time I saw him in *For Me and My Gal*. He was a dancing guy and he was not doing ballet. See, I started to be a ballet dancer and I was really good until I started growing and growing and growing and growing and then I simply did not look like a ballet dancer. I knew I had to do something else. I saw Gene Kelly on the screen and he was not wearing tights. He was wearing clothes, just like Fred Astaire. So, the two of them were my influences. Fred Astaire actually more because he was so thin and he looked very tall. He wasn't tall but he looked very tall on the movie screen to my young eyes. Of course, Gene Kelly was just so incredible, his acrobatic and sports background. He was sexy and Fred Astaire was elegant. So, it was a mix between the two that kept me jumping back and forth.

Fred Astaire's choreography was otherworldly. Kelly was meat and potatoes, but Gene would also direct and choreograph. They worked hard and long. Then on shooting days, a lot of the shooting was on that famous beautiful red floor that they had at MGM, which was polished to a high sheen and which was killer for dancing—killer on your body. They did not have sprung floors for them. Oh my God! Floor texture is so important. Of course, they wanted the floors to look beautiful in the movies. Gene Kelly's floors were always beautiful, but I kept thinking about every time he would come up and come down. He was on a cement floor because that is what was underneath.

And if that wasn't bad enough, dubbing taps is awful. I have been through that process myself and it is terrible because you do not have any room to dance. Here in a little tiny space close to the microphone, holding the earphones on your head, and trying to match the sounds but not being able to do the dance. You cannot jump all around and land and turn. You cannot do all of that when you are dubbing. It is really, really hard.

On *Hello, Dolly!* Gene had us over to his house for dinner, which was great, and then on location he had us over to his rented home. He was just a real guy, so helpful, and he was under a lot of pressure working with Barbra Streisand on the picture. It was not a pleasant actor-director relationship because she did everything she wanted to do. We would arrive on the set and get a scene all blocked out, how we are going to do it; and Gene figured out he is going to shoot it, and then he would say, "Send for the dreaded Barbara."

She would come in and change everything because she did not want to be photographed from a particular side, and she did not want to have the shot over her shoulder, and she did not want to walk through *that* door, she wanted to walk through *this* door, and she would just rehash the whole thing. And what did Gene do? Bend as much as he could to make it comfortable for her because she was the star.

He always used to say, "Okay, let us make a beautiful thing." I remember him talking about the color of the grass up in Garrison, New York [where some of *Hello, Dolly!* was shot] because it did not look right. He said, "Why can it not look like *l'herbe verte*?" He'd lapse into little bits of French because he spoke it very well. That was an interesting thing—when he could not express himself in English, he would speak French.

When I tested for the part of Ambrose in *Dolly!*, Gene asked me if I could dance and I said yes. He said, "Oh, good. Here, do this. We will get it down on film." And he made up a dance and taught it to me and he did it all on his left side. I said, "Oh, could we do it from my right side? I do everything from that side." He said, "Don't worry. I do everything on the left side and I can always reverse it." So, he would choreograph it on the left side and then reverse it because I am right-handed.

During filming he came up to me one time and said, "Tommy, dance better." It just floored me and I knew exactly what he meant—to give it that extra oomph! I was going full-out but he said, "Dance better." Great direction. It was simple, clear, beautiful. I've used it myself.[5]

MICHAEL FEINSTEIN

Singer, songwriter, pianist, and archivist Michael Feinstein is the foremost ambassador and interpreter of the Great American Songbook. A former assistant to Ira Gershwin, in 1988, Feinstein won a Drama Desk Special Award for celebrating American musical theater songs. In 2007, he founded the Great American Songbook Foundation, dedicated to celebrating the art form and preserving it through educational programs, master classes, and the annual High School Songbook Academy. Feinstein is a multi-platinum-selling and five-time Grammy-nominated recording artist and is currently artistic director for the Center for the Performing Arts in Carmel, Indiana.

Summer Stock is very much of its time. Being that—a time capsule—it covers a certain optimism by utilizing an old idea of an old showbiz story. It's a fine example of the MGM factory at its most efficient. Yet from that vantage point, not necessarily knowing that it was one of many films that were turned out on the MGM assembly line, it's remarkably good and holds up on its own. *Summer Stock* doesn't have a weighty message, though it's filled with brilliant moments. Though perhaps not a classic, it contains classic moments. Knowing that television was coming in and the studio system was about to fall apart, they were starting to feel the need to up their game and how to figure out just how to do that. *Summer Stock* is a worthy film and one that I enjoy watching.

I think Judy is wonderful in the film. She had this visceral or natural ability to bring to life whatever she was doing. I don't find any wear and tear in the film. I haven't seen it in a long time, but I did happen to see the "Friendly Star" sequence the other night as I was passing through somewhere and I stopped to watch it. I think that her innate gifts are intact in *Summer Stock* despite what was happening with her.

And Gene in *Summer Stock* is at his most Gene-ius! Being a brilliant man and an intellectual, and one of the architects of the modern musical film, Gene, unlike Fred Astaire, could sometimes be a bit hammy in performance. But, because he was so charming, it was often very endearing. It's just that sometimes his facial expressions feel a little like pandering which seems unnecessary to me in the context of the rest of his work. That nitpicking may seem antithetical to the sublime nature of his choreography and is, perhaps, minor. I think that when one deals with perfection on the level of Gene's, it gives one, perhaps, permission to nitpick because the overall achievement is so great. But make no mistake: I think that he was truly extraordinary.[6]

SARAH URIARTE BERRY

On Broadway, Sarah Uriarte Berry is perhaps most noted for creating the role of Franca in the Lincoln Center Theater's production of The Light in the Piazza, *for which she received Drama Desk and Outer Critics Circle nominations. Prior to that, she appeared as Belle in Disney's* Beauty and the Beast, *Eponine in* Les Misérables, *and as Diana in the Tony Award- and Pulitzer Prize-winning* Next to Normal. *She also appeared in the title role of New York City Opera's production of Rodgers & Hammerstein's* Cinderella. *In addition, Berry has toured extensively in her one-woman show,* For the Love of Judy, *which celebrates the music and life of Judy Garland.*

Okay, I was five. It was in the 1970s. We had a black-and-white television where I lived and I watched *The Wizard of Oz*. I had no idea that it was in color. And years later, when I saw it . . . I think I saw it in a movie theater. Oh my God! It was mind-blowing. I had kind of a weird childhood. My parents were divorced when I was three and my mother became a missionary. I was sent to live on a farm without my parents when I was from age five to eight. So, for me, especially, watching this little girl who was on this farm and she didn't have her mom or her dad, I really connected to that.

I just felt like, here's this little girl. She has brown hair, she has braids, and she's just like me. So, I really related to her because of that. And then, I remember even at age five thinking that it was the most beautiful voice I had ever heard. I mean, I started listening to music when I was probably fifteen months old. My mom played all the MGM albums, all the Disney albums, Barbra Streisand, Julie Andrews, and Ella Fitzgerald—I mean everything. There's tons of music in my life. I just remember at five years old watching Judy and thinking, "This is the most perfect thing I've ever seen."

I sort of became a Judy fanatic. In high school I lived in Fresno. My grandmother, Wanda, lived there and I would go to her house because she had air-conditioning. We did not. And she had tons of Judy albums, the actual albums that you would buy as they came out. I put the albums on. I would lie on the carpet and I would just listen and memorize every inflection. I would spend hours trying to become that voice.

Judy is still relevant because she's a phenomenal actress. It's occurred to me that so many of those MGM performers, and Broadway performers for that matter, have a great look and they have beautiful voices, but Judy infused such brilliant acting chops and how to really convey a lyric. She knew how to tell a story. She knew how to take a song and go into the song and surround herself with the song so that it really felt like it was coming out of her being. It was her producing this from her own soul. A lot of the time, you can see the acting; you can see the manipulation when a performer is singing. It's really hard to catch her doing that.

I teach singing over Zoom, private voice lessons, and I talk about Judy often. I tell my kids to watch her. I say, "You need to watch her because she's not putting voice first. She's putting the lyric first." She also happens to have this glorious flawless instrument that's God-given. When you see something that is absolutely rooted in honesty and truth and it's so flawlessly executed, that's what lasts. Every era has its tinkerers and its conquerors and you forget those people. And every era has artists that are truly great; they are the ones that last.

Judy could sing in an alto register and a mixed register. She even had soprano notes. I mean, she just used whatever part of her voice was suitable to communicate the music which, I think, is genius. No matter how silly and goofy the melody, she somehow was able to tap into it and try to connect with what the composer was trying to communicate through the notes.

She could take whatever was thrown at her and she could figure out how to make it work and how to make it honest. Also, I think she completely let down her guard and let everything that was inside just bubble up and she wasn't afraid of connecting to that part of herself; to let it come through the work. So many people try to manufacture that, and she just let it happen.[7]

MIRANDA GARRISON

Miranda Garrison is an actress and choreographer best known for choreographing dozens of films and television shows, including the two-part TV mini-series Life with Judy Garland: Me and My Shadows, *starring Judy Davis. Garrison was a dancer in the 1980 film* Xanadu, *which featured Gene Kelly.*

Gene was so clever in the "squeaky board" dance in *Summer Stock* because he wanders in with pedestrian body movement; just a guy alone with an optimistic whistle and he ends the number like that. He was a man's man—a scrappy can-do guy—and he had that Irish charm and that smile and you knew he was a good guy but that he would tease the ladies. And always the girl had to say "no" like she's got a little "Marian the Librarian" thing going on, but through Gene's charm she warms up, like Judy Garland eventually did.

And let's not forget the hours and hours it took to create that "squeaky board" solo. He would have come to the plate already a master tap dancer, but to make something look like it's off the cuff, easy-breezy like that? And then to coordinate the camera movement! I'd love to know how they did the squeak—we're bringing in props; we're bringing in the costume department; we're bringing in the cameraman; we're bringing in the choreographer almost as writer—it's a full-blown narrative, that little scene.

I was with Gene during the American Zoetrope experience [the now-defunct film studio created in the late 1970s by directors Francis Ford Coppola and George Lucas]. He was professional to the bones and did not suffer fools well. He was highly intellectual and multilingual.

I think both Fred Astaire and Gene Kelly will be icons forever, especially, going forward via YouTube. I taught for ten years at USC and I would show film clips and the young people absolutely loved Gene Kelly. I don't think he'll ever go away and I dare anybody in their deepest depression to go on YouTube and watch the title number from *Singin' in the Rain* and not just feel completely transformed into joy.

Gene really represented something that, sadly, I don't see very much in evidence right now in America. He represented the best of the 1950s; the scrappy guy, optimistic, still playful, all the hope in the world, encompassing some of the best feeling that America has produced.[8]

JOAN ELLISON

Joan Ellison is a critically acclaimed concert singer specializing in the Great American Songbook. She has made a specialty of reviving Garland's repertoire from Judy's Hollywood years to her Carnegie Hall concert and television show, including restoring Garland's original song orchestrations. Ellison almost always includes "Get Happy" from Summer Stock *in her concert set.*

My parents bought me *The Wizard of Oz* album—that's really dating myself. But I had the album; this was in the early 1970s, and I just fell in love with the whole thing, but especially "Over the Rainbow." I mean there was music on at home, but really that was the first time I had that kind of a vocal model, and something about that song and that singer just really spoke to me. I think it was the longing in the song and just the quality of her voice and I just decided I wanted to be a singer at that point and that was that. I gotta say, though, I saw it on a black-and-white TV and I remember being terrified of the Wicked Witch of the West. I would run and hide under the couch; it was that bad.

I think Judy's a-once-in-possibly-500-years artist. I don't think we're going to see that kind of artist again just because of what her God-given gifts were and the upbringing and the hours she logged and the training she got. First of all, just the quality of Judy's voice is so unique and so direct. I feel like when she sings there are no barriers between the song and her whole life experience. You can't see the seams anywhere. She has a tremendous amount of musicality and she puts it all together in a way that is uniquely her and uniquely expressive and that can just melt through any barriers the audience may have and it just goes straight into your heart. It bypasses everything else and shoots straight in. I don't know how she learned to do that and I'm not sure she knew how she learned to do that, but it's magical and unique.

As far as "Get Happy" is concerned, in *Summer Stock* it is pure joy and so understated. She doesn't overplay it one tiny bit. It's all style and the staging and performance of it elevates the song way above what was maybe originally on the paper. It's so ageless and I don't know how it could have been improved on. I mean, there's nothing I could think of—the costuming, that backdrop with the pink and the white clouds, and the dancers. It's hard not to watch Judy because your eyes are glued to her, but if you make yourself watch the other things going on around her, those dancers are incredible, and the choreography is so inventive.[9]

MIKHAIL BARYSHNIKOV

Considered one of the greatest dancers of our time, after a spectacular career with the Kirov Ballet in Leningrad, Baryshnikov came to the West in 1974, settling in New York City as principal dancer with American Ballet Theatre (ABT). In 1978 he joined New York City Ballet, where he worked with George Balanchine and Jerome Robbins. A year later he was appointed artistic director of ABT where, for the next decade, he introduced and shepherded a new generation of dancers and choreographers. As an actor he has performed widely on and off Broadway, as well as in television and film, receiving a Tony Award nomination and a Drama Desk Award nomination for Metamorphosis, *and a Best Supporting Actor Academy Award nomination in 1977 for the ballet movie* The Turning Point.

I vaguely remember seeing bits of *An American in Paris* when I was in my twenties and when I was still in the Soviet Union. I didn't know anything about American movies, or tap, or anything American really, but I recall being impressed with how open, how accessible Gene Kelly seemed onscreen—"a normal Joe" as I later came to understand.

Gene was great looking, smart, had an impeccable technique, and he was always authentic. He was also intensely creative. He made dance the star of so many stories. And no wonder the "squeaky board and newspaper" solo is his favorite. It's inventive, relaxed, and ingenious in its simplicity and casualness. It's also as fresh now as when it was filmed. Amazing!

There'll certainly be scholars writing fat books about American movie musicals and Kelly will be part of that conversation, but I think as long as people can see him on screen he'll continue to be relevant. People don't forget that kind of brilliance. I have to say that I had the privilege to get to know him a little towards the end of his life, and with all that talent and star power, he was one of the most generous and warm people I've had the pleasure to know.[10]

MARILYN MICHAELS

Marilyn Michaels is best known for people she isn't. *As a singer and mimic, she's famous for her penetrating impressions of, among others, Barbra Streisand, Dinah Shore, Diana Ross, Eartha Kitt, and Judy Garland. Throughout a long career, Michaels has appeared alongside hosts as diametrically opposite as Ed Sullivan and Howard Stern and on such TV shows as* The Kopykats, The Love Boat, Regis and Kathie Lee, *and* Hollywood Squares, *to name just a few.*

I can't recall when I first saw or heard Judy, but in the early 1950s she was performing at the Palace Theatre and my uncle took me to see her—box seats, no less! That made a big impression on me; even though she was hoarse, the audience still went wild. It is difficult to name the mysterious quality that goes into making a star. Many try to put it into words and it's not easy, it's something indefinable, special, a charisma, and in Judy's case, talent that consisted of that throbbing voice that cuts into your soul as well as the intelligence that comes with being a superb comedienne and actress who could tap into her deepest self. All these qualities went into making Judy that adored icon.

The main thing that *Summer Stock* has going for it is "Get Happy," because Judy was wrestling with a weight problem then and would for many years. She was a tiny individual and any extra poundage was impossible on the screen. Screen actors must be very buff and very thin. There is so much anorexia in this profession (read Diane Keaton's book). So Judy, having lost weight, finally got to where she looked great and did the number which was possibly the first time she looked stylish *and* sexy. Couple that with a great vocal and choreography, and a set that was equally stylish (slashes of pinks and blacks), and you had movie magic.

Judy could work with anyone if she was feeling well, and up to it. She was brilliant with James Mason in *A Star Is Born* and at her most charming and seemingly relaxed with Fred Astaire in *Easter Parade*, which is my main happy, go-to movie. Her comic timing and charm are on full display in that film. The "Couple of Swells" number she did with Fred as a hobo—more magic. Who else could have done that with such gamine charm?

Her TV shows showcase her vocal powers and, later in life, her intense emotional problems, with the addictions, added to her fragility, which is a sad statement. But like many icons, their personal lives become part of their persona. Addictions die hard and the pressure is always there. Each time you walk out on that stage, you are under a microscope.[11]

MANDY MOORE

Moore is a four-time Emmy nominee and world-class director, choreographer, and dancer best known for her work on the television reality show So You Think You Can Dance *and, most recently, the smash-hit movie* La La Land. *Moore also choreographed David O. Russell's Oscar-nominated film* Silver Linings Playbook *with Bradley Cooper and Jennifer Lawrence.*

I think you would have to be dead inside not to think that Gene's dancing in *Summer Stock* is incredible. I think a lot of the movement he does—say, an attitude turn or triple pirouettes or a barrel jump turn—or a lot of the tap rhythms are still things that are done today, and he does them very well. So, I think for that part of it people would recognize his dancing and see it for its technical greatness, if for nothing else. But I also think he was a magnetic performer.

The DNA of the storytelling of the dance is what I really believe is what draws people in and why people love numbers like his "squeaky board" or "Dig-Dig-Dig Dig for Your Dinner," or "The Portland Fancy" duet he does with Judy. Who is to say if another person did it, it would be as strong? probably not. But I would still think those numbers would be incredible even with someone other than Gene Kelly because the storytelling is so strong in them. He, of course, makes them—particularly his solo with the board and newspaper—like, out of this world. But do I think people would be surprised to think that it was filmed seventy years ago, are you kidding me? Like, really, who is doing anything even remotely like that now? I'll tell you who—nobody![12]

VICTORIA MORRIS

Victoria Morris is the president and CEO of Lexikat Artists, a managing agency specializing in theatre directors, writers, and choreographers. As one of the entertainment industry's first dance agents, during the commercial dance market explosion in Los Angeles and the advent of MTV, Morris represented young and innovative dance talent from around the world. She serves on the board of directors of Broadway Dreams and is a consultant for the Miracle Project. As a dancer, Morris worked with Gene Kelly in the 1980 film Xanadu.

My knowledge of Gene Kelly actually deepened when I did *Xanadu* because we were told at one of the first rehearsals that Gene Kelly was going to be in the movie. At the time, you didn't have Google or anything like that. Everybody went to the library, did whatever we could do and watched his old movies. Kenny Ortega [choreographer of *Xanadu*] was a huge fan of Kelly's.

For me, the story about Gene Kelly is twofold. One, I think, in a way, he was mesmerized by this new dance scene that was upon us then and that he was thrown into for the shoot of *Xanadu*. Also, he had to tap dance with Olivia [Newton-John]. Olivia was not a great tap dancer. I have to say that he was very patient there. By the time we were shooting the finale, I think he was looking around. It was such chaos and madness. It was a typical 1980s film set; a lot of stuff going on. I'm not so sure he appreciated all that. He really wanted everyone to be very disciplined and grateful for the fact that they were working and doing this film, and to take it more seriously. There were probably 120 or more extras around at any time. It was a little bit like *The Wizard of Oz*. There were all these people that were day-players. I think that he probably enjoyed the film, but I also think that he was just really baffled by the whole scenario.

For a lot of us, this was our first film. There's lots of time on a film set where there's nothing going on but there was just drugs, sex, and rock 'n' roll happening everyplace you looked. There was cocaine on the set. It was a typical 1980s musical set, really. I'm not saying that it was bad. I'm just saying even myself as an eighteen-year-old, I was looking around going, "Whoa, this is fun!" There were lots of parties. It was a set on the Universal lot and it was very chaotic.

If I looked at what was going on through Gene's eyes, he was clearly on a lot of sets, musical sets during his era, I'm sure they were chaotic, too. I also think that he was a star and he had a lot of control. But he didn't have control in *Xanadu*. I don't know why he did the movie. I think it's great that he did. My guess is that he did it as a favor for Kenny.

For me, one moment stood out during filming. A lot of people—kids that were not professionals—were on the set. Anytime they saw a camera, all they wanted was to be in the shot. They weren't thinking of the greater good of the project the way Gene always did. I could tell that just by being in his presence. I was standing there. He just looked at me and he said, "Just don't pad your parts, kids." I still remember that because I thought, "Gosh, what does he mean by that? It's Gene Kelly and he said something to me!" It was a lesson that less is more when you're in front of the camera.

I think the thing about Gene is that he was constantly pushing the boundaries of what you could do, not only as a dancer but as an artist. He was an American dance innovator. But it's not like what we have today. The world is different and larger. If a TikTok video goes viral in this day and age, it's not going to create a Gene Kelly. I think that anyone that you show older clips to of Gene, they're going to be impressed; they can't *not* be impressed. But I don't know if they'd grasp that he was a conceptual artist. You can't call him just a dancer. That was one of his tools, but he was a conceptual artist. He was curious all the time. He was never going to rest on his laurels. I don't know if he was ever satisfied; I don't think he was.

Gene was an idea generator. He would go into a studio or wherever and try to figure out what he was doing and how he was going to film something. I think his era was exciting. The sky was the limit for him. If somebody said, "Hey, can you dance on top of this giant sphere?" Gene would have figured out how to do that. He was a puzzle-solver.[13]

KEYS DATES IN THE MAKING OF *SUMMER STOCK*

December 1948	MGM options Sy Gomberg's original screenplay; Judy Garland and Gene Kelly are announced for the lead roles in the movie to be called *Summer Stock*.
February 1949	June Allyson now named as one of the leads (replacing Garland) of *Summer Stock*.
June 14, 1949	Garland again announced as the star of *Summer Stock*.
August 1949	Garland attends pre-production meetings for the film.
October 1949	Rehearsals for *Summer Stock* begin.
October 13, 1949	The first recording sessions for the film begin. "If You Feel Like Singing, Sing" and "(Howdy Neighbor) Happy Harvest" are recorded.
October 31, 1949	After missing six of the first twenty days of pre-production work on *Summer Stock*, Garland receives a "warning letter" from MGM. She asks to be released from working on the film but MGM studio chief Louis B. Mayer convinces her otherwise.
November 21, 1949	Filming begins. "If You Feel Like Singing, Sing," is the first number shot.
December 1949	Additional songs are composed for the film ("You Wonderful You," "All for You," and "Heavenly Music"), pushing back the production schedule.
Mid-February 1950	Garland "wraps" her work on *Summer Stock*.
Early March 1950	It's decided that another number (a "show-stopper") is needed for the film, and the Harold Arlen–Ted Koehler song "Get Happy" is chosen.
March 15, 1950	Garland returns to the studio to record and film "Get Happy."

April 1950	Kelly films his solo dance with the squeaky board and newspaper.
April 5, 1950	*Summer Stock* wraps production.
May 11, 1950	A preview screening of *Summer Stock* is held in Los Angeles.
August 31, 1950	*Summer Stock* is released nationwide to mostly favorable reviews.
September 11, 1950	While on a shopping trip to New York City, Garland attends a late-night screening of *Summer Stock* at the Capitol Theatre. After the film, she exits the theater to thunderous applause and cheering fans follow her car. Next day, Garland tells columnist Earl Wilson that the response was "astonishing and wonderful."
September 29, 1950	Garland is released from her MGM contract and leaves the studio after fifteen years and twenty-eight feature films.

THE CAST AND PRODUCTION CREW OF *SUMMER STOCK**

METRO-GOLDWYN-MAYER
PRESENTS
SUMMER STOCK
RELEASED ON AUGUST 31, 1950
RUNNING TIME: 109 MINUTES
COLOR BY TECHNICOLOR
TITLE IN THE UK: *IF YOU FEEL LIKE SINGING*

CAST

Judy Garland (Jane Falbury)
Gene Kelly (Joe D. Ross)
Eddie Bracken (Orville Wingait)
Gloria DeHaven (Abigail Falbury)
Marjorie Main (Esme)
Phil Silvers (Herb Blake)
Ray Collins (Jasper G. Wingait)
Nita Bieber (Sarah Higgins)
Carleton Carpenter (Artie)
Hans Conried (Harrison I. Keath)

*Many on this list did not receive screen credit

Members of the stock company

Bridget Carr
Jeanne Coyne
Carol Haney
Jean Adcock
Joanne Tree
Rena Lenart
Joan Dale
Betty Hannon
Elynne Ray
Marilyn Reiss
Dorothy Tuttle
Carol West
Arthur Loew Jr.
Eugene Freedley
Dick Humphreys
Don Powell
Joe Roach
Albert Ruiz
Jimmy Thompson
Johnny Duncan

Erville Alderson (Zeb)
Paul E. Burns (Frank)
Eddie Dunn (Sheriff)
Jack Gargan (Clerk)
Almira Sessions (Constance Fliggerton)
Kathryn Sheldon (Amy Fliggerton)

Showgirls

Bette Arlen
Bunny Waters
Alice Wallace
Meredith Leeds
Lorraine Crawford

Dancers

John Brascia
Luigi Faccuito
Bert May

Boys

Michael Chapin
Teddy Infuhr

Prospective Producers of "Fall in Love"

Cameron Grant
Jack Daley
Reginald Simpson

Townsmen

Roy Butler
Henry Sylvester
George Bunny
Frank Pharr
Slim Gaut
Jimmie Horan
Dick Johnstone
Al Kunde
Alan Sewall

Townswomen

Nora Bush
Ann Kunde

Margaret Bert (woman at barn dance)
Joe Ploski (man at barn dance)

Pete Roberts (vocal dubbing)
Maurice "Muzzy" Marcelino (dubbed Gene Kelly's whistling in the squeaky board/newspaper dance)

Production Crew

Joe Pasternak (producer)
Charles Walters (director)
George Wells and Sy Gomberg (screenplay)
Sy Gomberg (story)
Harry Warren (music)
Mack Gordon (lyrics)
Harold Arlen, Ted Koehler, Saul Chaplin, and Jack Brooks (additional songs)
Johnny Green and Saul Chaplin (musical directors)
Nick Castle (choreographer)
Robert Planck (director of photography)
Henri Jaffa and James Gooch (Technicolor color consultants)
Cedric Gibbons and Jack Martin Smith (art directors)
Albert Akst (film editor)
Conrad Salinger and Skip Martin (orchestrations)
Douglas Shearer (recording supervisor)
Edwin B. Wills (set decorations)
Alfred E. Spencer (associate set decorator)
Walter Plunkett (costumes)
Helen Rose (Gloria DeHaven's costumes)
Sydney Guilaroff (hair stylist)
Helene Parish (hair stylist)
William J. Tuttle (makeup artist)
Dorothy Ponedel (makeup artist)
John Truwe (makeup artist)
Al Jennings (assistant director)
Joseph Ruttenberg (photographer)
Otto Dyar (still photographer)
Harkness Smith (camera operator)
Alfred Spencer (associate set director)
Lew Roberts (gaffer)
Robert Franklyn (orchestrator)

John A. Williams (sound)
Bob Osgood (co-director of square dance sequences)
Hugh Boswell (production manager)
Les Martinson (screenplay supervisor)
Tom Long (grip)
Uan Rasey (musician, trumpet soloist)

ACKNOWLEDGMENTS

WRITING A "MAKING OF" BOOK LIKE THIS, WE WERE CONFRONTED AT THE outset by a major challenge: Unlike the Arthur Freed–produced musicals at MGM, which had voluminous archives attached to them detailing budgets, shooting days, and containing other illuminating interoffice memoranda and correspondence, there was a distinct paucity of information related to *Summer Stock*. Producer Joe Pasternak did not preserve personal papers relating to any of his films. So telling the story of *Summer Stock* was like assembling a jigsaw puzzle from various pieces scattered not across a table but in different rooms—a daunting prospect to be sure, and one we could never have accomplished without the dedicated effort of an army of individuals who shared their time, expertise, and perspectives on *Summer Stock* and the many artists associated with the film.

In addition, we came to find out that a worldwide pandemic presents unforeseen obstacles—and a few opportunities. As researchers and writers, it has afforded us ample time (as we, along with most of the rest of the world, were hunkered down for months on end) to sit at our keyboards and write. It also freed up some normally extremely busy people for phone, Zoom, and email interviews. For the curators who worked with us, the pandemic provided unique challenges; they had to access needed information, in many cases remotely, when libraries and other research venues were shut down. Like the movie musical itself, writing a book of this kind takes a collaborative effort, and we're eternally grateful to all the people who've helped us tell the story of this film.

First, to dancer and choreographer extraordinaire Savion Glover, who discovered the joys of *Summer Stock* and shared that discovery with our readers; Tom Early, who scouted for us the location in the San Fernando Valley where Judy Garland performed the "Happy Harvest" number; John Fricke, the world's foremost authority on Judy Garland, who encouraged our taking on this project and who took the time over some long, memorable meals in New York City to share his insights and expertise; Brent Phillips, biographer of director Charles Walters, for his insights; George Feltenstein, historian at Warner Bros., who has done so much to keep the flame of these classic films burning bright with a new generation of fans; Jamie Harris, who made so many invaluable connections for us, not the least of which are Lorna Luft and Savion Glover; Scott Brogan, Garland historian and purveyor of the Judy Room (www.thejudyroom.com); the incomparable Michael Feinstein, singer, pianist, and expert on Golden Age musicals and the men and women who interpreted the Great American Songbook; and Howard Mendelbaum, photo archivist and owner of Photofest.

A special thanks to the curators, researchers, and librarians who fielded our endless requests for information: Franklin Robinson, the National Museum of American History at the Smithsonian; Christina Jensen, the DeGolyer Library at Southern Methodist University; Dr. Sandra Garcia-Myers, USC Cinematic Arts Library and Archives; Ned Comstock (retired) from USC; Emily Wittenberg, the American Film Institute; Kristine Krueger, Margaret Herrick Library, Academy of Motion Picture Arts and Sciences; Claudia Thompson, American Heritage Center, University of Wyoming; Jane Parr, Howard Gotlieb Archival Research Center, Boston University Libraries; the Media History Digital Library, led by Eric Hoyt; and the Wisconsin Center for Film and Theater Research.

To the following who aided us in ways great and small, we are in your debt: Richard Glazier, Cynthia Brideson, Paula Ehrenfeld, Connie Francis, Lorna Luft, Mario Cantone, Leslie Caron, Paula Prentiss, Twyla Tharp, Susan Stroman, Mikhail Baryshnikov, Tommy Tune, Brenda Buffalino, Michael Chapin, Stephanie Powers. Joan Ellison, Miranda Garrison, Brett Halsey, Kim Lundgreen, Ben Vereen, Nick Castle Jr., Kerry Kelly Novak, Katherine Blake, Mandy Moore, Victoria Morris, Roxanne Messina Captor, Christiane Noll, David Jenkins, Corey John Snide, Jennifer Berzin, Jeff Pasternak, Roger Gordon, Trilby Conried, Marilyn Michaels, Michael Troyan, Frank Santopadre, Kelli Marshall, Julia Riva, Jean-Paul Riva, Richard Eyer, Bill Biss, Jack Campey, Sam Scalamoni, Chris Gomberg, Earl Hess, Pratibha Dabholkar, Craig Damon, Pamela Cooper, Ron Roberts, Huong Hoang, Chris Yogerst, Ivy Faulkner, and Margaret O'Brien.

And we wouldn't have been able to provide so many firsthand accounts and insights into the production of *Summer Stock* if it wasn't for these one-of-a-kind talents who are no longer with us and who, over the past forty-plus years, were kind enough to share their time with two classic film fans from the Midwest: Gene Kelly, Harry Warren, Charles Walters, Eddie Bracken, Carleton Carpenter, André Previn, Esther Williams, Kathryn Grayson, Jo-Carroll Denison, Hal Prince, Fayard Nicholas, Harold Nicholas, Vincente Minnelli, Cyd Charisse, Robert Stack, Alice Faye, Mel Tormé, Nick Perito, Burton Lane, Stanley Donen, and Milton Berle.

Big thanks to Dan Augustine, who designed the eye-catching book cover.

Lastly, to our editor at the University Press of Mississippi, Emily Bandy, and the team that has supported this project every step of the way, Pete Halverson, Jordan Nettles Rueff, Shane Gong Stewart, and Will Rigby: Many thanks.

APPENDIX I

SETTING THE TEMPO

Johnny Green and the MGM Orchestra

IN ACCEPTING THE 1985 AFI LIFE ACHIEVEMENT AWARD, GENE KELLY SPOKE about all the people who contributed to making MGM musicals unparalleled and without peer. Of the men who arranged the music, Kelly said, "If they weren't around, all our dances would've been flat!" Kelly certainly had people like Johnny Green in mind when he made his remarks.

Perhaps more than anyone else, Green is responsible for the lush, swinging sound of MGM musicals during their heyday in the late 1940s and early 1950s. Conductor of Metro's orchestra for the recording of the music tracks of *Summer Stock*, Green's prowess with a baton and as the studio's music director (he assumed both posts at MGM in 1949) partly sprang from the fact that he was also a songwriter—and a good one. "Body and Soul" and "I Cover the Waterfront" are two of his tunes.

We reached out to American songbook expert Michael Feinstein to tell us why Green was such an integral contributing factor to the sound (and success) of so many Golden Age MGM musicals, including *Summer Stock*:

• • •

Johnny Green was a good friend of mine and I spent a lot of time with him in his later years. He was very proud of the work that he did at MGM because he fundamentally changed the entire music department in a way that was quite extraordinary. But Johnny was a man with a very healthy ego and it sometimes got in the way. And in retrospect, people seem to focus more on his emotional makeup rather than his extraordinary achievements as a musician. For example, Uan Rasey, the great first trumpet at Metro, never forgave Johnny for some of his behavior at the studio. And indeed Johnny himself later regretted the way he had treated people when he became head of the music department. He was filled with regret and literally in tears. Rasey plays the raucous "Chocolat" trumpet solo that begins the Toulouse-Lautrec section of the ballet in *An American in Paris* and he likely played the trumpet break on "The Portland Fancy" in *Summer Stock*.

But putting all of that aside, Johnny accomplished a number of things at MGM. He recognized that the orchestra had a makeup that included some players who were not at the top of their game. The sad thing is that he retired some of them when they were only weeks or a couple of months away from getting their retirement package. And that was unfortunate. The result of his restructuring—the orchestra itself was considered to be one of the two finest orchestras in Hollywood [the other being Twentieth Century-Fox]. Johnny had an innate ability to hear orchestral colors and sounds and translate them from his imagination into reality. So, he knew how to create a certain mood, musically. That was a perfect skill set to have for the movie industry.

Johnny's desire to restructure the orchestra was part of his vision for the MGM music department. In the late 1940s, of course, music was changing a great deal and MGM was sometimes slow to keep up with the changing musical tastes. For example, Nathaniel Finston (MGM music director) left the studio, from what I can figure, because of a dispute over the overall style of the music being featured in motion pictures then. Finston was part of the "old school" and preferred operetta and classical music and didn't like the encroachment of swing music, which was becoming the standard sound of musicals even in the mid- to late-1930s. Finston left and MGM was, in certain ways, adrift and trying to find its musical identity, although one wouldn't believe or consider that when watching (and listening to) the Arthur Freed musicals. But there was no clear direction from the top as to what the sound or style of the MGM musical should be. And when Johnny came in, he had a very clear vision about the sound and the feel of musicals.

Once Johnny became head of the MGM music department, he instituted other changes that are reflected, for example, in the conductor books that are only the surviving examples of MGM musical scores. The conductor books notated all the orchestration for all the numbers or songs in any MGM film. Before Johnny came in, the books were comparatively rudimentary, in contrast to the very detailed conductor scores that Johnny had the copyists create.

So he was meticulous and methodical and demanded a higher standard in the way the music department was run and the way the librarians worked—in the way it was all prepared. Sometimes it was a bit excessive when, for example, Johnny, for all the motion pictures that he personally worked on as a conductor or composer, had custom score paper printed with the name of the film in the lower corner. That insistence resulted in a lot of surplus score paper after the films were completed which ended up in piles in his home and lived there many years after the films themselves had became a dim memory.

Johnny acoustically redesigned the famous soundstage at MGM. I don't know where that ability or knowledge about acoustics came from, but he understood how to create the best orchestral sound and was heavily involved in the recording process and the way that the sounds of the orchestra were captured on film. He was also a pioneer in the switch from optical film to recording on magnetic film, which all happened around that time. I believe it was *An American in Paris* that was the first film that actually used magnetic recording. Johnny was at the forefront because he had more knowledge of the technical side of recording and how it affected the music than most other people. Johnny was largely self-taught and so it's extraordinary that he was able to realize all of that latent ability.

He slaved over creating scores. Orchestration did not come easily for him. He was not facile as compared, for example, to Al Sendrey, who was a very facile though largely uncredited orchestrator. Sendrey became Johnny's main musical amanuensis and would help realize Johnny's short scores, his sketch scores, and turn them into full-blown scores, just to save time. So, Johnny also became a hero to composers at MGM because Metro had a habit (or a policy, if you will) of when a film was in preview, they didn't wait for it to be scored; they would have their stock music librarian score the film for previews, and often the producers would want to keep some stock music scores, making it very difficult for composers to create their own score after the producers had fallen in love with the stock score.

I forget the name of the man who was in charge of the stock library, but he literally knew these hundreds and even thousands of different musical cues and could slot in the different kinds of music needed for any given underscore cue. Johnny stopped that because he was a champion of the creative process and didn't want composers to have to go through the humiliation of having to deal with producers who wanted to keep a canned score versus an original one. He also famously rescued David Raksin's theme from *The Bad and the Beautiful* [1952] by suggesting a change in the instrumentation at the recording session that turned it from a failed main title to an iconic one. Specifically, with *Summer Stock*, knowing that Skip Martin's first job at MGM was scoring "Get Happy," that would have come under Johnny's responsibilities. And so it is certainly to his credit that he brought Skip to MGM, who then went on to define, with Conrad Salinger, the MGM sound throughout the 1950s.

Johnny was also very meticulous about the assembly of main titles and even got involved in the construction of a song where he made suggestions. For example, in Cole Porter's song "I Love You, Samantha" from *High Society*, he asked Porter about changing some notes. Porter agreed and the changes made the song better. The song "Be My Love" from *The Toast of New Orleans* did not have a musical tag; that is the iconic part of that number and it was Johnny's suggestion. So, it is my educated guess that Johnny was very involved in bringing the *Summer Stock* score to fruition through the travails of Mack Gordon being fired and having Saul Chaplin involved in writing the extra songs, because Johnny was the guy where the buck stopped! And so, even though the score of *Summer Stock* is patchwork—not all the work of one composing team—it is all of a piece and that would be as much Johnny's doing as it would be anyone else's.

I hope this ramble helps illuminate the musical atmosphere that pervaded MGM when *Summer Stock* was being made.

APPENDIX II

ARRANGEMENTS HAVE BEEN MADE

Conrad Salinger and Skip Martin and the "MGM Sound"

NO OTHER FILM STUDIO DURING HOLLYWOOD'S GOLDEN AGE TOOK MUSICALS more seriously or did them better than MGM. The luster of those movies owes a huge debt to the thick rank of below-the-line experts who worked diligently behind the scenes and, in the bargain, rarely registered name recognition with the moviegoing public. That's certainly true of the men and women who provided the musical accompaniment to Metro musicals great and small: the gifted musicians who comprised the MGM orchestra and the talented individuals who took the melodies of such greats as George Gershwin, Cole Porter, Irving Berlin, and Harry Warren and arranged and orchestrated them into what has been described as the "MGM sound"—a unique aural stamp that was instantly recognizable.

Two of those unsung heroes responsible for bringing MGM musical scores to life worked together on *Summer Stock*—Conrad Salinger (August 30, 1901–June 17, 1962) and Skip Martin (May 14, 1916–February 12, 1976).

Salinger, called Connie by his friends and colleagues, was born in Brookline, Massachusetts, in 1901, and took an early interest in music, graduating from Harvard and then studying at the prestigious Paris Conservatoire. Although he provided arrangements for several Broadway productions in the 1930s, it is his work in movies where Salinger excelled.

In Hollywood in 1937, Salinger began working freelance as an arranger for composer Alfred Newman at Twentieth Century-Fox. His first MGM assignment came a year later when he orchestrated "The Jitterbug" for *The Wizard of Oz,* a number cut from the film but from which the recording and grainy archival footage survives. At the time, producer Arthur Freed was building his musical "unit" in the early 1940s, and at the urging of Freed's right-hand man Roger Edens, Salinger signed a long-term studio contract with the studio and would play a big part in creating the distinctive MGM musical sound over the next two decades. Salinger's contributions as an arranger include the musicals *Meet Me in St. Louis, Summer Stock, Royal Wedding, An American in Paris, Show Boat, The Band Wagon, Seven Brides for Seven Brothers*, and *Gigi*.

Author Hugh Fordin rated Salinger's orchestration of "The Trolley Song" from *Meet Me in St. Louis* a masterpiece: "It conveyed all the color, the motion, the excitement that eventually was going to be seen on the screen . . . Salinger always maintained sonority and texture in his writing, which made his a very special sound and style that has never been equaled in the American movie musical."[1]

According to Fordin, most musical directors, arrangers, and orchestrators working during that period operated via the maxim: "The bigger the orchestra, the larger the vocal group—the bigger and better the sound." In Fordin's estimation, Salinger's writing sounded best with thirty-six or thirty-eight musicians.[2]

Jack Campey, the artistic director and principal conductor of the United Kingdom–based Studio Orchestra, a sixty-five-to-eighty-piece professional symphony orchestra dedicated to the performance of music from film, theater, and television, called Salinger the "best" of all the Hollywood orchestrators:

> There is no doubt that Salinger's musical contribution helped define the MGM musical. There wouldn't have been the opening vamp to *Singin' in the Rain*, or the buzz and excitement of "The Trolley Song" in *Meet Me in St Louis*. He was as much theatrical as he was musical. He always understood the assignment and took it to places that many thought weren't possible. It is incomprehensible to think of an MGM musical without acknowledging his craft and genius. There's never been anyone quite like him since.
>
> Salinger had a vast orchestral palette. Although not as adept at doing jazz as Skip Martin was, it was his lush extended ballet sequences [the "An American in Paris" ballet and the "Broadway Melody" ballet from *Singin' in the Rain*] that were his trademark. He

> was able to take a simple melody and stretch it out into some of the most lavish orchestral sequences, taking the number to places that were almost transcendent. He pushed the orchestra players to the limit; for example, French horns would be up in the stratosphere, playing soaring countermelodies. On the other hand, the string voicing could go from dense division creating a plush cushion of sound, to delicate gentle playing. He mastered his craft studying in France during the 1920s, and the impressionist styles/orchestration of Ravel and Debussy are rife within his arrangements. His orchestrations and arrangements are full of color and deep texture.[3]

When Johnny Green began his decade-long tenure as musical director of Metro and head of the studio orchestra in 1949, he expanded the number of musicians to a full symphonic complement.*

Salinger easily adapted to these changes, as is reflected in his orchestrations during that period. As musicals faded in audience popularity and the studio system collapsed, Salinger continued to work, mostly in television, until his untimely death in 1962 at the age of sixty-one.

Lloyd Vernon "Skip" Martin was born in Robinson, Illinois, in 1916 and along with Salinger would be the driving force in creating the lush orchestrations that informed MGM musicals, including *Summer Stock*. Before coming to work at MGM, Martin was one of the architects of the swinging sound that defined the big band era that peaked between 1935 and the end of World War II. Martin, who died in 1976 at the age of seventy, worked with Count Basie, Charlie Barnet, Benny Goodman, and Glenn Miller, often doubling as an arranger and alto sax player. His biggest chart-topper was his arrangement of the Irving Berlin standard "I've Got My Love to Keep Me Warm" for Les Brown in 1949, although it was recorded in 1946.[4]

Johnny Green brought Martin to MGM in 1949 just as he was expanding and revamping the sound of the MGM orchestra. Martin's first assignments at the studio were for two Joe Pasternak productions: *Duchess of Idaho* (1950), starring Esther Williams, and *Summer Stock*. In quick succession, Martin

*Two jazz musicians at MGM during this period of change were clarinetist Gus Bivona and trombonist Jack Teagarden. Bivona was a longstanding MGM staff musician who had gigged with Benny Goodman, Les Brown, and Tommy Dorsey and later would be sidekick to comedian Steve Allen. Teagarden, along with Benny Goodman, Glenn Miller, Gene Krupa, and Jimmy Dorsey, was in the legendary 1927 pit band (the Red Nichols Orchestra) for the Gershwins' *Strike Up the Band* on Broadway, and later recorded a series of popular Dixieland albums. Both musicians were featured on the *An American in Paris* soundtrack and may have contributed uncredited work on *Summer Stock*.

contributed arrangements to scores of musicals, notably *An American in Paris, Royal Wedding, Singin' in the Rain, The Band Wagon, Kiss Me Kate* (1953), *Funny Face* (Paramount, 1957), and *Silk Stockings* (1957).

Two of Martin's orchestrations—both showcasing Judy Garland—personify the jazzier sound he brought with him to MGM: "Get Happy" from *Summer Stock* and "The Man That Got Away" from Garland's Warner Bros. comeback, *A Star Is Born*, released four years after *Summer Stock* and her exit from MGM.

"André Previn told me that Skip Martin's arrangements for MGM always sounded to him like it was the Les Brown Band, which was not a criticism on any level," said Michael Feinstein. "Skip brought a muscularity and swagger to the swing arrangements at MGM that had not existed previously, not on that level. Once Skip arrived, we have a very different kind of swing sound that inhabited the musical life or the overarching feel or sound of MGM. When Garland made 'A Star Is Born,' I would wager that she specifically requested that Skip do the arrangements because it would have been Ray Heindorf's (arranger/conductor at Warner Bros.) job, but it was Skip who did all of those charts."[5]

Campey added:

> Skip Martin was the big band specialist at MGM. If there was a jazzy, brassy number, then it would be assigned to him. Skip added that big band sound to the orchestra, bringing in additional players to the brass sections to make it a four trombones and four trumpets setup for recording sessions of his arrangements (the contracted orchestra at MGM was three and three). He knew exactly how to write for brass and big band in general from his years as an arranger with Les Brown. His brass lines are bold and heavy, his sax lines suave and fluid. He had an impeccable sense of rhythm and pulse, and was the choreographer's dream in that sense. Fred Astaire loved dancing to his arrangements (even more than to Salinger's). Just listen to "Shine on Your Shoes" from *The Band Wagon* or "Clap Yo Hands" from *Funny Face*, both Skip Martin arrangements that fully zing and ping. Strings in his arrangements are really secondary and provide a lush velvet cushion for the big band of orchestra to sit and dance upon.

Both "Get Happy" and "The Man That Got Away" include brilliant brass licks and punctuations throughout that are trademarks of Skip's sound. "The Man That Got Away" demonstrates it's not just the loud/shout choruses he was good at. The beautiful trombone cup mute solo at the beginning and end of this number is haunting and nostalgic. The song itself goes through swings in moods from sensitive melancholy to confident and proud—just genius; bold and punchy; from raucous to refined—jazz![6]

APPENDIX III

SUMMER STOCK FROM VINYL ALBUM TO DIGITAL CD

LIKE THE FILM ITSELF, THE SOUNDTRACK OF *SUMMER STOCK* HAD ITS OWN distinct path from when it was first released on vinyl as a long-playing record in 1950 to the latest and most comprehensive reissue of the music tracks as part of the Rhino/Turner Entertainment CD that came out in 2001. Following is our Q&A with George Feltenstein,[1] WarnerMedia Library historian, and as much a venerated presence at Warner Bros. as the logo'd water tower that looms over the studio lot in Burbank. George produced the Rhino/Turner *Summer Stock* CD and is the answer man for all questions concerning the film's iterations on vinyl and CD.

• • •

Authors: Can you detail for us a bit about the MGM record of *Summer Stock* before Rhino Records produced—actually, *you* produced—their comprehensive CD version of the soundtrack? When was *Summer Stock* first released as a vinyl soundtrack? We seem to remember having a reissue version of the soundtrack in the 1970s when it was also paired with *In the Good Old Summertime* as a vinyl double album. We know that *Summer Stock* sheet music was published in 1950 when the movie came out.

Feltenstein: The first release of the music from *Summer Stock* was as a soundtrack "album" on MGM Records at the time of the film's release in 1950.*

*In addition to the MGM contract that Judy Garland signed on November 21, 1946, she also inked a separate contract with the studio on June 21, 1950, granting her royalties for her solo recordings from *Summer Stock*: "(Howdy Neighbor) Happy Harvest," "If You Feel Like Singing, Sing," "Friendly Star," and "Get Happy." This agreement applied to three different kinds of recordings that were available at that time: singles (one side only), double-sided (one song on each side), and long-playing records containing more than two numbers. The royalties for these formats varied but ranged from 2½ to 5 percent of 90 percent of total retail sales worldwide. The contract also stipulated that for a period of five years, Garland could not re-record these songs for a different label.

There was a 10" LP album, a four-disc 78 RPM album, and a four-disc 45 RPM album. This was at the time the vinyl LP was in its infancy, most people still had older 78 RPM phonographs, and RCA had introduced its competitor to Columbia Records' LP format, the 45 RPM album. The original issue had eight songs from the film:

1. "(Howdy Neighbor) Happy Harvest"—Judy Garland
2. "You Wonderful You"—Gene Kelly
3. "Friendly Star"—Judy Garland
4. "Heavenly Music"—Gene Kelly and Phil Silvers
5. "If You Feel Like Singing, Sing"—Judy Garland
6. "Mem'ry Island"—Gloria de Haven and Pete Roberts (voice double for Hans Conried)
7. "Dig-Dig-Dig Dig for Your Dinner"—Gene Kelly (assisted by Phil Silvers)
8. "Get Happy"—Judy Garland

Of those eight songs, most were presented in their complete form as seen/heard in the film. "Happy Harvest" had a verse that was ultimately not used in the final film. "Heavenly Music" had some edits as well, as did "Dig-Dig-Dig Dig for Your Dinner."

It has to be understood that Jesse Kaye, the original producer of the MGM soundtrack albums, took creative license with having to fit each song to the limits of a 45 or 78 RPM single. In addition, he would make creative choices, such as adding drumbeats where a film had taps.

Summer Stock was later released as a 12" LP in 1955 with *The Pirate*. Six songs from each film were included on the album. "Heavenly Music" and "Mem'ry Island" were removed for this reissue.

The album was out of print for many years thereafter. In 1972, MGM Records was sold by the studio to Polygram, along with a ten-year license on the MGM soundtrack with royalties paid to MGM. In 1973, the new owners of MGM Records saw an opportunity to reissue many of the MGM soundtrack LPs in a series of releases called "Those Glorious MGM Musicals." *Summer Stock* was reissued on a two-disc set not with *In the Good Old Summertime*, but with *Everything I Have Is Yours* and *I Love Melvin*. The eight tracks on the original 1950 release were presented on this set. Twelve of these two-disc sets were released, and sold well, especially after the 1974 release of *That's Entertainment!* brought new interest in MGM musicals. After the ten-year license expired, the rights to the soundtracks reverted to MGM, who licensed them to CBS Songs, Inc., along with the sale of the MGM publishing companies. In the United States, the MGM soundtracks were briefly reissued by MCA Records, and there was a *Summer Stock/Lovely to Look At* album on LP and cassette issued in the 1980s.

The next *Summer Stock* release was in 1990 through CBS Special Products (soon to be renamed Sony Music Special Products). This was a more "complete" album in that the songs were taken seemingly from composite tracks of the film itself (my guess is that they used laserdiscs as an audio source). Six additional tracks were added, including the "Overture," "The Portland Fancy," Gene Kelly's "Newspaper Dance" to "You Wonderful You," Kelly and Garland's reprise of "You Wonderful You," and the finale reprise of "(Howdy Neighbor) Happy Harvest." These albums were curiously produced, and were laden with dialogue, sound effects, footsteps, and the like. The CBS Songs license that made these MGM soundtrack releases possible expired, and was briefly extended by Turner Entertainment until the Rhino/Turner soundtrack joint venture was ready to begin.

Authors: How did your involvement with producing the Rhino *Summer Stock* soundtrack CD come about?

Feltenstein: That is a perfect segue from the end of the last answer. I had always been frustrated by the lack of definitive MGM musical soundtracks. Either you had the MGM Records versions, which were often truncated or altered, or you had these bad-sounding CBS/Sony CDs in the early 1990s lifted off videotapes or laserdiscs. When I first started working at MGM, I learned that most of the original pre-recordings for the studio's films were still extant, and I thought it was an untapped goldmine to make this music available properly. It took many years to get there. The studio transferred most of the recordings from the optical era [pre-1950/51] to quarter-inch reel-to-reel tapes at a not-optimum speed. This was done over a ten-year period, and since it came from nitrate film, not everything had survived when transferred to tape.

Further, MGM had recorded much of their music using multiple microphones in order to get a balanced-mix monaural track. There was no thought of stereophonic recording or a playback process yet for such a thing (with the exception of Disney's experiment with RCA for *Fantasia*, called Fantasound).

However, I began to borrow these tapes and listen to them on weekends over a series of years. It became clear to me that it might be possible to create stereophonic mixes from these "angles," making the prospect of soundtrack recordings anew on CD even more exciting. It also explained for me why, as a child, when I saw *That's Entertainment!* for the first time in theaters, it was the 70mm blowup version with six-track stereo sound, and certain musical numbers such as "On the Atchison, Topeka and the Santa Fe," had actual separation between orchestra, lead vocal, and chorus. And yet I knew even at that early age that stereophonic sound in films didn't arrive until the early 1950s through magnetic recording, yet I knew what I was hearing was genuine stereo. I could not figure it out, and didn't until adulthood and my going through these tapes and understanding how they recorded these songs. Not all songs were done that way, FYI. Some were done with just one microphone, including a great deal of *The Wizard of Oz*.

So we did a test of "The Trolley Song" using the three channels of Judy Garland's vocal, the orchestral channel, and the choral channel. Because of computerized technology we were able to create true stereo and have no "drift" from the tape sources. That led to the creation of releases on VHS & Laserdisc of *Meet Me in St. Louis* and *Ziegfeld Follies* with stereophonic audio mixes, and pairing them with CDs from the stereo mixes (where available). We marketed the CDs as MGM Records and tried to get Turner (who now owned the library) to let us [MGM/UA Home Video, who had the Turner-owned old MGM library under license after Turner bought MGM] release more soundtracks, but they saw bigger money opportunities so they shopped a deal around and made an arrangement for a joint venture with Rhino. I was not a part of this until a year later when I left MGM/UA at the end of my contract there and joined Turner, which had just been bought by Warner Bros. I had oversight of the joint venture by that point [1996].

Authors: Did you make the determination about releasing the comprehensive music tracks on the *Summer Stock* CD?

Feltenstein: Yes.

Authors: Why is incidental music, music not connected to any number, included on the *Summer Stock* CD, such as "Tractor Busted/New Machine" or "Wet Feet?"

Feltenstein: Our goal was to try to include underscoring on these albums wherever possible, especially if it made for a good listening experience. The surviving *Summer Stock* recordings were incomplete. There are many films from the period from 1946–51 where the nitrate tracks either disappeared or decomposed and were not transferred. This was in the early sixties.

Authors: Where did you obtain the music tracks? We suppose that Warner's has rights to them and they are warehoused somewhere. Is that true?

Feltenstein: The music tracks were stored in underground tunnels on the MGM lot until Turner bought MGM's library, and the material had to be moved off the lot. The tapes made from the optical nitrate were sent to a large warehouse MGM had bought near the studio that became Turner's property, and all the MGM lot elements were stored there until Time Warner bought Turner Broadcasting in 1996, and all the material stored at Turner was either sent to the Warner Bros. lot in Burbank or to underground storage in Hutchinson, Kansas (the "salt mines" you may have heard about).

Authors: Were you on site when the tracks were recorded or transferred to Rhino? How did that work, exactly?

Feltenstein: Yes, they were not transferred to Rhino. By the time I did the *Summer Stock* album, the tapes were in the Warner Bros. Kansas storage. They were shipped to our engineer's studio, where they were transferred into Pro Tools, and cleaned up and edited.

Authors: The "You Wonderful You" (newspaper dance reprise) contains Gene Kelly's tap sounds, which are marvelous. Why was the decision made to include them on that track but omit tap sounds on "Dig-Dig-Dig Dig for Your Dinner" and "The Portland Fancy"? We've always wondered about that because the tap stuff adds a real percussive flavor to the soundtracks whenever they're included, like in Fred Astaire's "Drum Crazy" number on the Rhino *Easter Parade* CD.

Feltenstein: It was an artistic choice. Too many times if someone was being lazy, they'd just transfer over tracks from the composite film with footsteps and sound effects. We wanted these albums to be "clean." However, there were indeed certain places where we felt the taps were essential to the enjoyment of the track. The newspaper dance is one of them. We did not feel the same about "The Portland Fancy" or "Dig-Dig-Dig Dig for Your Dinner." When doing *Broadway Melody of 1940*'s "Begin the Beguine," we cut the taps back in where there were holes, but we felt it important that the music be heard, and yet I also agree that the taps are often integral to the aural experience. So we have taken different approaches on each film, each track.

Authors: What do you think about the Rhino *Summer Stock* CD? Are you pleased with how it came out? What do you like or maybe dislike about the version?

Feltenstein: I was very happy with it, considering that the surviving materials were incomplete or in rough shape. For example, we used the MGM Records version of "If You Feel Like Singing, Sing" because the quality was better; the same for "Get Happy." Unfortunately, there were very few that survived with multi-angles. Ironically, the deleted "Fall in Love" duet with Silvers and DeHaven was the only vocal I can recall that survived enough to get a stereo mix. We also found an orchestral tag that let us put the last few seconds of "Happy Harvest" in stereo. It comes "alive" all of a sudden. But I would say we only had about 35 percent of the original recording masters.

First day of filming on *Summer Stock*. Left to right: Chuck Walters, Judy Garland, Vincente Minnelli (Garland's husband at the time), Joe Pasternak. USC Cinematic Arts Library.

Jane's farm after Joe Ross's troupe "invades." Left to right: Carleton Carpenter (with broom), Marjorie Main (with cow on leash), Gloria DeHaven and Hans Conried (seated back-to-back), Phil Silvers (shouting), Jeanne Coyne (in shorts and black top), and Nita Bieber (reading book). Courtesy of Kim Lundeen Collection.

Shooting "Dig-Dig-Dig Dig for Your Dinner." Left to right: Jeanne Coyne, Gene Kelly, Nita Bieber, and Phil Silvers. Note open-face lights suspended above the set. USC Cinematic Arts Library.

Marjorie Main and Judy in an early scene from *Summer Stock*. Courtesy of Photofest.

Phil Silvers and Eddie Bracken, up close and personal in a scene from *Summer Stock*. Courtesy of Photofest.

Seated around Jane Falbury's dinner table. Left to right: Gene Kelly, Al Jennings (assistant director on *Summer Stock*), Judy Garland, and Chuck Walters. Courtesy of Photofest.

Judy and Gene in between takes on the set of *Summer Stock*, with director Chuck Walters behind them. Courtesy of Photofest.

Director Chuck Walters showing Phil Silvers how he should look after wrecking the tractor. USC Cinematic Arts Library.

Eddie Bracken cutting up cast and crew on the set of *Summer Stock*. Courtesy of Scott Brogan Collection.

Rehearsing "The Portland Fancy." Left to right: Judy Garland, choreographer Nick Castle, and Gene Kelly. Courtesy of Nick Castle Jr.

Nick Castle has an idea! Courtesy of Nick Castle Jr.

Nick Castle cracking up Gene Kelly. Courtesy of Nick Castle Jr.

Judy's daughter Liza Minnelli having a heart-to-heart chat with director Chuck Walters during a visit to the *Summer Stock* set. Courtesy of Photofest.

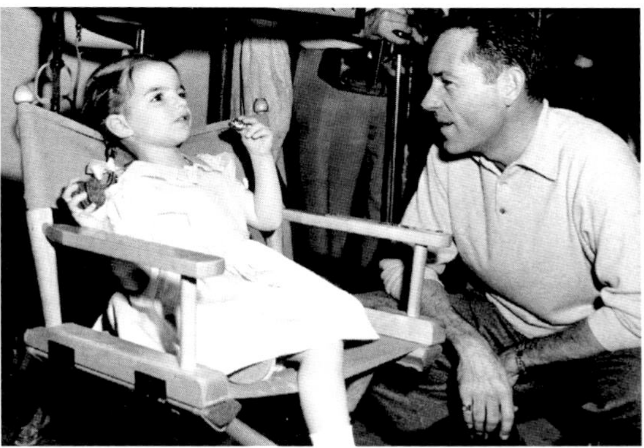

Gene Kelly "channeling" Buster Keaton in his "squeaky board/newspaper" dance. Note the wooden riser that figures prominently in the number. Courtesy of Photofest.

Shooting Judy Garland in "Get Happy." That's the back of Chuck Walters's head in the foreground. Courtesy of Scott Brogan Collection.

Judy and Gene perform "All for You" in the show-within-a-movie finale in *Summer Stock*. Courtesy of Kim Lundeen Collection.

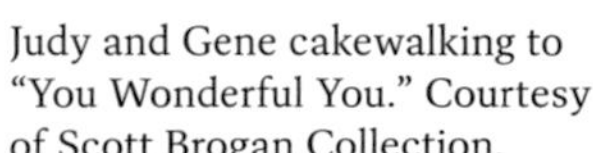

Judy and Gene cakewalking to "You Wonderful You." Courtesy of Scott Brogan Collection.

Phil Silvers and Gene Kelly in their hillbilly "Heavenly Music" number. Courtesy of Photofest.

Judy in hillbilly costume (although she never appeared in the "Heavenly Music" number) visits Spencer Tracy and director Vincente Minnelli on the set of *Father of the Bride*. Courtesy of Photofest.

Summer Stock composers Mack Gordon (left) and Harry Warren with a proclamation from the city of Chattanooga, TN, naming them "Honorary Citizens." Courtesy of Harry Warren Entertainment.

Summer Stock sheet music display in the window of G. Schirmer, Inc., with an offer of free tickets to see the film at Manhattan's Capitol Theater to the first ten people who buy the soundtrack album. Courtesy of the Margaret Herrick Library, Academy of Motion Picture Arts and Sciences.

A long queue waiting to buy tickets for *Summer Stock*. Courtesy of the Margaret Herrick Library, Academy of Motion Picture Arts and Sciences.

Theater advertising display of fans sending their "Good Wishes" to Judy Garland upon the release of *Summer Stock*. Courtesy of USC Cinematic Arts Library.

The Madame Alexander collectable doll of Judy Garland in her "Get Happy" costume from *Summer Stock*. From the author's personal collection.

NOTES

INTRODUCTION: WHY *SUMMER STOCK*?

1. Authors' email exchange with Harold Prince, February 22, 2019.
2. Brian Seibert, *What the Eye Hears: A History of Tap Dancing*, 289–90.
3. AFI Tribute to Gene Kelly, May 7, 1985.

I. THE STUDIO: MGM: DREAM FACTORY IN TRANSITION

1. "Film Needs Cited at MGM Meeting," *Los Angeles Times*, February 11, 1949.
2. Authors' interview with Milton Berle, February 23, 1995.
3. Alex Block, *Blockbusting: A Decade-by-Decade Survey of Timeless Movies Including Untold Secrets of Their Financial and Cultural Success*, 225, 320.
4. Gene Kelly interview, Gerold Frank Archives, University of Wyoming, American Heritage Center, date unknown.
5. Authors' interview with Esther Williams, May 1996.
6. Dore Schary interview, Gerold Frank Archives, University of Wyoming American Heritage Center, July 7, 1972.
7. "The Monster of MGM: How Louis B. Mayer Terrorized Hollywood's Women Long Before Harvey Weinstein," *The Telegraph*, London, October 10, 2017.
8. Authors' interview with Lorna Luft, November 2, 2020.
9. Scott Eyman, *The Lion of Hollywood: The Life and Legend of Louis B. Mayer*, 444.
10. Eyman, *The Lion of Hollywood*, 411.
11. "Louis B. Mayer: Lion of Hollywood," *Time*, December 7, 1998.
12. Fredrik Logevall, *JFK: Coming of Age in the American Century, 1917–1956*, 630–31.
13. Howard Strickling interview, Gerold Frank Archives, University of Wyoming, American Heritage Center, February 25, 1973.
14. Authors' interview with Kathryn Grayson, April 1995.

II. THE STORY: IT'LL MAKE *OKLAHOMA!* LOOK LIKE A BUM

1. *Summer Stock* Review, *Los Angeles Times*, August 12, 1950.
2. *Screenwriter Quarterly*, Fall 1996.

III. THE TALENT: IT'S UP TO YOU—YOUR BLOOD AND GUTS

1. Charles Walters interview, Gerold Frank Archives, University of Wyoming, American Heritage Center. February 19, 1973.
2. Authors' interview with John Fricke, September 24, 2021.
3. Authors' interview with Fricke, September 24, 2021.
4. Authors' interview with Burton Lane, October 1994.
5. John Fricke, *Judy Garland: A Legendary Career*, 100.
6. Arthur Freed interview, Gerold Frank Archives, University of Wyoming, American Heritage Center, July 18, 1972.
7. Authors' interview with John Fricke, September 24, 2021.
8. Vincente Minnelli interview, Gerold Frank Archives, University of Wyoming, American Heritage Center, July 20, 1972.
9. "Judy Garland's Own Story: They'll Always Be an Encore," *McCall's*, January 1964.
10. "Judy Garland's Own Story," *McCall's*, January 1964.
11. Arthur Freed interview, Gerold Frank Archives, University of Wyoming, American Heritage Center, July 18, 1972.
12. Authors' interview with Vincente Minnelli, August 5, 1981.
13. Authors' interview with John Fricke, September 24, 2021.
14. Authors' interview with Margaret O'Brien, 2014.
15. Vincente Minnelli interview, Gerold Frank Archives, University of Wyoming, American Heritage Center, July 20, 1972.
16. Authors' interview with Kerry Kelly Novick, July 20, 2019.
17. Authors' interview with André Previn, July 23, 2016.
18. Gene Kelly interview Gerold Frank Archives, University of Wyoming, American Heritage Center, date unknown.
19. James Goode, "Judy," *Show Business Illustrated*, October 31, 1961.
20. "Judy Garland," Biography.com.
21. Arthur Freed interview, Gerold Frank Archives, University of Wyoming, American Heritage Center, July 18, 1972.
22. John Gruen, "Over the Rainbow and into the Valley Goes Our Judy," *New York World Tribune Magazine*, April 2, 1967.
23. Authors' interview with Charles Walters, September 2, 1980.
24. Saul Chaplin interview, Gerold Frank Archives, University of Wyoming, American Heritage Center, December 24, 1973.
25. Andrew Britton, *Talking Films: The Best of the Guardian Film Lectures*, 199.
26. "An American in Style," *New York Times*, April 17, 1994.
27. "Gene Kelly Knew What the Camera Could Do for the Dance," *The Telegraph*, August 24, 2012.
28. "Gene Kelly Dancing on Film and Strolling Down Memory Lane," *New York Times*, June 1, 1980.
29. Authors' interview, Lorna Luft, November 2, 2020.
30. Authors' interview, Luft, November 2, 2020.
31. "An American in Style."
32. "An American in Style."
33. "It Must Be Love," *Modern Screen*, April 1950.
34. Earl Hess and Pratibha Dabholkar, *Gene Kelly: The Making of a Creative Legend*, 189–90.

35. Authors' interview with Fayard Nicholas, May 6, 1998.
36. Authors' interview with Harold Nicholas, November 20, 1993.
37. "Gene Kelly Dancing on Film and Strolling Down Memory Lane."
38. Authors' interviews with Stanley Donen, September 4, 1980, May 4, 2014.
39. "Talking to Gene Kelly," *Disney Channel Magazine*, March–April 1988.
40. Authors' interviews with Gene Kelly, Beverly Hills, June 23, 1978, March 29, 1994.
41. Authors' interviews with Kelly, Beverly Hills, June 23, 1978, March 29, 1994.
42. Authors' interviews with Kelly, Beverly Hills, June 23, 1978, March 29, 1994.
43. Authors' interview with André Previn, July 23, 2016.
44. "Gotta Dance!" *New Yorker*, March 24, 1994.
45. Authors' interviews with Gene Kelly, June 23, 1978, March 29, 1994.
46. Authors' interview with Cyd Charisse, April 1996.
47. Authors' interview with Vincente Minnelli, August 5, 1981.
48. Authors' interview with Leslie Caron, November 8, 2013.
49. Authors' interviews with Gene Kelly, June 23, 1978, March 29, 1994.
50. Authors' interview with Christiane Noll, November 23, 2020.
51. Authors' interview with Eddie Bracken, 1997.
52. Authors' interview with Bracken, 1997.
53. "Eddie Bracken, 87, Comedy Star on Film and Broadway," *Los Angeles Times*, November 16, 2002.
54. "Bring on Eddie Bracken," *Movieland Magazine*, August 1943.
55. "Eddie Bracken Dies at 87; Acted in Sturges Comedies," *New York Times*, November 16, 2002.
56. Eddie Bracken interview, Southern Methodist Oral History Program, July 31, 1986.
57. "Eddie Bracken Dies at 87; Acted in Sturges Comedies."
58. Bracken interview, Southern Methodist Oral History Program, July 31, 1986.
59. Bracken interview, Southern Methodist Oral History Program, July 31, 1986.
60. "Eddie Bracken Dies at 87; Acted in Sturges Comedies."
61. "Eddie Bracken Dies at 87; Acted in Sturges Comedies."
62. Authors' interview with Eddie Bracken, 1997.
63. John Fricke, *Judy: A Legendary Film Career*, 282.
64. Gloria DeHaven biography, IMDb.
65. "John and Gloria Payne Upset Over Separation," *Los Angeles Times*, May 1, 1948.
66. "Movie Musicals: Remembering," *New York Times*, June 13, 1996.
67. "Gloria DeHaven, Hollywood Actress—Obituary," *London Telegraph*, August 17, 2016.
68. "It's Her 50th Year in Show Business," *Toronto Star*, April 2, 1989.
69. *Toronto Sun* article, 1944.
70. "Alias Gloria DeHaven, A Delightful Dish on the Hollywood Menu," *Movieland*, September 1944.
71. "Old Friends O'Connor, DeHaven Team Up," *Philadelphia Inquirer*, October 25, 1996.
72. "Gloria DeHaven Loses $200,000 in Jewels to Burglar," *Los Angeles Times*, October 27, 1980.
73. "It's Her 50th Year in Show Business."
74. "Marjorie Main: Good for a Lot of Laughs," *Indiana Historical Society*, Winter 2000.
75. "Crude But Comical," *Hollywood Magazine*, February 1942.
76. "Marjorie Main: Good for a Lot of Laughs."
77. "Marjorie Main 'Ma Kettle' Enjoyed Hoosier Roots," *Post-Tribune*, November 25, 2020.
78. "Crude But Comical."

79. “Crude But Comical.”
80. “Hedda Hopper’s Hollywood,” *Los Angeles Times*, August 7, 1941.
81. “Marjorie Main: Good for a Lot of Laughs.”
82. Authors’ interview with Brett Halsey, 2021.
83. Authors’ interview with Richard Eyer, 2021.
84. Authors’ interview with Carleton Carpenter, February 25, 2019.
85. “Crude But Comical,” *Hollywood Magazine*, February 1942.
86. “Marjorie Main: Good for a Lot of Laughs.”
87. Authors’ interview with Jo-Carroll Dennison, 2020.
88. Official bio, The British Phil Silvers Appreciation Society.
89. Official bio, The British Phil Silvers Appreciation Society.
90. Official bio, The British Phil Silvers Appreciation Society.
91. Official bio, The British Phil Silvers Appreciation Society.
92. Phil Silvers with Robert Saffron, *The Last Laugh Is On Me: The Phil Silvers Story*, 92.
93. “Phil Rolls with the Punches,” *Los Angeles Times*, December 2, 1966.
94. Silvers with Saffron, *The Last Laugh Is On Me: The Phil Silvers Story*, 123.
95. Official bio, The British Phil Silvers Appreciation Society.
96. Authors’ interview with Jo-Carroll Dennison, 2020.
97. “Divorce Won by Wife of Phil Silvers,” *Los Angeles Times*, May 9, 1950.
98. “Phil Silvers: Behind Bilko’s Bluff,” *Los Angeles Times*, May 12, 1963.
99. “Phil Silvers Tells Friars of Gaming Disease,” *Los Angeles Times*, August 8, 1968.
100. Authors’ interview with Stephanie Powers, 2020.
101. “Berle’s Tribute Marks Memorial for Phil Silvers,” *Los Angeles Times*, November 4, 1985.
102. Ray Collins bio, Peoplepill.com.
103. Ray Collins bio, Peoplepill.com.
104. Ray Collins bio, Imdbpro.
105. Ray Collins bio, Peoplepill.com.
106. Nita Bieber bio, IMDb.
107. Brent Phillips interview with Nita Bieber, September 23, 2008.
108. Authors’ interview with Ivy Faulkner, July 20, 2021.
109. Authors’ interview with Carleton Carpenter, February 25, 2019.
110. Authors’ interview with Carleton Carpenter, February 25, 2019.
111. “Carleton Carpenter Turns 90,” *The Spectrum*, July 7, 2016.
112. “Carleton Carpenter Turns 90.”
113. “Carleton Carpenter Turns 90.”
114. “Actor Carleton Carpenter on His Unfulfilled Gay Love Story, Losing Debbie Reynolds and Cary Grant’s Visit to His Dressing Room,” *Boyculture.com*, February 20, 2017.
115. Suzanne Gargiulo, *Hans Conried*, 72–73.
116. Gargiulo, *Hans Conried*, 72–73.
117. Authors’ interview with Trilby Conried, January 22, 2021.
118. Authors’ interview with Trilby Conried, January 22, 2021.
119. Authors’ interview with Trilby Conried, January 22, 2021.
120. Conried interview, Southern Methodist University, November 30, 1973.
121. Conried interview, Southern Methodist University, November 30, 1973.
122. Conried interview, Southern Methodist University, November 30, 1973.
123. “Hans Conried Merits Great Actor Term,” *Los Angeles Times*, January 31, 1960.
124. Conried interview, Southern Methodist University, November 30, 1973.

125. "Hans Conried, 66, An Actor on Stage, TV and in Movies," *New York Times*, January 6, 1982.
126. Conried interview, Southern Methodist University, November 30, 1973.
127. Ed Sikov, *On Sunset Boulevard: The Life and Times of Billy Wilder*, 123–24.
128. Authors' interview with Jeff Pasternak, 2020.
129. "Pasternak: The Man Who Out-Disneyed Disney," *Los Angeles Times*, January 9, 1980.
130. "Pasternak: The Man Who Out-Disneyed Disney."
131. Earl Wilson column, *New York Post*, 1958.
132. Saul Chaplin, *The Golden Age of the Hollywood Musicals and Me*, 123.
133. Authors' correspondence with Paula Prentiss, 2020.
134. Authors' interview with Connie Francis, July 2, 2020.
135. Joe Pasternak, *Easy the Hard Way*, 257.
136. AFI Tribute to Gene Kelly, May 7, 1985.
137. United States Holocaust Memorial Museum, www.ushmm.org.
138. Database of Auschwitz prisoners, Auschwitz Memorial and Museum, www.auschwitz.org.
139. Pasternak, *Easy the Hard Way*, 155.
140. Pasternak, *Easy the Hard Way*, 130.
141. Authors' interview with Connie Francis, July 2, 2020.
142. Authors' interview with Robert Stack, March 18, 1994.
143. Authors' interview with Kathryn Grayson, April 1995.
144. "Obituary: Joe Pasternak," *The Independent* (London), September 19, 1991.
145. "Pasternak: The Man Who Out-Disneyed Disney."
146. Authors' interview with Esther Williams, 1994.
147. Authors' interview with Jeff Pasternak, 2020.
148. Authors' interview with Connie Francis, July 2, 2020.
149. Authors' interview with Jeff Pasternak, 2020.
150. Authors' interview with Connie Francis, July 20, 2020.
151. Brent Phillips, *Charles Walters: The Director Who Made Hollywood Dance*, 1.
152. "Charles Walters: In the Background Director Behind Many Top MGM Tuners," *Daily Variety*, November 4, 1975.
153. Authors' interview with Brent Phillips, July 18, 2021.
154. Phillips, *Charles Walters: The Director Who Made Hollywood Dance*, 2.
155. Charles Walters interview, Gerold Frank Archives, American Heritage Center, University of Wyoming, February 19, 1973.
156. Authors' interview with Charles Walters, September 2, 1980.
157. Authors' interview with Charles Walters, September 2, 1980.
158. Authors' interview with Charles Walters, September 2, 1980.
159. Authors' interview with Charles Walters, September 2, 1980.
160. Authors' interview with Charles Walters, September 2, 1980.
161. Authors' interview with Charles Walters, September 2, 1980.
162. Authors' interview with Lorna Luft, November 2, 2021.
163. Charles Walters interview, Gerold Frank Archives.
164. Charles Walters interview, Gerold Frank Archives.
165. Charles Walters interview, Gerold Frank Archives.
166. Charles Walters interview, Gerold Frank Archives.
167. Authors' interview with Charles Walters, September 2, 1980.
168. Authors' interview with Charles Walters, September 2, 1980.

169. Charles Walters interview, Gerold Frank Archives.
170. Authors' interview with Brent Phillips, July 18, 2021.
171. Authors' interview with Charles Walters, September 2, 1980.
172. Authors' interview with Charles Walters, September 2, 1980.
173. Authors' interview with Charles Walters, September 2, 1980.
174. Authors' interview with Charles Walters, September 2, 1980.
175. Mary Whiteley, "Charles Walters Teaches at USC," *USC Spectator*, Spring 1982.
176. Authors' interview with Charles Walters, September 2, 1980.
177. Tony Thomas, *Harry Warren and the Hollywood Musical*, 276.
178. Warren Interview, Southern Methodist University, August 23, 1977.
179. Authors' interview with Harry Warren, August 31, 1980.
180. Thomas, *Harry Warren and the Hollywood Musical*, 5.
181. Authors' interview with Nick Perito, 1993.
182. Authors' interview with Alice Faye, 1993.
183. Authors' interview with Harry Warren, August 31, 1980.
184. Authors' interview with Mel Tormé, 1993.
185. Authors' interview with Harry Warren, August 31, 1980.
186. Warren Interview, Southern Methodist University, August 23, 1977.
187. Warren Interview, Southern Methodist University, August 23, 1977.
188. Warren Interview, Southern Methodist University, August 23, 1977.
189. Warren Interview, Southern Methodist University, August 23, 1977.
190. Warren Interview, Southern Methodist University, August 23, 1977.
191. Warren Interview, Southern Methodist University, August 23, 1977.
192. Warren Interview, Southern Methodist University, August 23, 1977.
193. Thomas, *Harry Warren and the Hollywood Musical*, 2.
194. Baker's Biographical Dictionary of Musicians.
195. Tony Thomas, *Harry Warren and the Hollywood Musical*, 165.
196. Thomas, *Harry Warren and the Hollywood Musical*, 117.
197. Baker's Biographical Dictionary of Musicians.
198. Authors' interview with Roger Gordon, February 25, 2021.
199. Harry Warren Oral History, American Film Institute, 1974.
200. "Mack Gordon Divorced: Songwriter's Wife Testifies He Said He Was Ashamed of Her," *New York Times*, February 26, 1936.
201. "Mack Gordon Returns Gift Perfume in Court," *Los Angeles Times*, October 15, 1948.
202. Authors' interview with Roger Gordon, February 25, 2021.
203. Authors' interview with Roger Gordon, February 25, 2021.
204. Harry Warren Oral History Project, Southern Methodist University, August 23, 1977.

IV. THE PRODUCTION: HOW DARE THIS LOOK LIKE WE'RE HAVING ANY FUN!

1. John Fricke, *Judy Garland: A Legendary Film Career*, 280.
2. Part of Synopsis, American Film Institute.
3. Alvin Yudkoff, *Gene Kelly: A Life of Dance and Dreams*, 204.
4. Yudkoff, *Gene Kelly: A Life of Dance and Dreams*, 204.

5. Gene Kelly interview, Gerold Frank Archives, University of Wyoming, American Heritage Center.
6. Clive Hirschhorn, *Gene Kelly: A Biography*, 190.
7. Vincente Minnelli with Hector Arce, *I Remember It Well*, 216–17.
8. Authors' interview with Kerry Kelly Novak, July 20, 2019.
9. Kelly interview, Gerold Frank Archives, University of Wyoming, American Heritage Center.
10. Kelly interview, Gerold Frank Archives, University of Wyoming, American Heritage Center.
11. Yudkoff, *Gene Kelly: A Life of Dance and Dreams*, 205.
12. Dore Schary Papers, Wisconsin Center for Film and Television Research, University of Wisconsin–Madison.
13. Yudkoff, *Gene Kelly: A Life of Dance and Dreams*, 205.
14. Edith Gwynn's syndicated Hollywood column, September 15, 1949.
15. "Argentine Actor Signed at Metro," *Los Angeles Times*, September 10, 1949.
16. "Eddie Bracken Does Summer Stock," *Los Angeles Times*, October 24, 1949.
17. "Silvers Rejoins Kelly," *Los Angeles Times*, October 17, 1949.
18. Fricke, *Judy Garland: A Legendary Film Career*, 284.
19. Star salaries, *Los Angeles Times*, January 13, 1949.
20. Fricke, *Judy Garland: A Legendary Film Career*, 284.
21. Charles Walters interview, Gerold Frank Archives, University of Wyoming, American Heritage Center, February 19, 1973.
22. Fricke, *Judy Garland: A Legendary Film Career*, 288.
23. Hugh Fordin, *The World of Entertainment! Hollywood's Greatest Musicals*, 278.
24. Arthur Freed interview, Gerold Frank Archives, University of Wyoming, American Heritage Center, July 19, 1972.
25. "Berkeley Off 'Gun'; Walters Gets Meg," *Hollywood Reporter*, May 4, 1949.
26. Gerold Frank, *Judy*, 253.
27. Vincente Minnelli interview, Gerold Frank Archives, University of Wyoming, American Heritage Center, July 20, 1972.
28. Minnelli interview, Gerold Frank Archives, University of Wyoming, American Heritage Center, July 20, 1972.
29. Frank, *Judy*, 255.
30. Frank, *Judy*, 256.
31. Carleton Alsop interview, Gerold Frank Archives, University of Wyoming, American Heritage Center, February 25, 1973.
32. Kelly interview, Gerold Frank Archives, University of Wyoming, American Heritage Center.
33. Frank, *Judy*, 264.
34. Frank, *Judy*, 265.
35. Brent Phillips, *Charles Walters: The Director Who Made Hollywood Dance*, 119.
36. Minnelli with Arce, *I Remember It Well*, 212.
37. Minnelli with Arce, *I Remember It Well*, 213.
38. Authors' interview with Charles Walters, September 2, 1980.
39. Authors' interview with Michael Troyan, August 19, 2020.
40. Charles Walters papers, Cinematic Arts Library, University of Southern California.
41. "George Wells (screenwriter)," Wikipedia.

42. Authors' interview with Katherine Blake, August 14, 2020.
43. Sam Staggs, *When Blanche Met Brando*, 130.
44. MPAA Correspondence, Margaret Herrick Library.
45. Bob Pondillo, "Joseph Breen," First Amendment Encyclopedia Online, https://mtsu.edu/first-amendment/.
46. Robert Koelker, *The Culture of American Film*, 121.
47. Koelker, *The Culture of American Film*, 121.
48. Richard Jewell, *The Golden Age of Cinema, Hollywood 1929–1945*, 137.
49. Script provided by the Boston University Libraries' Howard Gotlieb Archival Research Center.
50. Charles Walters papers, Cinematic Arts Library, University of Southern California.
51. Walters papers, USC.
52. Minnelli with Arce, *I Remember It Well*, 216.
53. Phillips, *Charles Walters: The Director Who Made Hollywood Dance*, 120.
54. "Poundage Nearly Costs Judy Garland a Role," *Los Angeles Times*, November 1, 1949.
55. "Poundage Nearly Costs Judy Garland a Role."
56. Hedda Hopper column, *Los Angeles Times*, January 12, 1950.
57. Arthur Freed interview, Gerold Frank Archives, University of Wyoming, American Heritage Center, July 18, 1972.
58. Carleton Alsop interview, Gerold Frank Archives, University of Wyoming, American Heritage Center, February 25, 1972.
59. Charles Walters interview, Southern Methodist Oral History Program, August 21, 1980.
60. Walters interview, Gerold Frank Archives, University of Wyoming, American Heritage Center, February 19, 1973.
61. Walters interview, Gerold Frank Archives, University of Wyoming, American Heritage Center, February 19, 1973.
62. Walters interview, Gerold Frank Archives, University of Wyoming, American Heritage Center, February 19, 1973.
63. Frank, *Judy*, 220.
64. Kelly interview, Gerold Frank Archives, University of Wyoming, American Heritage Center, date unknown.
65. Betsy Blair, *The Memory of All That*, 207–8.
66. Walters interview, Gerold Frank Archives, University of Wyoming, American Heritage Center, February 19, 1973.
67. Authors' interview with Eddie Bracken, 1994.
68. Eddie Bracken interview, Southern Methodist Oral History Program, July 31, 1986.
69. Bracken interview, Southern Methodist Oral History Program, July 31, 1986.
70. Bill Biss, *Buzz* interview with Gloria DeHaven, 2013.
71. Kelly interview, Gerold Frank Archives, University of Wyoming, American Heritage Center, date unknown.
72. Kelly interview, Gerold Frank Archives, University of Wyoming, American Heritage Center, date unknown.
73. Kelly interview, Gerold Frank Archives, University of Wyoming, American Heritage Center, date unknown.
74. Dore Schary interview, Gerold Frank Archives, University of Wyoming, American Heritage Center, July 7, 1972.
75. David Shipman, *Judy Garland: The Secret Life of an American Legend*, 247.

76. Frank, *Judy*, 267.
77. Phil Silvers, *This Laugh Is on Me*, 171.
78. Silvers, *This Laugh Is on Me*, 172.
79. Authors' interview with Carleton Carpenter, February 25, 2019.
80. Authors' interview with Michael Chapin, September 2, 2020.
81. Eddie Bracken interview, Southern Methodist Oral History Program, July 31, 1986.
82. Gerald Clarke, *Get Happy: The Life of Judy Garland*, 266.
83. Joe Pasternak, *Easy the Hard Way*, 231.
84. Harry Warren interview with the AFI, August 12 and November 29, 1973.
85. Max Wilk, *They're Playing Our Song*, 124.
86. Hirshhorn, *Gene Kelly: A Biography*, 190.
87. Meredith and Dorothy Ponedel, *About Face: The Life and Times of Dottie Ponedel*, 124.
88. Authors' interview with Charles Walters, September 2, 1980.
89. Fordin, *The World of Entertainment: Hollywood's Greatest Musicals*.
90. Earl Wilson, "Judy Garland Cheered on Broadway at 1.a.m.," *San Francisco Examiner*, September 7, 1950.

V. THE MUSICAL NUMBERS: A BRILLIANT CREATION!

1. Authors' interview with Michael Feinstein, August 31, 2021.
2. Authors' interview with Michael Feinstein, August 31, 2021.
3. Authors' interview with Michael Feinstein, August 31, 2021.
4. Authors' interview with Tom Early, August 31, 2020.
5. David Shipman, *Judy Garland: The Secret Life of an American Legend*, 248.
6. Brent Phillips, *Charles Walters: The Man Who Made Hollywood Dance*, 121.
7. Gerald Clarke, *Get Happy: The Life of Judy Garland*, 265.
8. Phil Silvers, *This Laugh Is On Me: The Phil Silvers Story*, 172.
9. Authors' interview with John Fricke, September 24, 2021.
10. Authors' interview with Scott Brogan, August 14, 2021.
11. Production Code files, the Academy of Motion Picture Arts & Sciences.
12. Mack Gordon Papers, Archives Center, National Museum of American History, Smithsonian Institution.
13. Harry Warren interview, American Film Institute, August 12–November 29, 1972.
14. Harry Warren interview, Southern Methodist University, August 23, 1977.
15. Brian Seibert, *What the Eyes Hears: A History of Tap Dancing*, 289–90.
16. John Fricke, *Summer Stock* DVD liner notes.
17. Authors' interview with Mandy Moore, October 3, 2020.
18. Authors' interview with Carleton Carpenter, 2018.
19. Authors' interview with Mandy Moore, October 3, 2020.
20. Authors' interview with Cory John Snide, October 14, 2020.
21. Authors' interview with Brenda Bufalino, August 30, 2020.
22. Authors' interview with Mandy Moore, October 3, 2020.
23. Tony Thomas, *Harry Warren and the Hollywood Musical*, 260.
24. Authors' interview with Gene Kelly, 1978.
25. Clive Hirshhorn, *Gene Kelly*, 191.
26. Hirshhorn, *Gene Kelly*, 194–95.

27. Authors' interview with Nick Castle Jr., March 7, 2019.
28. Brent Phillips, *Charles Walters: The Director Who Made Hollywood Dance*, 122.
29. *Performing Arts Encyclopedia*, Library of Congress.
30. NPR interview with Fayard Nicholas, January 25, 2006.
31. Authors' interview with Nick Castle Jr., March 7, 2019.
32. "Tap Dance in America: A Short History," Library of Congress.
33. Authors' interview with Mandy Moore, October 3, 2020.
34. Authors' interview with Corey John Snide, October 14, 2021.
35. Marshall and Jean Stearns, *Jazz Dance: The Story of American Vernacular Dance*, 188.
36. Hirshhorn, *Gene Kelly*, 91.
37. Authors' interview with Corey John Snide, October 14, 2021.
38. Authors' interview with Mandy Moore, 2020.
39. Clive Hirshhorn, *Gene Kelly*, 195.
40. Brent Phillips, *Charles Walters: The Man Who Made Hollywood Dance*, 123.
41. Authors' interview with Michael Feinstein, August 31, 2021.
42. Saul Chaplin interview, Gerold Frank Archives, American Heritage Center, University of Wyoming, December 24, 1973.
43. Tony Thomas, *Harry Warren and the Hollywood Musical*, 264.
44. Thomas, *Harry Warren and the Hollywood Musical*, 297.
45. Harry Warren interview, American Film Institute, August 12 and November 29, 1972.
46. Brent Phillips, *Charles Walters: The Director Who Made Hollywood Dance*, 123–24.
47. Authors' interview with Michael Feinstein, August 31, 2021.
48. David Shipman, *Judy Garland: The Secret Life of an American Legend*, 248.
49. Authors' interview with Joan Ellison, October 23, 2020.
50. Authors' interview with Lorna Luft, 2020.
51. Andrew Britton, *Talking Films: The Best of the Guardian Film Lectures*, 195.
52. Authors' interview with Brenda Bufalino, August 30, 2020.
53. Authors' interview with Mandy Moore, October 3, 2020.
54. George Stevens Jr., *The Great Moviemakers of Hollywood's Golden Age at the American Film Institute*, 529.
55. Authors' interview with Mandy Moore, October 3, 2020.
56. Authors' interview with Brenda Bufalino, August 30, 2020.
57. Authors' interview with Corey John Snide, October 14, 2020.
58. Authors' interview with Corey John Snide, October 14, 2020.
59. Authors' interview with Lorna Luft, November 2, 2020.
60. Gene Kelly interview by Roddy McDowall, PBS, 1979.
61. BBC interview with Gene Kelly, 1974.
62. Authors' interview with Kerry Kelly Novak, 2014.
63. Authors' interview with Nick Castle Jr., March 7, 2019.
64. Harry Warren, American Film Institute interview, August 12 and November 29, 1972.
65. Authors' interview with Tommy Tune, August 27, 2020.
66. Britton, *Talking Films: The Best of the Guardian Film Lectures*, 196.
67. Stevens, *The Great Moviemakers of Hollywood's Golden Age at the American Film Institute*, 525.
68. Authors' interview with Brent Phillips, July 18, 2021.
69. Authors' interview with Mandy Moore, October 3, 2020.
70. "Gene Kelly Knew what the Camera Could Do for Dance," *The Telegraph*, August 24, 2012.
71. Authors' interview with Michael Feinstein, August 21, 2021.

72. Chaplin, *The Movie Musical and Me*, 126–27.
73. Saul Chaplin profile, Songhall.org.
74. Saul Chaplin interview, Southern Methodist Oral History Program, July 29, 1976.
75. Max Wilk, *They're Playing Our Song*, 225.
76. Clive Hirschhorn, *Gene Kelly*, 29.
77. Brent Phillips, *Charles Walters: The Man Who Made Hollywood Dance*, 125.
78. Hirschhorn, *Gene Kelly*, 192.
79. Michelle Vogel, *Marjorie Main: The Life and Films of Hollywood's Ma Kettle*, 176.
80. Saul Chaplin interview, Gerold Frank Archives, American Heritage Center, University of Wyoming, December 24, 1973.
81. Authors' interview with Michael Feinstein, August 31, 2021.
82. Authors' interview with Michael Feinstein, August 31, 2021.
83. Authors' interview with Charles Walters, September 2, 1980.
84. Gerold Frank, *Judy*, 273.
85. Saul Chaplin, *The Golden Age of Movie Musicals and Me*, 127–28.
86. Brent Phillips, *Charles Walters: The Director Who Made Hollywood Dance*, 125.
87. David Shipman, *Judy Garland: The Secret Life of an American Legend*, 250.
88. Phillips, *Charles Walters: The Director Who Made Hollywood Dance*, 126.
89. Edward Jablonski, *Harold Arlen: Happy with the Blues*, 44.
90. Max Wilk, *They're Playing Our Song*, 143.
91. Vincente Minnelli and Hector Arce, *I Remember It Well*, 217.
92. Frank Billecci, *Irene: A Designer from the Golden Age of Hollywood, The MGM Years, 1942–49*, 102.
93. Billecci, *Irene: A Designer from the Golden Age of Hollywood, The MGM Years, 1942–49*, 102.
94. Authors' interview with Lorna Luft, November 2, 2020.
95. Authors' interview with Michael Feinstein, August 31, 2021.
96. Authors' interview with Michael Feinstein, August 31, 2021.
97. Production Code materials, Margaret Herrick Library, Academy of Motion Picture Arts and Sciences.
98. Mack Gordon papers, National Museum of American History, Smithsonian Institution.
99. John Fricke, *Summer Stock* CD liner notes.
100. Authors' interview with George Feltenstein, September 16, 2021.

VI. MARKETING, REVIEWS, REVENUE, AND REVIVALS: THE VOICE OF GARLAND AND THE FEET OF KELLY ARE AT HIGH TIDE IN *SUMMER STOCK*

1. *Boxoffice*, September 14, 1950.
2. "Critics Cheer Judy Garland in Latest Film," *Boston Globe*, August 6, 1950.
3. Howard Gottlieb Archival Research Center, Boston University.
4. *Boxoffice*, November 4, 1950.
5. "The Screen in Review," *New York Times*, September 1, 1950.
6. "The New Film," *Pittsburgh Post-Gazette*, September 1, 1950.
7. "That Judy's in Top Form," *Los Angeles Evening & Herald Express*, August 12, 1950.
8. *Milwaukee Journal*, August 31, 1950.
9. "*Summer Stock*, Tired, but Pleasant," *Miami News*, September 15, 1950.
10. "Added Weight and Slacks Do Judy No Good," *Chicago Daily Tribune*, September 5, 1950.

11. *Asheville Citizen-Times*, October 1, 1950.
12. *Ekstra Bladet*, September 18, 1951.
13. "Chin Up, Judy! New Film's Great," *Minneapolis Tribune*, August 19, 1950.
14. "Judy Garland, Gene Kelly and the bittersweet joys of puttin' on a show," *avclub.com*, February 26, 2021.
15. *Variety*, September 6, 1950.
16. *Variety*, September 14, 1950.
17. H. Mark Glancy, "MGM Film Grosses, 1924–1948: The Eddie Mannix Ledger," *Historical Journal of Film, Radio and Television* 12, no. 2 (1992).
18. Glancy, "MGM Film Grosses, 1924–1948: The Eddie Mannix Ledger."
19. E. J. Mannix Ledger, Howard Strickling Collection, Margaret Herrick Library, Academy of Motion Pictures Arts and Sciences.
20. "Earnings Reports of Corporations," *New York Times*, January 23, 1952.
21. "*An American in Paris* (musical)," Wikipedia.
22. Authors' interview with Roxanne Messina Captor, November 13, 2020.
23. "Summer Stock gives its Audience lots of Reasons to Get Happy," *Monterey County Weekly*, September 7, 2000.
24. Authors' interview with Roxanne Messina Captor, November 13, 2020.
25. *Playbill.com*, October 2, 2009.
26. *Playbill.com*, September 16, 2009.
27. Authors' interview with Sam Scalamoni, September 13, 2021.
28. Email exchange between authors and Dan McMahon, Goodspeed Opera House.
29. "Summer Stock into MGM Series," *Hollywood Reporter*, November 13, 1978.
30. Authors' interview with Warner Bros. executive George Feltenstein, September 16, 2021.
31. "The Bonus View," *High-Def Digest*.

VII. STRAIGHT UP ALL THE WAY

1. "Judy Garland Slashes Throat after Film Row," *Los Angeles Times*, June 21, 1950.
2. "Judy Garland Slashes Throat after Film Row."
3. "Judy Garland Slashes Throat after Film Row."
4. "The Brutal Truth about Judy Garland," *Modern Screen*, September 1950.
5. David Shipman, *Judy Garland: The Secret Life of an American Legend*, 260.
6. Shipman, *Judy Garland: The Secret Life of an American Legend*, 260.
7. Gerald Clarke, *Get Happy: The Life of Judy Garland*, 276.
8. Authors' interview with Brent Phillips, July 18, 2021.

VIII. TAKING STOCK: WHO'S DOING ANYTHING REMOTELY LIKE IT NOW? I'LL TELL YOU WHO—NOBODY!

1. Authors' interview with Lorna Luft, November 2, 2020.
2. Authors' interview with Kerry Kelly Novick, July 20, 2019.
3. Authors' interview with Ben Vereen, 2020.
4. Authors' interview with Mario Cantone, July 14, 2020.
5. Authors' interview with Tommy Tune, 2020.

6. Authors' interview with Michael Feinstein, August 31, 2021.
7. Authors' interview with Sarah Uriarte Berry, October 12, 2020.
8. Authors' interview with Miranda Garrison, September 13, 2020.
9. Authors' interview with Joan Ellison, October 23, 2020.
10. Authors' interview with Marilyn Michaels, November 23, 2020.
11. Authors' interview with Marilyn Michaels, November 23, 2020.
12. Authors' interview with Mandy Moore, October 3, 2020.
13. Authors' interview with Victoria Morris, October 8, 2020.

APPENDIX I: SETTING THE TEMPO: JOHNNY GREEN AND THE MGM ORCHESTRA

1. Authors' interview with Michael Feinstein, August 31, 2021.

APPENDIX II: ARRANGEMENTS HAVE BEEN MADE: CONRAD SALINGER AND SKIP MARTIN AND THE "MGM SOUND"

1. Hugh Fordin, *The World of Entertainment*, 102.
2. Fordin, *The World of Entertainment*, 102.
3. Authors' interview with Jack Campey, October 8, 2021.
4. Wikipedia.
5. Authors' interview with Michael Feinstein, August 31, 2021.
6. Authors' interview with Jack Campey, October 8, 2021.

APPENDIX III: *SUMMER STOCK* FROM VINYL ALBUM TO DIGITAL CD

1. Authors' interview with George Feltenstein, 2021.

SELECTED BIBLIOGRAPHY

Billecci, Frank. *Irene: A Designer from the Golden Age of Hollywood: The MGM Years, 1942–49*. Atglen, PA: Schiffer, 2015.

Blair, Betsy. *The Memory of All That: Love and Politics in New York, Hollywood and Paris*. New York: Knopf, 2003.

Block, Alex. *Blockbusting: A Decade-by-Decade Survey of Timeless Movies, Including Untold Secrets of Their Financial and Cultural Success*. New York: It Books, 2019.

Britton, Andrew. *Talking Films: The Best of* The Guardian *Film Lectures*. London: Fourth Estate Classic House, 1992.

Chaplin, Saul. *The Golden Age of Movie Musicals and Me*. Norman: University of Oklahoma Press, 1994.

Clarke, Gerald. *Get Happy: The Life of Judy Garland*. New York: Random House, 2000.

Donnelley, Paul. *Judy Garland*. London: Haus Publishing, 2007.

Edwards, Anne. *Judy Garland: A Biography*. New York: Simon and Schuster, 1975.

Eyman, Scott. *The Life and Legend of Louis B. Mayer*. New York: Simon and Schuster, 2005.

Fordin, Hugh. *The World of Entertainment! Hollywood's Greatest Musicals*. New York: Doubleday and Company, 1975.

Frank, Gerold. *Judy*. New York: Da Capo Press, 1975.

Fricke, John. *Judy: A Portrait in Art and Anecdote*. New York: Bulfinch, 2003.

Fricke, John. *Judy Garland: A Legendary Film Career*. Philadelphia and London: Running Press, 2010.

Gargiulo, Suzanne. *Hans Conried*. Jefferson, NC: McFarland, 2002.

Griffin, Mark. *A Hundred or More Hidden Things: The Life and Films of Vincente Minnelli*. Philadelphia: Da Capo Press, 2010.

Harvey, Stephen. *Directed by Vincente Minnelli*. New York: HarperCollins, 1990.

Hess, Earl, and Pratibha Dabholkar. *Gene Kelly: The Making of a Creative Legend*. Lawrence: University Press of Kansas, 2020.

Hirschhorn, Clive. *Gene Kelly: A Biography*. New York: St. Martin's Press, 1985.

Jablonski, Edward. *Harold Arlen: Happy with the Blues*. New York: DaCapo Press, 1986.

Jewell, Richard. *The Golden Age of Cinema, 1929–1945*. Hoboken, NJ: Blackwell, 2007.

Koelker, Robert. *The Culture of American Film*. Oxford: Oxford University Press, 2014.

Logevall, Fredrik. *JFK: Coming of Age in the American Century, 1917–1956*. New York: Random House, 2020.

Minnelli, Vincente. *I Remember It Well*. New York: Doubleday, 1974.

Pasternak, Joe. *Easy the Hard Way*. New York: G. P. Putnam's Sons, 1956.

Phillips, Brent. *Charles Walters: The Director Who Made Hollywood Dance*. Lexington: University Press of Kentucky, 2014.

Ponedel, Meredith, and Dorothy Ponedel. *About Face: The Life and Times of Dottie Ponedel: Make-Up Artist to the Stars*. Albany, GA: BearManor Media, 2018.

Schechter, Scott. *Judy Garland: The Day-by-Day Chronicle of a Legend*. New York: Cooper Square Press, 2002.

Schmidt, Randy. *Judy Garland on Judy Garland*. Chicago: Chicago Review Press, 2014.

Seibert, Brian. *What the Eyes Hears: A History of Tap Dancing*. New York: Farrar, Straus and Giroux, 2015.

Sennett, Ted. *Hollywood Musicals*. New York: Abradale Press, 1985.

Shipman, David. *Judy Garland: The Secret Life of an American Legend*. New York: Hyperion, 1993.

Sikov, Ed. *On Sunset Boulevard: The Life and Times of Billy Wilder*. Jackson: University Press of Mississippi, 2017.

Silvers, Phil. *This Laugh Is on Me: The Phil Silvers Story*. Englewood Cliffs, NJ: Prentice-Hall, 1973.

Stearns, Marshall, and Jean Stearns. *Jazz Dance: The Story of American Vernacular Dance*. New York: Macmillan, 1968.

Stevens, George, Jr. *The Great Moviemakers of Hollywood's Golden Age at the American Film Institute*. New York: Vintage Books, 2006.

Thomas, Tony. *The Films of Gene Kelly*. Secaucus, NJ: Citadel Press, 1974.

Thomas, Tony. *Harry Warren and the Hollywood Musical*. Secaucus, NJ: Lyle Stuart, 1975.

Vogel, Michelle. *Marjorie Main: The Life and Films of Hollywood's "Ma Kettle."* Jefferson, NC: McFarland, 2011.

Wilk, Max. *They're Playing Our Song*. Wickford, RI: Moyer Bell, 1991.

Yudkoff, Alvin. *Gene Kelly: A Life of Dance and Dreams*. New York: Watson-Guptill, 2002.

INDEX

ABOUT THE AUTHORS

Photo courtesy of the authors

DAVID FANTLE, mostly in collaboration with Tom Johnson, has been interviewing, writing, and speaking about Hollywood's Golden Age stars for more than forty years. Their work has appeared in media outlets throughout the world. Fantle's career also includes more than three decades as an award-winning marketing and public relations professional, including a tenure as Deputy Tourism Secretary for Wisconsin. He resides in Milwaukee, Wisconsin, and is an adjunct professor in film, pop culture, and public relations at Marquette University.

TOM JOHNSON began his collaboration with David Fantle in 1978 as a student journalist at the University of Minnesota by co-writing an award-winning arts and entertainment column for the *Minnesota Daily* called "Entertainment Ltd." Johnson, who lives in Los Angeles, was a senior editor at Netflix and has written movie reviews and features for E! Online, *Moviefone*, and *People* magazine, among other publications. Johnson's entertainment writing has been recognized with a Minnesota Newspaper Association achievement award and a National Hearst Foundation award for news writing.

Fantle and Johnson's *Hollywood Heyday: 75 Candid Interviews with Golden Age Legends* was a best-seller on Amazon and winner of the National Indie Excellence Award as Best Book of 2018 (entertainment category).